MW01057030

7 LEADERSHIP LESSONS OF D-DAY

Lessons from the Longest Day—June 6, 1944

JOHN ANTAL

CASEMATE

Philadelphia & Oxford

Special thanks to COL (Ret.) Fran Fierko for his work in editing the manuscript. As a very good friend, and gatekeeper for good grammar, you are the best! And thanks to my readers, COL (Ret.) Rick Jung, COL (Ret.) JP Hogan, LTC (Ret.) Tim Vane and CSM (Ret.) Edward Braese. —JFA

Published in the United States of America and Great Britain in 2017 by
CASEMATE PUBLISHERS
1950 Lawrence Road, Havertown, PA 19083, USA
and
The Old Music Hall, 106–108 Cowley Road, Oxford OX4 1JE, UK

Copyright 2017 © John Antal

Hardcover Edition: ISBN 978-1-61200-529-4
Digital Edition: ISBN 978-1-61200-530-0

A CIP record for this book is available from the Library of Congress and the British Library

Printed and bound in the United States of America
Typeset in India by Lapiz Digital Services, Chennai

For a complete list of Casemate titles, please contact:

CASEMATE PUBLISHERS (US)
Telephone (610) 853-9131
Fax (610) 853-9146
Email: casemate@casematepublishers.com
www.casematepublishers.com

CASEMATE PUBLISHERS (UK)
Telephone (01865) 241249
Fax (01865) 794449
Email: casemate-uk@casematepublishers.co.uk
www.casematepublishers.co.uk

Contents

To the Greatest Generation who defeated German Fascism and the follow-on generations who continue to defend Liberty.

Their leadership made all the difference. They did not hesitate; they did not equivocate; they did not plea-bargain with the Nazis. They rallied against evil, faced the fire, changed the world, and decided the fate of countless generations.
We must learn from their example.

This photo, taken at 7:40 a.m. on June 6, 1944, by Robert F. Sargent, a chief photographer's mate in the United States Coast Guard, is titled "Taxis to Hell—and Back—Into the Jaws of Death." The Landing Craft, Vehicle, Personnel (LCVP), or Higgins boat, has grounded some distance out from Omaha Beach, beach sector Easy Red, Normandy, on June 6, 1944. The men are wading toward the long stretch of open sands. These troops are believed to be members of the 1st Battalion, 16th Infantry, landing in waist-deep water when the tide was through the lower obstacles. In the distance, an M4A3 Duplex Drive (DD) tank (No. 9, from Company A, 741st Tank Battalion) is on the edge of the tidal flat.

Why Leadership Matters

*"A mighty endeavor, a struggle to preserve our Republic, our religion,
and our civilization, and to set free a suffering humanity."*
President Franklin D. Roosevelt

"We will accept nothing less than full victory."
General Dwight D. Eisenhower

June 6, 1944 has been called the "Day of Days."

It was a different time than today. World War II was a desperate time, when nations were in the throes of cascading chaos, war, and death on a scale that is nearly unimaginable today. It was a time when ruthless totalitarianism was on the march and winning. It was a time when brave men and women stood in defiance of tyranny and their leadership made all the difference.

The invasion of Normandy on June 6, 1944 was an immense undertaking involving nearly 6,939 Allied ships, 11,590 aircraft and 156,000 troops. The military term "D-Day" refers to the day when a combat operation is to start, and "H-hour" is the exact time the operation commences. This concept permits military strategists to plan for an operation in advance, even when the exact date and time of the action are still unknown. D-Day will, however, forever be associated with the invasion of Normany—the largest and most famous amphibious operation in the history of war. D-Day is also the largest night airborne operation ever conducted.

In the waning hours of June 5, 1944, American and British para-troopers were flying in hundreds of aircraft over the English Channel to embark on the "Great Crusade" against Fascism and to defeat the Nazis' gospel of hate. The courageous "All Americans" of the 82nd (US) Airborne Division, the "Screaming Eagles" of the 101st (US) Airborne Division, and the "Red Devils" of the (British) 6th Airborne Division were the vanguard of an immense military force that was to enter the continent of Europe and bring about the defeat of Nazi Germany.

On D-Day, at 5:50 a.m., the vast Allied naval armada began the bombardment of targets on the five designated Allied assault beaches: from west to east, the American beaches code-named Utah and Omaha; and the other Allied beaches, code-named Gold (British), Juno (Canadian), and Sword (British). The dawn was shattered by the fury of thousands of guns, bombs, and rockets from battleships, cruisers, destroyers, and smaller craft. Overhead, thousands of aircraft, including large formations of B-17 and B-24 and Lancaster bombers, dropped their lethal payloads at 6 a.m. on German defenses along the coastline. H-Hour, the time when the first wave hit the beach at Omaha and Utah, was 6:30 a.m. The British and Canadians were scheduled to land at their designated beaches an hour after the Americans.

Although some found themselves all alone on D-Day, most fought in small teams. Squads, tank crews, gun crews, sections, platoons, batteries, companies, battalions, regiments, and brigades were thrown into this desperate fight, and all had designated leaders, or leaders who rose to the occasion and took charge. These leaders had a tremendous challenge: to lead by example through the melee of surprise, fear, disorder, and death; to keep a calm head at a time when it was reasonable to lose all sense of composure; to forge ahead when anyone with any sense wanted to run and hide. Some leaders fell short that day; but many did not and their leadership turned chaos into victory. It did not matter what insignia or badge of rank they wore on their sleeve or their collar. Leadership is not about position, rank or title; it is about action. Leaders led by example and pulled their teams forward. Some were killed in the act of leading, and when that happened, other leaders stepped up to fill the gap.

The leaders profiled in this book are extraordinary. Some of them are well known, while others are barely mentioned in the history books. All made a dramatic difference in the fight to break Hitler's grip on occupied Europe during World War II. All understood that they had a mission to accomplish, and that, if they failed to lead, that mission would fail and more of their men would die. Why they led, why they were leaders at all, is a fundamental question that is as different as each of these individuals. There is, however, a fundamental characteristic that they all had in common. When things did not go as planned, when everything started to turn into chaos, they didn't hesitate to lead. They were there, decided to act, adapted, and overcame the challenges. They were leaders. They recognized that leadership was the only way to get through the storm of death and the only antidote to conquer the disease of fear and paralysis.

Fear, and its handmaiden paralysis, has destroyed more projects, plans, enterprises and possibilities than any other in human history. When fear is gripping everyone, when paralysis and inertia reigns, leaders must rapidly recognize the symptoms of the disease and act. Learning how to overcome fear and paralysis involves accustoming the mind to think and focus on courage. Leaders who understand this have learned how to stop thinking about what they can't do, and focus on what they can do. This is as true for you in your daily life—with your family, school or business—as it was during the dramatic events of D-Day. Understanding what others have done when the situation was significantly more difficult provides a comparison that can develop a resilient mind. You can generate this somatic and psychological resilience through practice (habit), study (knowledge), and leadership exercises (experience). The sum of knowledge and experience is wisdom. If thoughts create action, are your thoughts resilient enough to drive on and overcome adversity? How can you raise your level of wisdom (knowledge plus experience) to lead more effectively?

This book is one journey down your personal path to raise your level of leadership. The seven leadership case studies in this book provide timeless examples that can help you open your mind to possibilities rather than limit yourself to past options. I have taken some creative license to reconstruct some conversations and scenes in this book, and in doing so, have kept to the known history of what was said and done in each occasion. This book is not meant to be a complete history of D-Day; nor does it cover the heroic leadership of the British, Canadian, Free French, New Zealand, Australian, Polish, Norwegian, Czechoslovak, Greek, Dutch, Danish, and members of the French Resistance who also participated in the Normandy assault and the ensuing battles for the lodgment areas. This book focuses on seven actions of the American contribution to D-Day and is a primer on how you can lead today, no matter what your occupation or role in life.

I am asked frequently what is the most powerful means to improve an understanding of leadership. The answer is simple: read. Reading is fuel for the mind. I know very few leaders who are uninterested in reading. Reading does more than lift meaning from the pages of a book; it has the possibility of upgrading how you think. Reading involves imagination and improves creativity. Reading improves judgment. Reading improves communication skills. Reading stories provides a window into other people's lives and this insight can improve your people skills. Reading improves self-awareness. Reading can reduce stress and improve focus. Focus is vital and rare. Mastering focus masters the mind. Reading, therefore, is fuel for the mind. Over 2,500 years ago, the great Chinese philosopher, Confucius said: "No matter how busy you may think you are, you must find time for reading, or surrender yourself to self-chosen ignorance." Galileo, the great astronomer, physicist, engineer, philosopher, and mathematician who lived during the 17th century, said: "Books give us superhuman powers."

If you read, you are more likely to lead. Reading can improve leadership awareness. Leadership awareness can increase the reader's leadership knowledge. Raising your knowledge level is the fastest way to leverage experience. Experience is the greatest teacher, but it is also the most expensive and time-consuming way to raise your leadership level. Combining knowledge with experience puts you on the fast track to raising your understanding of leadership. Leadership knowledge, combined with leadership experience can produce wisdom. Read to lead.

Last, and most importantly, if you wish to improve your understanding of leadership, read about the people who led in difficult times. D-Day, June 6, 1944, and the battles that followed, provide an extraordinary leadership laboratory for anyone willing to pick up a book, watch a movie or listen to a podcast. The soldiers, sailors, airmen and coast guardsmen of the Allied Expeditionary Force who ran into the jaws of hell on D-Day confronted evil face to face and did not falter. They gave us freedom. They made a tremendous investment in our liberty. Words cannot explain the depths of what they did for us and what we owe them for their sacrifice. We owe them the world we live in today. If they had faltered or failed, Western civilization would be tragically and horribly different, liberty and religion crushed, and hundreds of millions of people would have died and been subjugated to totalitarian oppression and slavery. We should act every day to earn their sacrifice. These lessons beckon to us today to learn the gift of leadership and liberty that the heroes of the Greatest Generation so aptly demonstrated for us.

Extraordinary leaders can transform the world. In the pages of this book, you will be exposed to the extraordinary stories of leadership of American soldiers who led teams to do impossible things. The lessons will illuminate truths about leadership that you can use regardless of your occupation, age or station in life. I challenge you to learn, adapt and grow your leadership every day. Use these "lessons learned" to refine or create your own personal definition of leadership. In the process, I guarantee that as your learning matures your awareness will improve and expand to fill your leadership potential.

John Antal

The Road to the Longest Day

"How horrible, fantastic, incredible it is that we should be digging trenches
and trying on gas-masks here because of a quarrel in a far-away country between
people of whom we know nothing. It seems still more impossible that a quarrel that
has already been settled in principle should be the subject of war."
Prime Minister Neville Chamberlain, in an address to
Great Britain on September 27, 1938

The dictator of the German Reich scowled. He looked across the room, identified his target, and then faked his best smile. His prey, the Prime Minister, looked quite the proper English gentleman. He wore an immaculately tailored three-piece suit and his eyes reflected the sincerity of a man totally dedicated to nonviolence. The dictator wore a martial-style brown Nazi party uniform, proudly displaying the distinctive red swastika armband on his left arm. He moved in for the kill. Like a wolf, baring his teeth before the strike, he walked up to the Prime Minister and extended his hand. The Prime Minister offered a nervous, weak grin and then shook the dictator's hand.

"I have come here to offer peace," the tall, thin Prime Minister offered, still holding the dictator's hand. "I earnestly hope we can do whatever it takes to avoid war."

A translator whispered into the dictator's ear. The dictator deftly smiled, while increasing the pressure of his grip on the Prime Minister's hand.

xii • 7 LEADERSHIP LESSONS OF D-DAY

The politicians had assembled in Munich, Germany, at a hastily organized conference to determine the fate of the tiny country of Czechoslovakia. The Germans wanted all Czechoslovak land where ethnic Germans lived to be ceded to the Nazi Reich. The Czechs had bravely refused. Germany, in response, threatened war. Britain and France, representing the major Western powers, hoped to negotiate a solution. With the horrible death toll of World War I—nearly 17 million dead and at least 20 million wounded just 20 years earlier—another war was unthinkable to the leaders of Britain and France. That was not, however, the case in the mind of the dictator.

The translator coughed. "Herr Hitler agrees. Peace is most welcome." Adolf Hitler, the Führer of Nazi Germany, then commenced a 30-minute soliloquy in German on the victimization of the German people, their need for strong leadership, and the obligation of the Western powers to understand the German requirement for unification and the advancement of the Aryan race. Prime Minister Neville Chamberlain, along with the French President Édouard Daladier, listened attentively through their interpreters. Without the Czechs present at the meeting, and without the consent of the Czechoslovakian government, Chamberlain and the French premier agreed to Hitler's demands. Czechoslovakia would surrender the Sudetenland, a large portion of land that bordered Germany, to the Nazis. In return, Hitler promised not to invade the rest of Czechoslovakia. After less than an hour of negotiations, Hitler signed the agreement, promising that the Nazis had no further territorial ambitions in Europe.

Chamberlain, visibly relieved at this "good" news, flew back to London from Munich with a copy of the signed treaty in his pocket. As he stepped from the British Airways airplane at Heston Aerodrome in London (east of today's Heathrow Airport), a large crowd and a bevy of press reporters greeted him. Standing at the microphone and holding the piece of paper in his hand, he declared:

> The settlement of the Czechoslovakian problem, which has now been achieved is, in my view, only the prelude to a larger settlement in which all Europe may find peace. This morning I had another talk with the German Chancellor, Herr Hitler, and here is the paper which bears his name upon it as well as mine. Some

of you, perhaps, have already heard what it contains but I would just like to read it to you: 'We regard the agreement signed last night and the Anglo-German Naval Agreement as symbolic of the desire of our two peoples never to go to war with one another again.'[1]

Later that evening, Chamberlain gave his report to Britain's King George VI at Buckingham Palace, and then made his way through throngs of joyous citizens who met him in front of the Prime Minister's office at Number 10 Downing Street. The crowd begged him to offer some words to express the moment they had all prayed for—peace. Chamberlain moved inside and then appeared at the first-floor window: "My good friends, for the second time in our history, a British Prime Minister has returned from Germany bringing peace with honour. I believe it is peace for our time. We thank you from the bottom of our hearts. Now I recommend you go home, and sleep quietly in your beds."

On October 3, 1939, the British House of Commons discussed the agreement Chamberlain had brought back from Munich. A vote was taken to approve the agreement. Not one Conservative voted against the agreement, with only a very small number abstaining. Winston Churchill vigorously disagreed with the Munich agreement and warned the House of Commons: "England has been offered a choice between war and shame. She has chosen shame, and will get war."

Fear is a reaction; courage is a decision. Chamberlain could have decided on courage, but he was gripped in fear of another horrific war. At this critical point in time, Chamberlain was the popular leader of the British Labour Party, the Prime Minister of the United Kingdom, and the leader of the largest empire in the world. He had become Prime Minister in 1937 and led the British Empire, which counted 20 percent of the world's population as its subjects (458 million out of 2.295 billion). Chamberlain did not want to be distracted by foreign policy and preferred to focus his attention on the internal development of the empire and the social and economic status of the British people. By 1938, Chamberlain was one of the most influential national leaders in the world. Great Britain had the largest empire, the greatest navy, and the British economy was emerging from the Great Depression—or the Great Slump as it was called in England—with an economy better than many other nations. Although the decade of 1928 to 1938 had hit Great Britain hard and unemployment was as high as 70 percent, the British economy fared better than most. When Chamberlain met with Hitler in Munich in 1938, unemployment had dropped to 13 percent. Great Britain was also the holder of the world's reserve currency and worldwide trade was conducted using the British Sterling. Most importantly, Great Britain was a victor in World War I, along with France, Italy, and the United States. World War I, "The Great War," had cost nearly every nation in Europe an entire generation of young men.

Chamberlain feared another war, but Adolf Hitler yearned for conflict. Hitler pushed and advanced his ideas and, where there was no resistance, he seized what he wanted. Hitler wanted Austria to be part of Germany and organized pro-Nazi agitators to hasten this outcome. The government of Austria wanted to put unification with Germany to a vote, but on March 11, 1938, a day before the vote was to be held, pro-Nazi elements conducted a *coup d'état* and took over the Austrian government. On March 12, Hitler conducted the "Anschluß" (political annexation) of Austria with Germany, marching his German troops into Austria. The British and French answered this provocation with meekly worded diplomatic protests. After all, what could the British and French do in the face of Hitler's determined moves? Fight? To them, this was unthinkable. Although the Versailles treaty that ended World War I forbade the unification of Austria and Germany, no European power was willing to fight Germany over this blatant violation.

Protests and sternly worded messages, however, would not stop Adolf Hitler. After Austria, Hitler turned his attention to Czechoslovakia. During the summer of 1938, Hitler supported pro-Nazi rebels in the Sudetenland and financed them to cause unrest. In the meantime, Hitler's minister of propaganda, Paul Joseph Goebbels, generated a torrent of stories that reported that Germans were being mistreated and persecuted by the Czechs. Goebbels' message was clear: all Germans should be a part of the new Nazi Reich.

Chamberlain heard the drums of war beating and hoped to avoid conflict by offering understanding, fair negotiation, and conciliation. He feared igniting a new slaughter and sought to avoid war at all costs. He believed any effort that avoided conflict was noble and worthy. The horrors of World War I were more than most Europeans could bear and more than Chamberlain could endure. The contemplation of a second—and possibly bloodier—war was inconceivable to him.

So, at Munich, Chamberlain acted out of fear. He feared that standing up to Hitler would cause a war. After all, didn't Herr Hitler have a point? The Germans who were living in the Sudetenland of Czechoslovakia wanted to live under German rule. The Sudetenland was the name the Germans used to refer to those areas of Czechoslovakia inhabited mostly by German-speaking citizens from areas that bordered Germany. Why should British and French young men die in a fight over who ruled the Sudeten Germans of Czechoslovakia?

The unintended consequence of his fear, however, sealed the fate of nations. Chamberlain met with Hitler at his Bavarian retreat at Berchtesgaden on September 15, 1938, where he agreed to give the Sudetenland to Germany. Daladier approved the deal on September 18. The Czech government was neither invited nor consulted in the September 18 meeting and did not learn the news until the 19th. Little Czechoslovakia felt betrayed by the two greatest powers in the world, Great Britain and France. Their liberty had been unilaterally surrendered for the "peace" of Europe.

On September 22, Chamberlain flew again to Germany to finalize the deal. More negotiations took place, but Hitler raised the stakes. He stated Germany would invade Czechoslovakia if the agreement was not signed within a few days. Hitler dominated the discussion and badgered Chamberlain and Daladier until they accepted his conditions. At a subsequent meeting on September 29, 1938, Chamberlain and Daladier met with Hitler to review a proposal from Fascist Italian dictator Benito Mussolini that suggested a peaceful solution to the Sudetenland problem. The proposal, which was supplied to Mussolini by the Nazis, became known as the Munich

Pact. Chamberlain agreed to the terms and signed the document on September 30, although it was dated September 29. Germany, France, the United Kingdom and Italy signed, but Czechoslovakia did not. The agreement compelled Czechoslovakia to surrender large portions of their country to Nazi Germany within 24 hours. The Czechoslovak government stood by, paralyzed by fear, as the German Army marched into the Sudetenland. Hitler had just conquered Czechoslovakia without firing a shot.

Chamberlain believed that he had averted a terrible war and that peace, even at the cost of Czechoslovakia, was the noble and right path. Of his meeting with Hitler, he said: "In spite of the hardness and ruthlessness I thought I saw in his face, I got the impression that here was a man who could be relied upon when he had given his word." When Chamberlain returned to London, he waved a piece of paper with Hitler's signature on it and told the reporters that he had secured "peace for our time." The British House of Commons burst into euphoria at the news of Chamberlain's success. Crowds of British citizens cheered Chamberlain as the savior of the world and a leader that would keep Britain out of war.

What we do in life echoes in history. As difficult as it was for Chamberlain to see it then, what happened in Munich on September 30, 1938 initiated a turn of events that resulted in World War II and the deaths of over 60 million people. The ripples of Munich still shape our world today.

Back in Germany, Hitler was smiling. His triumph at Munich was a huge bluff. Hitler did not know it, but he had narrowly averted his own demise. Many leaders in the German Army were nervous over Hitler's reckless behavior. They knew that Germany was not ready for a major war, and many on the German General Staff stridently wanted to avoid a conflict with Great Britain and France. Senior leaders of the German Army planned to arrest and overthrow Hitler if the British and French stood firm and opposed the annexation of the Sudetenland. When Chamberlain and Daladier melted under Hitler's pressure and submitted to the terms of the Munich Pact, the opposition to Hitler in the German Army quickly receded. It is difficult to oppose a dictator when he is winning. If Chamberlain and Daladier had stood up to Hitler and made him back down, displaying courage instead of fear, their actions could have generated one of the greatest alternative outcomes in history.

Chamberlain and Daladier, however, were not made of such stern stuff. Hitler viewed them as weak leaders whom he could bully at will. Threats were his most useful weapon and he used them to his advantage. Later he would say: "Our enemies are little worms. I saw them at Munich."

On March 15, 1939, Hitler met with the Czechoslovak president in Berlin and demanded he surrender his country to Germany. The Czechoslovak president had a heart attack during this session and eventually submitted. Hitler broke the promises of the Munich Pact and his forces stormed into the remainder of Czechoslovakia, which quickly fell without a fight. From the historic Prague Castle, Hitler proclaimed Czechoslovakia as part of the greater German Reich. Great Britain and France vigorously protested Germany's brazen act of conquest, but did nothing more than that. Eleven months later, on September 1, 1939, Hitler's armies invaded Poland. Finally, shamed into action, Britain and France felt they had no choice but to declare war on Germany. The British and French put their military forces on high alert along the French border, but did nothing to help the beleaguered Poles. Soviet Russia, in a stunning surprise, joined Germany and attacked Poland from the east. Democratic Poland fell to the combined Nazi-Soviet attack in 35 days. On April 10, 1940, while the British and French Armies sat idle along the French, Belgian, and Dutch borders, the Nazis launched a stunning attack on Denmark and Norway, using troops in "Trojan Horse" freighter ships and airborne troops supported by the German Air Force (the *Luftwaffe*). Denmark was overrun in just days and Norway subsequently succumbed two months later. While the fighting was going on in Norway, on May 10, 1940, Hitler attacked Belgium, Holland, Luxembourg, and France. In 43 days of rapid assaults, the Nazis defeated the combined British and French forces in a blitzkrieg (lightning war). The British missed total disaster by frantically evacuating their beaten troops from the Dunkirk beaches to England in a massive sealift. The French surrendered and became part of the Nazi empire. The little piece of paper that Chamberlain signed in Munich on September 30, 1938, did little to help the conquered people of Europe and clearly did not deliver on Chamberlain's promise of "peace for our time."

Communist Russia, led by another ruthless dictator, Joseph Stalin, was subsequently attacked by their German allies on June 22, 1941 and was rapidly pushed to the brink of defeat. By late 1941, Hitler's empire stretched from the shores of France to the Parthenon in Greece and to the gates of Moscow. On December 7, 1941, Nazi Germany's ally, the Empire of Japan, executed a surprise attack on the United States at Pearl Harbor, Oahu, Hawaii, killing 2,403 military personnel and 68 civilians, leaving a further 1,178 military personnel and at least 35 civilians wounded. The Japanese attack badly damaged the US Pacific Naval Fleet, sinking, among others, four battleships. That same day, the Japanese attacked US forces in the Philippines, and Guam, while simultaneously attacking British and Dutch forces across the Pacific. Hitler, who held true to his alliance with the military dictatorship of Imperial Japan, obligingly declared war on the United States.

In 1941, the United States was not ready for war. The US Army was ranked 19th in the world and was smaller than the army of Romania. Only three divisions in the US Army were considered combat ready and these lacked the modern equipment—especially tanks—that was the key ingredient of the German Army's (the Wehrmacht's) success. The Army Air Corps (the United States Air Force did not become a separate service until 1947, after World War II) was struggling to train pilots on mostly obsolete aircraft. Only the United States Navy was truly a force to be reckoned with but was focused primarily on the Pacific with its major base at Pearl Harbor, Hawaii.

The surprise Japanese attack on Pearl Harbor in the early morning hours of December 7, 1941 crippled America's fighting forces in the Pacific and shocked the American people. American naval and aircraft losses were heavy. All eight American battleships anchored at Pearl Harbor, the pride of the US Navy, were damaged, with four being sunk, along with the loss of three cruisers and three destroyers. Although the US Navy's aircraft carriers escaped the attack, 188 Army and Navy aircraft were destroyed. Most tragically, 2,403 Americans were killed, with another 1,178 wounded.

President Franklin D. Roosevelt, in his address to Congress on December 8, 1941, stated: "Hostilities exist. There is no blinking at the fact that our people, our territory, and our interests are in grave danger. With confidence in our armed forces—with the unbounding determination of our people—we will gain the inevitable triumph—so help us God."

On December 11, 1941, when Hitler declared war on the United States, America's ability to fight a global war against the Axis powers of Imperial Japan and Nazi Germany looked impossible. Impossible, however, was not a word in the American dictionary and America rose to the challenge. Almost immediately after the Pearl Harbor attack, Americans shook off isolationism, rolled up their sleeves, and decided to lead. It took tremendous effort, organizational skills, and sacrifice by a united America to raise the Army, Army Air Forces, Navy, Marines and Coast Guardsmen required to turn the tide against this vicious totalitarian onslaught.

As Nazi Germany pushed the Russians to the gates of Moscow, the Western Allies, primarily the British Commonwealth and American forces, began attacking Hitler's legions on the western periphery of the Nazi Empire, first in Africa in 1942, then in Sicily and Italy in 1943. By late 1943, the Germans were defeated by the Russians at Stalingrad and the Red Army began pushing the Germans westward, back towards Europe. In the mountains of Italy, the Germans fought the combined American, British, Canadian, and other Allied nations' forces to a standstill, blocking Churchill's "soft underbelly" approach to attack Nazi-occupied Europe. The Allies then knew that they had to invade the European continent somewhere along the coast of France to secure a decisive victory.

Hitler knew this as well. With his forces under immense pressure fighting legions of Russians on the Eastern Front, he sought to conduct an economy of force effort in the West by relying on fixed fortifications to deter the American and British allies from attempting a seaborne invasion. On March 23, 1942, Hitler ordered the creation of a series of 15,000 defensive bunkers and steel- and concrete-reinforced fighting positions along the western coast of Europe to stop any attack by Allied forces from the sea. The Nazis created an impressive belt of fortifications termed the "Atlantic Wall" which stretched from Norway in the north to the French–Spanish border to the south. The Germans forced 260,000 local workers into service to pour 17 million cubic meters of concrete, reinforced by 1.2 million tons of steel, to construct the bunkers and hardened gun emplacements of the Atlantic Wall. In addition to these defensive positions, the Germans planted millions of anti-invasion obstacles designed to rip apart landing craft. They reinforced these obstacles by sowing millions of antipersonnel and antitank land mines. Behind these formidable defenses were thousands of additional bunkers for troops to shelter in prior to launching local counterattacks on the beaches. In addition, fast moving combined arms units, equipped with tanks, assault guns, mobile artillery, and antiaircraft guns, were positioned nearby in order to conduct powerful striking operations to defeat the invaders at the water's edge. Hitler's Atlantic Wall was one of the largest, and most imposing, combat engineering projects of all time.

An initial attempt to raid the coast of France and pierce the Atlantic Wall was made on August 19, 1942 by a force of 5,000 Canadians, 1,000 British, and 50 US Army Rangers at Dieppe, on the shores of northern France, after a naval bombardment involving 237 ships. The operation started going awry from the beginning, when the landing force ran into a small German naval convoy. The German defenders quickly regrouped, pinned the invasion forces to the beaches with intense artillery, mortar, and machine-gun fire, and then slaughtered them as the Canadians, British, and Rangers attempted to break out. After 10 hours, the raid was in shambles, with heavy casualties. With the total annihilation of the invasion force looming, the commander of the raid, British Admiral Louis Mountbatten, withdrew the survivors. The casualties among the largely Canadian force were horrific. Nearly 60 percent of the landing force was killed, wounded or captured. The Germans took 1,945 Canadian prisoners. Almost all the Canadian tanks

The D-Day Decision was made on June 4, 1944 by General Dwight D. Eisenhower with the help of his senior subordinate commanders. This photo shows the key commanders. Standing from left to right are Lieutenant General Omar Bradley, Admiral Sir Bertram Ramsey, Air Chief Marshal Sir Trafford Leigh Mallory and Lieutenant General W. Bedell Smith. Seated from left to right are: Air Chief Marshall Sir Arthur Tedder, General Eisenhower and General Sir Bernard Montgomery. (National Archives)

and vehicles that accompanied the assault were left on the beach. Film of the Allied disaster, depicting bodies on the sands, burning tanks, and forlorn Allied prisoners, were shown in every movie theater in the Reich to rally the German population. The Germans quickly declared Dieppe a tactical victory that proved the invincibility of the Führer's Atlantic Wall.

Knowing the skill of the German Army and strength of the German coastal defenses, the Allies then prepared for the greatest invasion in history. The operation, code-named *Overlord*, would involve the greatest naval armada, the largest fleet of aircraft, and more ground troops than the Western Allies had ever assembled. *Overlord* employed nine divisions in the initial assault to seize the five Normandy beaches. A total of 160,000 men were to move across the English Channel to land on the beaches and pierce the Atlantic Wall on D-Day. The beaches were code-named, from west to east, Utah, Omaha, Gold, Juno, and Sword. The American beaches were Utah and Omaha. President Roosevelt and Prime Minister Winston Churchill jointly selected 53-year-old American General Dwight David Eisenhower to command the entire Allied operation. Roosevelt and Churchill also agreed that all operational issues of the Allied invasion effort would be decided by Eisenhower as Supreme Commander of the Allied Expeditionary Forces (SHAEF) without political interference or micro-management.

Learning from the unsuccessful Dieppe raid, Eisenhower continued preparations for the invasion. Every detail was meticulously planned and painstakingly rehearsed. Operation *Neptune* was the codename for the amphibious and airborne component of *Overlord* that would crack Hitler's Atlantic Wall and form a lodgment on the continent of Europe. A brilliant deception effort, code-named Operation *Bodyguard*, was executed to make the Germans believe that the invasion would be at the closest point between England and France, at the Pas-de-Calais. By May 1944, the Allied invasion force was ready. One and a half million American soldiers had arrived in England. Millions of tons of equipment and supplies had been delivered as well. Eventually, nearly three million Allied soldiers were equipped, trained, and prepared. The undertaking was tremendous, but the outcome was hardly assured. In fact, the chances of success against Hitler's forces defending the impressive Atlantic Wall, as the Dieppe raid seemed to prove, were slim. If the Allies failed to maintain surprise and the landings were defeated with heavy casualties as at Dieppe, it would take another year to prepare and launch a second invasion, providing the Germans even more time to improve their already impressive defenses. Eisenhower knew he had only one chance to get it right.

After more than two years of planning and preparation, Operation *Overlord* was ready to begin. The invasion was initially scheduled for May 1, 1944. Eisenhower subsequently determined additional troops and landing craft were needed and D-Day was shifted to June 5, 1944.

On June 4, 1944, at 2 a.m., Eisenhower was briefed that the weather report for June 5 was dire. One of the worst storms in 20 years was pummeling the Channel. The forecast called for high winds and huge waves. The weather officer predicted that if a landing were attempted on June 5, many of the landing craft would be swamped; there would be little chance of accurate naval gunfire support and scant probability of air operations. The invasion could be postponed to June 6, or June 19, but no other dates between June 6 and 19 had the required moon and tide requirements. Eisenhower listened, asked the advice of his senior commanders, and decided to cancel the invasion for the morning of June 5. At 4 a.m. on June 5, Eisenhower would receive the crucial weather forecast briefing and be faced with the fateful decision on whether to "go" or "not go" on June 6.

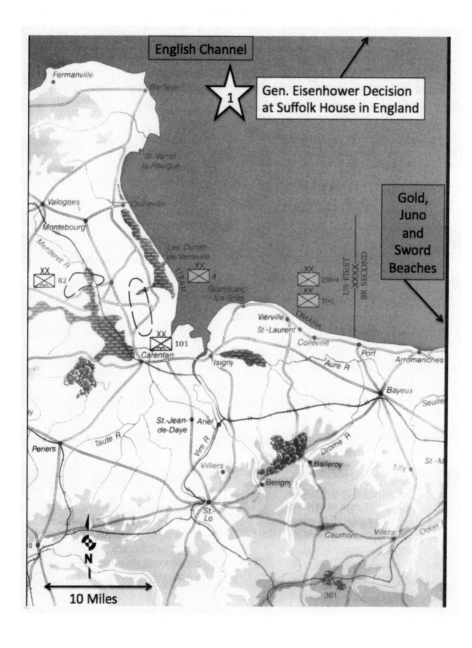

CHAPTER I

Making the Decision

Leadership

"The one quality that can be developed by studious
reflection and practice is leadership."
General Dwight D. Eisenhower

"Never take counsel of fear."
General Thomas J. "Stonewall" Jackson

The weather was foul. Everyone was in a dark mood. The man seated at the head of the table took a deep drag from a cigarette. He was smoking too much these days and getting too little sleep. Maybe that's why he looked older than his 53 years. He did not worry much about himself. Mostly, he opined about the weather.

The weather in May had been beautiful, with clear skies over the French coast. His forces were ready, but last minute changes to the plan involving Utah Beach required more landing craft and the decision to launch the invasion was postponed to June. The weather in June had turned miserable. It had rained every day. He had postponed the invasion once already. Initially planned for June 5, the weather forecast he was issued on June 4 was so terrible that he was forced to postpone the invasion in the hope of better conditions. The weather prediction for June 5 turned out to be true. The seas were so rough that day that many of the Allied ships had to seek safe harbors for fear of being swamped. Timing in war is everything, and everything was coming down to this moment and his decision.

People doubted that he could do what he had been asked to do. Some of those people were sitting at the table with him and some were waiting in the wings. The previous day, June 4, he had briefed the leader of the Free French Forces in exile, General Charles de Gaulle. The dour Frenchman lectured him for an hour about the miscalculations of the invasion plans. He listened patiently but put these doubts aside. His mission was clear: "You will enter the continent of Europe and, in conjunction with the other united nations, undertake operations aimed at the heart of Germany and the destruction of her armed forces."[1]

He mulled over in his mind the words he would use if his plan failed. "Our landings in the Cherbourg-Havre area have failed to gain a satisfactory foothold and I have withdrawn the troops. My decision to attack at this time and place was based on the best information available. The troops, the air and the Navy did all that bravery and devotion to duty could do. If any blame or fault attaches to the attempt, it is mine alone."[2]

The air was damp with moisture. Outside the building, a hard, driving rain assailed the glass windows of Southwick House, an elegant three-story English manor located north of Portsmouth in Hampshire, England. Southwick House served as the advanced command post of the Supreme Headquarters Allied Expeditionary Forces (SHAEF), providing space for the operations staff and for meetings of the senior commanders and staff. Spartan living quarters were located nearby. The Supreme Commander lived in a specially designed trailer and his staff slept in prefabricated metal Quonset huts or tents. As the principal Allied headquarters, SHAEF coordinated the immense duties of inter-service and inter-Allied policy, plans, and operations to prosecute the war against Nazi Germany.

The time was 4 a.m., Monday, June 5, 1944. The leaders were assembled in the library of Southwick House. A fierce storm, with near hurricane winds and drenching rain, beat against manor's roof and walls. If the invasion were to take place on June 6, Eisenhower had to make the decision in the next few minutes.

Eisenhower sat at the head of a long rectangular table in the library, flanked by his subordinate commanders. Behind him was a hearth with a glowing fire; on the mantel, a clock continued to tick the seconds by, accentuating the intensity of the moment and adding to the pressure.

Two US soldiers stood guard outside the room, each armed with a .45-caliber Thompson submachine gun. The tension was as thick as the armor of a German Tiger tank.

At the table, to Eisenhower's right, was Lieutenant General Omar Bradley, Commander in Chief, First US Army Group; Admiral Sir Bertram H. Ramsay, Allied Naval Commander in Chief, Expeditionary Force; and Air Chief Marshal Sir Arthur W. Tedder, Deputy Supreme Commander, Expeditionary Force. At his left was General Sir Bernard L. Montgomery, Commander in Chief, 21st Army Group; Air Chief Marshal Sir Trafford Leigh-Mallory, Allied Air Commander, Expeditionary Force; and Lieutenant General Walter Bedell Smith, Eisenhower's chief of staff. According to Smith, "All the commanders were there when General Eisenhower arrived, trim in his tailored battle jacket, his face tense with the gravity of the decision which lay before him. Field Marshal Montgomery wore his inevitable baggy corduroy trousers and sweatshirt. Admiral Ramsay and his chief of staff were immaculate in navy blue and gold." The chief meteorologist was standing, facing Eisenhower and ready to brief. A slight smile crossed his lips. "I think we have found a gleam of hope for you, sir."

The weather briefing lasted for 15 minutes.

"So, what you are telling me, Stagg, is that we *may* have a brief period of barely tolerable weather?" Eisenhower responded.

Group Captain James M. Stagg, Operation *Overlord*'s senior weather adviser, nodded. Stagg had served in the Royal Air Force in the 1930s but was a civilian weatherman recruited to help plan for Operation *Overload*. Due to a disagreement between the US and British over Dr. Stagg's non-military status, Stagg was converted to the rank of group captain, Royal Air Force Volunteer Reserve. In a previous briefing, Stagg had explained to Eisenhower that the decision to "go" would be made on the meteorological advice given three days before D-Day (D-3). Stagg knew that the necessary operational orders would have to be issued on D-2, and that once the movement was begun, no postponement would be possible after D-1. "Yes sir," Captain Stagg replied in a heavy Scottish accent, looking down at the latest weather report in his hand. "Atmospheric surface pressure is rising steadily. This indicates a forecast of a window of marginal weather for the Normandy coast for at least 18 hours, possibly as long as 24 hours, on June 6. Wind swells in the Channel at 5–6 feet, decreasing to 3–4 feet with 3–4-foot wind waves near the invasion beaches. The weather on June 7 remains uncertain."

"How firm is your forecast?" General Montgomery asked.

"Very firm, sir," Stagg replied, "but not all the SHAEF meteorologists agree with me."

"And the waves will permit us to get the landing craft to shore?" General Bradley added.

"The morning will be fair," Stagg said. "Good weather may last through the afternoon."

"Only 18 hours?" Eisenhower inquired.

"Yes, sir. I can predict 18 hours of marginal weather from midnight on the 5th of June to the evening of the 6th of June with accuracy," Stagg answered, standing firm. "Twenty-four hours if we are lucky, but no more than 18 hours."

"Marginal weather?" Air Chief Marshal Tedder interjected. "Eighteen hours?"

"It's the best forecast I can offer," Stagg replied nervously. "There is a brief improvement in the conditions. The storm front is moving faster than we originally expected. The tide and wave swells are within margin, but cloud coverage could impede bombers from seeing their targets."

"If you decide to go on Tuesday, June 6, we will have to give the order to the Omaha and Utah beach forces in the next half hour," Admiral Ramsay added. Ramsay was in command of over 5,000 vessels involved in the invasion, ranging from naval combatants, landing craft and ships, naval auxiliaries, to merchant vessels. He clearly understood the time-and-space factors involved in maneuvering such a large and diverse naval force. "As you know, the Americans have the farthest to go."

Eisenhower knew that Ramsay was right. The specific planning requirements for the invasion at Normandy offered only 10 days a month for a successful amphibious landing. The Germans knew the invasion was imminent, although they did not know the exact time and location. General Erwin Rommel, one of Germany's finest generals and the man in charge of the German defenses in Normandy, had been improving the defenses of the Atlantic Wall all along the coast of continental Europe and Scandinavia. Rommel had increased the construction of German fortifications and ordered thousands of cleverly designed anti-invasion obstacles sown on every available landing beach. Rommel had guessed that the Allies would land in high tide and had rigged thousands of beach obstacles with deadly Teller mines. These devices were antitank mines, but they also served as excellent anti-landing craft mines. Each 20-pound Teller mine was loaded with 11 pounds of explosives. At high tide, the boats would not see the submerged obstacles and, if they hit a mine, the landing craft would be blown out of the water. Many of these Teller mines also had anti-handling devices that would explode the device if Allied engineers tried to disarm them. Eisenhower's planners learned about the beach obstacles and determined that they had to be mitigated. They planned for the landings at low tide, to permit Allied landing craft commanders the ability to identify and circumvent these deadly beach obstacles.

The low tide for the Normandy beaches occurred in the spring and then only for a few days each month. If these small windows were not used for the invasion, then the casualties from the beach obstacles alone could spell doom for the Allied landing forces.

"We have nearly a quarter of a million men on ships, landing craft, airfields, and naval embarkation points," Lieutenant General Walter Bedell Smith, Eisenhower's chief of staff, offered. "We can't keep them waiting indefinitely. And the longer we wait, the more likely the Germans will discover our plan. The next time the moon and tide will be right will be on the 19th of June."

Eisenhower nodded. These initial invasion troops were just the tip of the spear to penetrate Hitler's Atlantic Wall. Nearly three million men were under arms in southern England. With so many troops quartered on the island awaiting word of the invasion, security was a major concern. German spies and reconnaissance flights were active. So far, Eisenhower believed that the Germans did not know the time or location of the invasion. Another postponement might negate that surprise.

Long ago, Eisenhower had earned the nickname "Ike." He preferred being called Ike; it set people at ease. He had a knack for getting along with people of dissimilar temperaments. This was certainly the case among the Allied leaders. Ike realized that he had to play a role to bring people together, not tear them apart. Disarming people with his genial manner was part of his style. Patience was his most powerful virtue. There was enough happening in a world at war that was upsetting. He never wanted an impetuous attitude to inhibit his leadership and his ability to influence the team to work together to accomplish the assigned mission.

Ike knew that if the weather in the Channel was too rough, then many of his landing craft might sink. Should he postpone the invasion in hope of better weather? It was a very difficult decision and his decision alone. As the Supreme Allied Commander, he would take sole responsibility for the outcome of the attack, but he also demanded that his senior officers speak their minds. These were the best military, naval, and air force leaders of their respective services and nations. He understood that he was leading a coalition of nations and the points of view of their key leaders had to be considered. This was not the Soviet Union or Nazi Germany, where one leader would make the decision, seldom ask for advice, and expect to be blindly obeyed. The opinions of these men mattered to him. The code name of the invasion may have been *Overlord*, but Ike was keen not to "Lord Over" anyone.

Ike knew the fate of the invasion was in his hands. He knew that he would have to roll the dice, make his play, and, if he chose wrongly, thousands would die. A bloody failure of the invasion of France could set back the war for years. By then, who knows what evil new weapons the Nazis might create. There was already intelligence evidence of a new, long-range missile program, dubbed *Vergeltungswaffen* or "vengeance weapons" by the Germans. There were also credible reports that Nazi scientists were developing a new kind of bomb, more powerful that anything the world had ever seen. If the invasion failed and the Germans could marry their missile program with a new powerful means of destruction, then the war might be prolonged for decades— or worse, be lost. General George C. Marshall, the US Chief of Staff of the Armed Forces in Washington, D.C. and the right-hand military man for President Franklin Roosevelt, had sent an officer to brief Ike about a secret project called "Manhattan" and fears that the Nazis might use "radioactive toxins" against Ike's invasion force. He was worried about the possibility of the Nazis using chemical agents, such as chlorine or mustard gas, as had been employed on the battlefields of World War I. If the Germans gassed his men on the beachheads, then casualties would be horrendous. To add to these concerns, the top-secret Ultra intelligence intercepts that allowed the Allied leaders to read the Germans' strategic command messages had detected movement of the German 91st Division into the 82nd Airborne's drop zone. Was this coincidence, or did the Germans know the invasion was coming to Normandy?

In short, Ike had a significant list of troubling information to consider.

Every general at the table looked at Ike, waiting for a decision. The clock ticked. Ike put on his best poker face. Normally, he worked hard to appear optimistic in the presence of his generals and the troops. Their load was heavy enough and he knew that he did not need to add to it by brooding, being depressed, or showing hesitation. Ike understood that both optimism and pessimism are infectious. He believed that they spread more rapidly from the higher echelons of command downward than in any other direction. If he leaned either way, too optimistic or too pessimistic, then he might influence his generals. Right now, he wanted their personal and clear assessments.

"Sir, I can speak for the airborne forces," Air Commander Trafford Leigh-Mallory, the commander responsible for transporting the British and American paratroopers for Operation *Overlord*, announced. "In this weather, we can expect heavy casualties."

"How heavy?" Ike asked.

"I estimate our losses could be as high as 75 percent in the 101st and 82nd Airborne Divisions," Mallory said without flinching.

Several of the officers sitting at the table sat back in their chairs. Air Marshal Tedder shook his head and looked down at the table as if seeing the dead bodies of the young men laid out in front of him. If the decision was made to go, then the plan called for the landing of over 13,100 paratroopers, most of them behind Utah Beach. Seventy percent casualties meant the deaths, incapacitation or capture of at least 9,750 of the Allies' best soldiers.

"Maybe you should cancel the para-drops," Tedder offered.

"Sir, with all due respect to the Air Marshal, I need those troops dropped behind Utah Beach," Lieutenant General Omar Bradley, Commander in Chief, First US Army Group, in command of all US forces landing on Omaha and Utah, announced. The paratroopers from the 101st and 82nd Airborne Divisions were scheduled to drop at night, five hours before the first Utah sea-borne landings. These para and glider troops were to fight their way toward the beach and clear the Germans from their prepared positions along the beach exits. "If the paratroopers don't drop to stop the Germans from moving armor and reinforcements to the beachheads, then they could smash Utah Beach and drive us into the Channel."

Ike listened intently, considered the faces of the six prestigious leaders seated at the table, but knew he had no choice, 75 percent casualties or not; Bradley was right. The success of the landings depended on the paratroopers stopping the Germans from reinforcing the beaches. Massing combat power was the critical factor. Utah was divided from the rest of the four beachheads by the Douve estuary. Utah, the beach furthest to the west, was the right flank of the invasion and the most vulnerable to counterattack. Most importantly, the 4th Infantry Division that was scheduled to land at Utah had the critical task of attacking toward Cherbourg to secure its vital deepwater port, as expeditiously as possible. If the Germans counterattacked Utah in force, and the paratroops were not there to block the German attack, then the landing could fail. The Germans could then roll up the other beachheads one at a time. If the risk of the airborne drops was high, it was a risk that had to be taken.

The invasion plan called for Allied ground forces to secure five beachheads along a 20-mile stretch of the Normandy coast. Gold and Sword were British. Juno was to be invaded by Canadian forces. Omaha and Utah were the American targets. The most western beachhead, Utah, located between the French villages of Pouppeville and La Madeleine, was the right flank anchor of the Allied offensive and separated from the other beachheads by the Douve River estuary. Sword, Juno, Gold, and Omaha beaches were nearly contiguous. Utah was dangling out on the western flank all by itself and ripe for a German counterattack, if the Germans could act swiftly. The paratroopers had the mission to seize key villages, positions, and road junctions to stop any German counterattack long enough for the 4th Infantry Division to establish itself on Utah. Then, the invasion forces would link up with the airborne troops and move inland to take key objectives that would guard the flank of the Allied invasion forces.

The operation that Ike was about to decide was the most complicated and daunting attack of the war. The written plan, the "Overlord Operations Order," had more words than Hemingway's 1940 novel, *For Whom the Bell Tolls*. The decision of where and when to invade Hitler's *Festung Europa* (Fortress Europe) involved a multitude of calculations, any one of which would impact the lives of countless thousands and quite possibly the fate of the war itself. In addition to their beach defenses and static forces manning these defenses, the Germans had 13 combat divisions in the vicinity of Normandy and an additional 44 divisions in northern France, Belgium, and the Netherlands to move against the Allied invasion.

Despite the beachhead defenses and the supporting mobile forces the Germans could throw at the invaders after they landed, Ike was planning to win. The Allies had several significant advantages over the defenders.

First, the Allies had complete naval supremacy of the English Channel and could dominate both the French coast and many miles inland with naval gunfire. The Germans had scattered their few ships and U-boats to escape roving Allied aircraft to more distant ports. Second, the Allies had gained absolute air supremacy over the entire *Overlord* area. The Luftwaffe had been badly crippled in the months prior to June 1944 in fierce air battles and had moved its aircraft deep into France and Germany to avoid total destruction by Allied fighters and bombers.

Ike knew that the success of the invasion depended on securing the initial landings and quickly moving inland to seize the nearest ports. There are few military operations as complex as an amphibious invasion, especially on this large a scale. The naval forces' mission included numerous tasks, including clearing the English Channel of German water mines, bombarding the German defenses, clearing the beach approaches of anti-landing craft obstacles, and then delivering the invasion force using hundreds of landing craft of various sizes. The Allied air forces had the task of maintaining air superiority over the debarkation ports, fleet, and beachheads, bombing the beach defenses, and interdicting German supply lines and routes of transportation. The ground forces had to plan for the landing of infantry, tanks, and engineers against well-prepared defenses where the Allied forces would be initially outnumbered and very vulnerable to counterattack and defeat.

To plan against German countermoves and to ensure a continuous flow of supplies, ammunition, and equipment to the invasion forces, the Allies planned on capturing the port of Cherbourg by D+15. Just in case Cherbourg was too hard a nut to crack, Allied engineers had created two massive concrete floating harbors, codenamed Mulberry, to establish ports off the US and British beaches. These Mulberries were the brainchild of British civil engineer-inventors and championed by the British Prime Minister, Winston Churchill. The *Overlord* plan called for the reinforcement of the five beachheads with an additional 500,000 combat troops and 100,000 vehicles ashore within 15 days of the initial landings.

To mask the *Overlord* operation from their German foe, the Allies had crafted and executed an elaborate deception plan, Operation *Bodyguard*, to deceive the Germans, and specifically Adolf Hitler, as to the timing, size, and location of the Allied invasion. The deception plan was designed to make the Germans believe that the Allied invasion would be launched from the Strait of Dover at the Pas-de-Calais, the closest point between England and France. At the Pas-de-Calais, the distance from England to France was only 21 miles. The Germans believed US Army General George S. Patton was the Allies' best general, and thus assumed he would command the Allied invasion of France. Instead, Patton had been put in command of the fictitious First United States Army Group consisting of fake troop units, rubber tanks, phony camps, and an actual radio network that generated thousands of false radio messages to phantom formations. German spies were caught and turned into double agents to feed misinformation to the Nazi high command. The deception plan seemed to be working, as the powerful German Fifteenth Army, the strongest German defenses, and the largest reserve forces were positioned in the Pas-de-Calais area.

The Allied plan was complex, detailed, and sophisticated. Very little had been left to chance. *Overlord* had been in the making for several years and involved an intense military—as well as political—debate among the Allied powers. The marshaling of the invasion force, shipping, equipment, and supplies had taken years of preparation. The location and date of the invasion required intense study of the moonlight conditions, cloud cover, tides, winds, waves, beach conditions, access to ports, and the employment of land, air, and sea forces. The mission had to remain secret and hidden from the Germans—an extremely difficult task, with thousands of planners involved in some aspect of *Overlord*. If the Germans discovered the time and location of the invasion, then they could mass their forces and crush the Allied attack. Ike knew that he had to get it right the first time, as there might not be a second chance. It is an understatement to say that it took a very high degree of leadership to orchestrate this mighty endeavor.

The weather, however, was beyond the control of mortal man.

"I agree with Bradley," Ike replied, looking at the Air Marshal. "It's not an easy decision to make, and I don't like it, but when we decide to go, the paratroopers must drop as planned."

"I concur," added General Sir Bernard Montgomery, Commander in Chief, 21st Army Group. "It should be all or nothing."

"Well, then, I guess it is all up to whether we can put our trust in Captain Stagg's weather report?" Admiral Sir Bertram H. Ramsay, Allied Naval Commander in Chief, Expeditionary Force, proclaimed. "I've seen these Channel storms change in the blink of an eye. If the swell is too much, our landing craft will be swamped and capsize. Can we really bet the entire invasion on this weather report?"

The room was silent.

"Thank you, Stagg. You've done your best," Ike announced.

Stagg nodded and exited the room.

It was time for a decision. With the hint of a wry smile, Ike held up his hand. "Gentlemen, please give me your advice. Go or no?"

Admiral Ramsay answered first. "I was against this earlier, but am prepared to resume the operation as planned. The weather is not what I prefer."

"I say go," General Montgomery offered without hesitation. "If Ramsay can get us there, we can do the rest. We must blast our way on shore and get a good lodgment before the enemy can bring sufficient reserves to turn us out. I would say, go!"

"Conditions are marginal. I am not happy with this," Air Marshal Leigh-Mallory answered. "I say delay the invasion."

Ike reached for the pack of cigarettes in his pocket. He took one and lit it with the stub of his previous cigarette that was nearly burned out in his hand.

Air Marshal Tedder was next. He looked at Leigh-Mallory, then at Ike. "Too chancy. We should delay."

General Bradley spoke next. "Go."

General Smith then answered, "It's a gamble, but a good gamble. Go."

Ike nodded, paused, and then looked at the clock. Taking in the scene, he understood the gravity of the situation. Three of his senior officers offered a "go." Ramsay was hesitant. Leigh-Mallory and Tedder, his two leaders who commanded the air operations, would prefer to postpone in hope of better weather. He had to carefully consider their counsel, as the air operation was as key to the success of *Overlord* as the naval and land operations. Of all the British officers present, only Montgomery was fully ready to go.

Ike stood up and turned to the six men at the table. All looked up at him, waiting for the decision. Ike warmed himself at the fire for a moment and then paced the room in silence.

The silence lasted for five full minutes.

He thought about the letter he would write if the invasion failed. He thought about the thousands of brave paratroopers who would jump from C-47 transport planes in the dark. He thought about the young men who would storm the beaches into withering German fire. He reweighed every argument for and against in his mind.

He did not take counsel of his fears.

"Okay," he said. "Let's go."

The tension in the room instantly evaporated. Ike's six senior officers cheered and immediately exited the library for their respective commands. The room grew silent as the officers exited. Eisenhower was left all alone. He sat down on a sofa at one end of the room. The soul-raking decision was taken. Now, it was in the hands of the young leaders and troops.

He kept busy all day with orders and then moved out to visit the troops. At approximately 8:30 p.m., June 5, just hours before the paratroopers of the American 101st Airborne Division were about to take off for their drop zones in Normandy, Ike visited the 502nd Parachute Infantry Regiment (PIR) at Greenham Common airfield, southeast of Newbury, Berkshire, just 55 miles west of London. Ike walked among the paratroopers, hoping to cheer them up, but discovered instead that they lifted his morale. These paratroopers were elite soldiers and were eager to go. Walking among these young, fit warriors, their faces blackened with charcoal, Ike saw no hesitation in their eyes. Photos were taken. The men gathered around him. He asked them where they were from and bantered a few jokes back and forth. He spent some time with one of the officers he had served with before the war, Lieutenant Colonel Robert G. Cole, the commander of the 3rd Battalion, 502nd PIR, and wished

The Supreme Commander, General Dwight D. Eisenhower, gives the order of the day, "Full victory—nothing else," to 1Lt. Wallace C. Strobel and men of Company E, 502nd Parachute Infantry Regiment (PIR), at the 101st Airborne Division's camp at Greenham Common, England, June 5, 1944, just hours before these men were to board C-47 transport aircraft to conduct a night-time combat parachute drop over Normandy, France, to kick-off the invasion of Nazi-held Europe. (NARA NWDNS-111-SC-194399)

him and his men good luck. No one could have known at the time, but the 502nd PIR jumped into Normandy with 792 paratroopers. After the Normandy fighting, when the 502nd was relieved and sent back to England on June 29, 216 men had been killed, a staggering 27 percent attrition rate.

After conversing with Cole and the troops, Ike traveled back to his trailer near Southwick House. Just after midnight, in the early hours of June 6, as the paratroopers were jumping over Normandy and the seaborne forces were heading toward the beaches, Ike sent an "Eyes Only" message to General Marshall:

> The weather yesterday which was [the] original date selected was impossible all along the target coast. Today conditions are vastly improved both by sea and air

The Pathfinders were the first to parachute into Hitler's Fortress Europe and were therefore considered the bravest of the brave. In this photo, a "stick" of US Army Pathfinders and USAAF flight crew stand in front of a C-47 Skytrain at RAF North Witham Airfield in Lincolnshire, England, prior to D-Day, June 1944. Each C-47 carried a stick of paratroopers. A "stick" was the term used by the military for the paratroopers carried in each C-47 and, on D-Day, consisted of anywhere from 12 to 19 paratroopers. Although the C-47 might take as many as 28 paratroopers on a training jump, the number of combat-loaded paratroopers in a "stick" on the D-Day jump was determined by the weight of each paratrooper and the distance the aircraft was expected to fly. (Wikimedia, Owen 1985)

and we have the prospect of at least reasonable favorable weather for the next several days. Yesterday, I visited British troops about to embark and last night saw a great portion of a United States airborne division just prior to its takeoff. The enthusiasm and obvious fitness of every single man were high and the light of battle was in their eyes. I will keep you informed.

Ike turned to his cot, laid down, and tried to catch an hour's rest. He knew that June 6, 1944 would be the Longest Day.

★ ★ ★

Leadership Lesson

Leadership is the art of influence. Eisenhower influenced the finest minds available to plan and direct the invasion. These were the best leaders and staff experts of their respective disciplines, branches of service, and nations. Their thoughts mattered to Eisenhower and he listened carefully to each of his advisors, taking stock of their guidance, opinions, and fears. Eisenhower believed in "diversity in counsel and unity in command," meaning that while he sought the counsel of others, he always intended to maintain control over the final decision. As Supreme Commander, he shouldered the awesome responsibility of the lives of every man and woman in the invasion force. He made sure that everyone knew that he would use every bit of advice and information his commanders and staff could provide him, but that when the decision was made, it would be his decision. Ike hastily wrote a note and put it in his pocket with the words that he would issue if the invasion failed. In that letter, he took full responsibility. That was the kind of leader Eisenhower was. (See Appendix C: Eisenhower's "In Case of Failure" note.)

It would have been perfectly understood if Eisenhower had delayed the decision to launch D-Day and waited for better weather. Making tough decisions with imperfect information is something all of us will face. In business, fortunes are won or lost because CEOs cannot decide in time. Eisenhower had more than fortunes involved in his decision; he had the lives of hundreds of thousands of people and the fate of the free world in his hands. If he had decided to delay, the next best day predicted was June 19. That date turned out to be the worst gale in a century and would have destroyed any invasion fleet of small landing craft as much as the kamikaze winds had destroyed the great Mongol invasion fleet of Japan in 1281. If the invasion were postponed until July 1944, then the Germans would have had more time to prepare and might have discovered the invasion plans. German Field Marshal Erwin Rommel would have sown more mines on the beaches and emplaced more anti-invasion obstacles. By July 1944, the Germans would have had plenty of V-1 rockets to launch at the invasion fleet, and by September they would have had the newer, more powerful V-2 rockets, ready to blast the invasion ports. If D-Day were delayed even longer the fall weather might have forced the invasion to be postponed until the early months of 1945. By then, Adolf Hitler might have developed an atomic bomb.

Eisenhower, therefore, had to make a decision based on the best information he had at the time. His leadership influenced everyone around him to give his or her very best efforts. His powers of persuasion were seldom equaled. His confidence influenced every member of his team, encouraging them to believe that the invasion would succeed. He always took his job seriously, but never took himself seriously. He didn't shine, he reflected, and always gave the credit to others. This inspired people to follow him. His courage influenced others to have courage. During the D-Day planning, passions ran high because the stakes were extreme, and there were many leaders with grave concerns that the weather or other factors would wreck the invasion, but Eisenhower's leadership made them all pull together as a team. That is a sterling example of leadership. What can you learn from Eisenhower's story of the decision to "go" on D-Day in your life? How can you apply Eisenhower's steady influence, listening skills and ability to think and reflect on what others are reporting to make better leadership decisions?

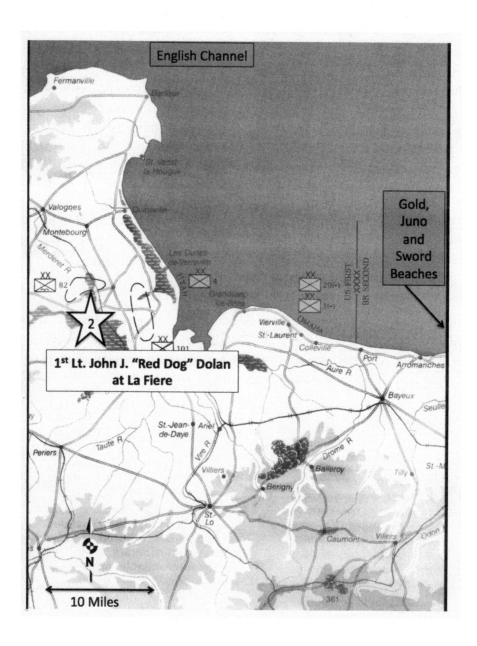

English Channel

Fermanville

Barfleur

St.-Vaast-
la-Hougue

Valognes

Ourneville

Montebourg

Merderet R.

Les Dunes-
de-Varreville

UTAH

4

Grandcamp-
les-Bains

XX 82

XX 101

2

1st Lt. John J. "Red Dog" Dolan
at La Fiere

XX 29(+)

XX 1(+)

US FIRST

XXXX

BR SECOND

Vierville

St.-Laurent

Colleville

OMAHA

Port

Aure R.

Arromanches

Bayeux

Seulle

Gold,
Juno
and
Sword
Beaches

St.-Jean-
de-Daye

Ariel

Taute R.

Vire R.

Drome R.

St.-M

Periers

Villiers

Balleroy

Tilly

Berigny

St.-
Lo

Caumont

Villers

Odon

N

361

10 Miles

CHAPTER 2

Taking and Holding the Bridge at La Fiére

Selflessness

"Soldiers, Sailors and Airmen of the Allied Expeditionary Force!
You are about to embark upon the Great Crusade, toward which we have striven
these many months. The eyes of the world are upon you. The hopes and prayers
of liberty-loving people everywhere march with you…"
Excerpt from General Dwight D. Eisenhower's Order of the Day
for the Invasion of Normandy, June 6, 1944

"Casualties to glider troops would be 90 percent before they ever reached the ground.
The killed and wounded among the paratroopers would be 75 percent."
Operation Overlord's *British air commander, Sir Trafford Leigh-Mallory in a*
conversation with General Eisenhower before the D-Day invasion.

First Lieutenant John J. "Red Dog" Dolan, the commander of A
Company, 1st Battalion, 505th Parachute Infantry Regiment, 82nd
Airborne Division, sat on a bench-seat inside a C-47 that was waiting to
take off from the airfield at RAF Spanhoe Airfield, in Northamptonshire,
England. The jump door of the C-47 had been removed and he was able
to see the endless line of C-47s taxiing in columns on the runway. The
sun had set and the sky was turning from gray to black. From his vantage
point, he could see a dozen C-47s just like his, filled with paratroopers
heading into the uncertainty of combat. He knew that hundreds of other
C-47s would soon be in the air, headed toward Normandy and their
rendezvous with Hitler's forces.

As he looked out the door, one of the C-47s opposite his aircraft suddenly exploded in a bright light and a loud blast. Stunned, he tried to understand what had happened. He recognized that the aircraft was from the battalion's headquarters company. The aircraft burst into flames and spun to the right, sliding off the landing field, as figures, some on fire, jumped out of the wreck and onto the tarmac.[1] A second huge explosion occurred as ammunition inside the aircraft cooked-off in a horrendous blast. The aircraft shuddered to a halt, broken and engulfed in black smoke. Dolan looked back at his men. The 18 paratroopers in his "stick" asked what had happened, some anxiously looking out the window. Dolan saw dead bodies scattered on the ground as his airplane passed the burning wreckage. The aircraft kept to the plan, inspite of the accident, and maintained the strict take-off schedule. "We're on our way to war," Dolan answered. "Be ready for anything."

Dolan shook his head and said a silent prayer for the poor bastards aboard the burning plane. Nothing could stop the invasion now, but it was a hell of an inauspicious start. His aircraft picked up speed and took off, followed in trail by many others.

A total of 821 Troop Carrier C-47s from the IX Troop Carrier Command prepared, loaded, and took off from 17 separate airfields in England. They conformed to an exact timetable that would launch each flight into the air, allow the pilots time to assemble in groups, and then move out in tight formation to each of their key coordination points. Each formation would fly in a "V of Vs," consisting of three planes in triangular Vs arranged in a larger V of nine planes. These formations followed a flight path that would take them over the invasion fleet, then west through the "back door," and finally across the Cotentin Peninsula from the southwest to reach their designated Drop Zones (DZ). This route was expected to surprise the Germans and protect the force from friendly fire. In Sicily, during Operation *Husky* in 1943, a flight of C-47s of the 82nd Airborne Division flew directly over the Allied fleet, as planned. The Navy and Coast Guard, however, did not get the word. Having been bombed by German planes earlier in the day, they were edgy and did not know that American planes would fly overhead just before dark. When they saw the unannounced aircraft, they opened up with everything they had and shredded the formations of C–47s carrying the 504th PIR, causing one of the worst friendly fire incidents of the war. Dolan hoped that would not happen today.

Dolan checked his watch. It was just past 10:30 p.m., British double-daylight savings time, which meant that nightfall was very late each evening. The sky darkened as his aircraft surged upward. The D-Day planners had decided that a night jump would save lives by decreasing the effectiveness of German flak and intervention by the Luftwaffe. As far as Dolan was concerned, that was fine. Dolan was a veteran of combat in Sicily and Italy and was used to night jumps. His men were well trained. Many of them had jumped with him at night, and he possessed a quiet confidence that he and his men could handle any situation.

Still, the explosion on the airfield was unnerving. What would the next 72 hours bring? Would he even live to know?

C–47 aircraft filled with Pathfinders from the 101st and 82nd Airborne Divisions preceded the main airborne invasion force. Twenty American C–47s of the IXth Troop Carrier Command Pathfinders Group took off at around 10 p.m. on June 5 from their base of North Witham, near Grantham, England. Their targets were Sainte-Mère-Église for the 82nd Airborne and Sainte-Marie-du-Mont for the 101st Airborne. These aircraft carried more than 200 Pathfinder paratroopers who had been expertly trained to be the vanguard of the invasion. They would jump into Normandy first to light the drop zones for the follow-on formations. These Pathfinders were critical to the success of the airborne mission. If the Pathfinders could not land, set up their Eureka light sets, and mark the drop zones before the main flights arrived, then the transport pilots would not know where to drop their sticks.

The main formations of the 101st and 82nd would follow the Pathfinders. The 82nd Airborne parachute elements were transported in 10 serials with a total of 369 aircraft. The 101st parachute units were transported in 432 aircraft to drop paratroopers over three regimental-sized DZs just behind Utah Beach. The route of the airborne invasion would take the massive formations of C–47s over the English town of Portland Bill, then southwest over the Channel, and then turn 90 degrees to enter the "back door" of Normandy, cross the Cotentin

This map depicts the airborne drop zones planned for the 82nd Airborne Division and 101st Airborne Division on the Cotentin Peninsula, Normandy, on D-Day, June 6, 1944. (CMH Map)

Peninsula near La-Haye-du-Puits, and head to their designated DZs. Dolan's DZ was "Drop Zone O" near Sainte-Mère-Église.

The formation of C-47s flew low over the English Channel to avoid detection by German radar and was guided by a series of beacon ships that were posted at strategic locations on the flight route. After the formation reached the last beacon ship, the C-47s climbed to higher altitude to avoid the flak located on the Channel Islands. The sky over the Channel became a dark purple. Earlier, in the waning dusk, Dolan observed the shadowy outline of hundreds of ships below him. They were a stirring testimony to the power of the great Allied invasion fleet that was sailing toward the coast of Normandy.

The powerful American air armada consisted of 821 Douglas C-47 Skytrains, a militarized version of the civilian DC-3 passenger plane. The C-47 Skytrain, nicknamed the "Gooney-Bird" by the Americans and the "Dakota" by the British, was the workhorse of the Allied air forces and the primary aircraft for delivering paratroopers over enemy territory. Dependable and versatile, the C-47 used two 1,200 horsepower Pratt & Whitney R-1830 radial engines, with three-blade propellers, to carry a payload of nearly 6,000 pounds almost 1,600 miles.

This capability came at a cost. The planes were not armed and relied on fighter escorts for their defense if they encountered enemy fighter planes. Unlike many fighter and bomber aircraft in the Allied air forces, the C-47 did not have self-sealing gas tanks. Enemy antiaircraft rounds could penetrate the thin skin of the C-47 as if it were made of paper, and if the gas tanks were hit, the high-octane aviation fuel would violently explode. The slow speed, low altitude, and the tight formations required to accurately drop paratroopers *en masse* on a relatively open and clear drop zone made these aircraft sitting ducks for enemy flak gunners. To enhance the survivability of the planes, *Overlord* planners were relying on a night-time airborne operation.

The aircraft could carry as many as 26 paratroopers on a training jump, but this was no training exercise. The D-Day C-47s were so over-weight with combat-loaded paratroopers that the number of jumpers was reduced to 15 or 18 per plane, depending on the weight of additional equipment. Many pilots worried about the excess load. They weighed each paratrooper before he entered their C-47, and then checked or reworked their flight-fuel-distance calculations. Each pilot knew that he had to make the run over Normandy, drop their paratroopers and equipment, and get back to England without delay, or risk ditching in the cold waters of the English Channel.

Pilots had to fly by vision alone, as there were no electronic aids for night formation, other than small wing and tail-lights. To maintain formation, pilots used the moonlight to see the faint blue lights of the aircraft to their front and flanks, or followed the glow of the other aircrafts' engine exhaust stacks and flame dampeners. If the formation hit clouds, the chances of a mid-air collision were high. The pilots had trained hard, in numerous night-training operations, to keep formation no matter what the flying conditions. To be able to discern friend from foe, every C-47 was adorned with newly painted invasion stripes: three white and two black stripes, each 2 feet (60cm) wide, around the fuselage behind the exit doors and from front to back on the outer wings. During the D-Day mission, the radios were set to "radio listening silence" to prevent the Germans from using their sophisticated radio listening systems to vector their deadly night fighters onto the vulnerable C-47s.

To improve the chances for success, the Allies had worked hard to remove the Luftwaffe from the equation. For nearly a year prior to D-Day, the Allied air forces had waged a strategic battle against the Luftwaffe to gain air supremacy over France and force the German air force away from any potential amphibious landing beaches. In March 1944, fully 56 percent of the available German fighters were lost, dipping to 43 percent in April (as the bomber effort switched to Germany's petroleum production), and rising again to just over 50 percent in May, on the eve of Normandy. Months of concentrated air warfare had given the Allies not only air superiority, but air supremacy as well.[2] Allied aircrew casualties to deliver this result were severe. Between April 1 and June 5, 1944, the Allied air forces flew 14,000 missions against German targets in Europe and lost nearly 12,000 airmen and 2,000 aircraft, but the Luftwaffe in the planned invasion areas was effectively destroyed. What was left of the German air forces moved farther to the east, out of the range of roaming American and British aircraft. These Luftwaffe aircraft were refocused on protecting cities inside the borders of Germany. With the Luftwaffe out of range of the Normandy beaches, a major requirement of the *Overlord* plan had been accomplished.

The Germans countered the loss of their aircraft by moving additional antiaircraft gun batteries into western France. These German "flak" units (the term "flak" is from the German *Flugabwehrkanone*, for "aircraft defense cannon") provided the only significant air defense in Normandy on D-Day. At the end of May 1944, only one anti-aircraft regiment—1st Flaksturmregiment of the III Flakkorps—was in Normandy and deployed between Isigny and Bayeux, which, unknown to the Germans, fell along the general path planned for the aircraft carrying the 82nd and 101st Airborne Divisions. Allied air planners had a good idea where the German flak units were, but did not think these units would be a significant threat to the night-time airborne drops.

As a result, the decision was made in May 1944 that heavy bombers would not precede the planes carrying the paratroopers of the 82nd and 101st Airborne to destroy any flak units. Bombers could have blasted the German antiaircraft defenses prior to the airborne drops, but there were only limited numbers of heavy bombers in the Allied air forces. It was decided to focus their efforts on bombing the beach defenses in preparation for the naval landings on the five Allied invasion beaches.

As the Pathfinder formation reached the western coastline of the Cotentin Peninsula, the pilots saw an ominous, dense cloudbank. Maintaining their course, they had no choice but to enter the cloudbank. Visibility decreased dramatically, creating exceptionally dangerous conditions for tight formation flying. As General Ridgway, the commander of the 82d Airborne Divison recalled:

> A few minutes inland, we suddenly went into cloud, thick and turbulent. I had been looking out the doorway, watching with a profound sense of satisfaction the close-ordered flight of that great sky caravan that stretched as far as the eye could see. All at once, they were blotted out. Not a wing light showed. The plane began to yaw and plunge, and in my mind's eye I could see the other pilots, fighting to hold course, knowing how great was the danger of a collision in the air.[3]

To avoid collision, driven by the inability to see the aircraft in front or to the flank, the formation began to break up. As though on cue, the Germans began firing antiaircraft machine guns and cannons at the incoming aircraft. Taking evasive action drove the transport aircraft further out of formation and caused them to stray off course. Despite these harrowing conditions, the brave pilots of the IXth Troop Carrier Command Pathfinders Group did their best to stay on their flight plans.

Dolan's aircraft crossed the French coast. When they eventually broke out of the cloudbank and flak, he could see the terrain below. The formation was only about 800 feet above the ground.

"Sound off for Equipment Check!" the jumpmaster bellowed.

The paratroopers in succession sounded off with their numbers until the final paratrooper in line shouted, "One okay!"

The jumpmaster shouted, "All okay!" and looked out the door.

Wild arcs of blue and green lights reached up from the ground and whipped through the moonlit night sky. The sight would almost be beautiful, if it were not so deadly, as the lights were tracers from German antiaircraft machine guns and cannons firing furiously upon the unarmed transport aircraft carrying the paratroopers. Wing to wing, the American aircraft flew through the dense enemy fire. A few aircraft were hit and burst into flame. Paratroopers jumped from the burning aircraft, some of them aflame, and plummeted to the ground.

German gunners looked up at the heavens in amazement as they shot furiously at hundreds of aircraft that seemed to fill the air as far as they could see. German searchlights swept their beams across the sky. The action was fast, and the planes kept coming.

"There were antiaircraft shells coming up in our direction, and our pilots took us right down on the deck," 24-year-old First Lieutenant Ray Grossman, C Battery, 456th Parachute Field Artillery Battalion, 82nd Airborne Division, recalled, referring to the night jump over Sainte-Mère-Église, "and they were making like fighter planes."

Dolan's plane took evasive action, jinking left and then right, climbing, and then diving fast to avoid enemy fire and collisions with other aircraft. Flak hit the plane like a shower of rocks against its metal skin, but the aircraft kept flying. Looking out the window, Dolan could see a C-47 on fire. The plane's engine was ablaze, and then the entire aircraft exploded. Tracers were all over the sky, streaking blue and green.

"Let's get out of here!" a paratrooper behind Dolan shouted.

"We wait for the green light," the jumpmaster replied. The C-47 was flying too fast to allow the paratroopers to exit. The heavily laden paratroopers were now standing, hooked up, and trying to keep their balance as the plane banked in the air.

Paratroopers in other aircraft observed the same chaotic spectacle. "The red warning light had been on for a few minutes, and as we came out of the cloudbank, the green light flashed on and the pilot yelled for me to get the troopers out," remembered Technical Sergeant W. E. "Bing" Wood, who was a C-47 aerial engineer during the D-Day jump. "The lieutenant's face looked ghastly in the green light as he felt my hand tap him on the shoulder. He gave a yell and sprang out the door followed by screaming, yelling troopers. The eighth or ninth trooper got stuck in the door—too much equipment, he couldn't get himself through—so I kicked him out. As soon as the last yelling trooper had gone out the door, I thumbed the mike and yelled 'All Clear' and yanked in the static cords," Woods continued. "All hell was breaking loose outside. Planes were blowing up in the air and the roar of exploding shells was deafening. The plane gave a lurch, and then headed toward the ground at an angle as the pilot stuck the nose and the left wing toward the ground to get the utmost of flying speed. At first, I thought we had been hit and was all ready to jump out the door. With one wing pointing almost directly at the ground and the throttles pushed solidly against the stops, we went barreling out as fast as the plane would go... We dropped our troopers at 2:06, right on the nose as far as time calculations.[4]

The plane came in low and fast, too fast, as "Red Dog" Dolan stood in the door waiting for the signal to jump. His nickname "Red Dog" was due to his brilliant red hair. He was from Quincy, Massachusetts, and was in college studying law when the war started. He left college and enlisted. As soon as he learned about the paratroops, he volunteered. He was a hard-nosed veteran of the fighting in Sicily and Italy with a reputation as a fighter and a proven leader.

He looked back at the men in his stick and knew they would measure up. His soldiers were a tough bunch. Able Company consisted of eight officers and 130 enlisted soldiers organized into three rifle platoons, 1st, 2nd and 3rd, and a 10-man headquarters section. He did not have an executive officer, but his first sergeant, Robert M. Matterson, was a first-rate, combat-proven noncommissioned officer. His platoon leaders were all combat veterans of Sicily and Italy and had his complete confidence and respect.

First Platoon was led by 2nd Lt. William A. Oakley. Oakley had been Brigadier General Jim Gavin's aide but requested permission to be transferred to lead a parachute rifle platoon. 2nd Platoon was led by 2nd Lt. George Wayne Presnell, and 3rd Platoon was commanded by 2nd Lt. Donald Coxon. Each platoon consisted of 40 men.

Dolan was proud of his paratroopers. They were physically fit, trained to a razor's edge, and combat ready. There was little hesitation among his men. They had trained for this mission for many months. Now, the show was on. All they wanted to do was to jump out of the aircraft and kill Nazis.

His mission was to assemble his rifle company after their jump and then seize and defend the bridge crossing the Merderet River on the D-15 road that ran from east to west from Sainte-Mère-Église. Once the bridge was seized, A Company was to block any German movement across the bridge and stop the enemy from counterattacking Sainte-Mère-Église and Utah Beach.

The C-47s of the 315th Troop Carrier Group in his serial were slightly off course, but had maintained their tight "V" formation, in spite of the vicious antiaircraft fire that greeted them. Up ahead, through the darkness, he could see a house on fire in the town that he recognized from countless hours of studying map and terrain models of Sainte-Mère-Église. He watched as a distant C-47 from another formation suddenly was riddled with tracers and exploded. More tracers shot toward his aircraft and the plane banked in reaction to the enemy fire, nearly knocking Dolan over. The green light popped on. "Go, go, go!" the jumpmaster shouted. Dolan jumped instantly, his men rapidly following him out of the door. He was never so glad to get out of a plane in his life. His parachute slammed open harder than he had ever felt before. He looked up, saw the chute fully deployed, then shifted his attention to the ground. In a second, the dark terrain was rushing up at him faster than he expected, and he hit the ground with a thud.

He slung his Thompson submachine gun over his shoulder, quickly gathered his parachute, and stowed it under a bush. The first man he linked up with was a Pathfinder who had helped light their drop zone. Dolan conferred with the Pathfinder, and in the moonlight quickly recognized the terrain and identified the D-15 road. From his study of the terrain models and maps, Dolan knew that the D-15 road ran east from Sainte-Mère-Église to the bridge at La Fiére. The La Fiére Bridge was Able Company's objective.

Dolan saw his men assembling. He posted the first men he met as security teams at the corners of a small field bordered by hedgerows. He then found one of his squad leaders and ordered him to rally the rest of the company as he surveyed the ground to determine his location. He quickly knew that the C-47 jockeys had put him and his company down in exactly the right place. One by one, the Able Company paratroopers converged on his position. Thankfully, there was no immediate enemy contact, although the sound of distant firing and explosions peppered the night air. It still took some time to assemble his men and equipment in the dark, but he had his company 90 percent accounted for in under an hour. It was just before dawn, June 6, 1944.

His leaders gathered around him. Dolan was a man of few words. When he did have something to say, his soldiers listened. They had learned to trust him both in training and in combat. Those who served with him in Sicily and Italy knew that he was an aggressive and skilled combat leader. If you wanted to stay alive, when Dolan talked, you listened.

"As you know, the landing at Utah Beach will happen in a few hours, at 0630 hours. We can expect to hear naval gunfire before then and the flyboys will be dropping some bombs. Don't let that bother you. Our job is to take the bridge," Dolan ordered. "You know what to do. We move 1st Platoon—Oakley, your lead—then company headquarters, 3rd Platoon, then 2nd. Any questions?"

There were none.

"Let's go," Dolan ordered.

Able Company moved out, with Oakley's 1st Platoon 10 yards in front of Dolan. On the way, Dolan met Major James E. McGinty. The soft-spoken 29-year-old McGinty was the executive officer and second in command of the 1st Battalion, 505th PIR. He had dropped in a field all alone and was looking for anyone in the 505th. McGinty, known as "Black Jack," was a 1940 graduate of West Point where he had excelled at boxing. He was known as an inspiring combat officer who had commanded G Company, 505th PIR, with distinction during the Sicily and Italy campaigns and was loved by his men for his fighting skill and leadership. Dolan was happy to link up with McGinty, who had recently been promoted and whom he had learned to respect during their training in England.

As the paratroopers moved forward in the dark, Dolan heard the noise of a motorcycle. His men hit the ground on both sides of the road, hiding to avoid contact, as were their orders. The German motorcycle passed by without noticing the Americans. Dolan stood up and signaled his men to continue the march.

The overcast sky began to drizzle. The men moved forward in the moonlight, but the hedgerows of Normandy with their thick sturdy walls of earth and trees soon made visibility as black as if moving in a forest. The sound of machine-gun fire echoed in the distance. In the dark, contact with Oakley's platoon was lost and Dolan sent the next platoon—Lieutenant Coxon's 3rd Platoon—forward. As they inched closer to the complex of stone buildings that made up the La Fiére farmhouse, they stopped at the edge of an open field. Dolan ordered his scouts forward. Coxon, leading by example, advanced with the two scouts. The men crawled through the hedgerow and right into a kill zone, covered by a German MG42 machine gun. The MG42 was morbidly nicknamed "Hitler's Buzz Saw" by American troops, as it was one of the fastest firing and most deadly machine guns ever made, delivering over 1,200 rounds a minute.

The MG42 let loose. In a matter of seconds, all three men were killed.

Second Lieutenant Robert E. McLaughlin, assistant platoon leader for 3rd Platoon, took over as Platoon Leader. He moved ahead with his radio operator and both men were hit. Having just lost five men, McGinty and Dolan carefully moved forward, with McGinty taking the lead as he always did. They moved farther down the hedgerow to see where they could break through to get an angle on the enemy gun in an attempt to flank it. As McGinty rushed forward, he was surprised by two Germans with MP40 submachine guns who popped up to fire at the end of the hedgerow. The Germans blasted away and McGinty was riddled with bullets before he could fire back. The young major fell and died instantly. Dolan instinctively jumped for cover into a nearby German foxhole. He fired into the bushes, peppering the hedgerow with .45 caliber bullets, killing one of the Germans who had hit McGinty. Other Germans returned fire. Every time Dolan tried to raise his head, a fusillade of bullets forced him to duck. Pinned down, he yelled for the rest of his men to stay back as he remained in the foxhole and fired his Thompson as best he could without exposing himself to enemy fire. After a long and tense wait, the Germans eventually stopped firing and withdrew.

Dolan was shocked by McGinty's death, but he knew that McGinty would expect him to accomplish his mission to secure the bridge. It was now nearly sunrise and firing could be heard in the surrounding area. Dolan could discern the rumble of huge explosions. The naval and aerial bombardment near Utah Beach was erupting right on time, but Dolan was behind schedule and he knew it.

With McGinty dead, Dolan was in charge. The Germans were firing from the La Fiére farmhouse located just southeast of the bridge, effectively holding up the entire operation. As long as the Germans held those stone buildings, they commanded the bridge. He knew that he must take the farmhouse first if he was to have any chance of blocking the expected German counterattacks that would come across the bridge to smash into the exposed flank of the 82nd Airborne Division. He could not let that happen.

Dolan heard small-arms fire from the far side of the farmhouse. The situation was chaotic as he tried to maneuver his men guided by the sound of gunfire. Later, military historian S. L. A. Marshall would explain why it took seven hours to take the La Fiére farm complex:

> Such tactical mishaps as occurred might be incomprehensible unless the development of the situation is examined in the light of the extreme difficulties of the ground. The area around the Manor de la Fiére [the farm complex] was strongly compartmented with high, box-like hedgerows, which for the most part were over-run with blackberry and other thorn bushes so that both observation and the opportunity for penetration were critically limited. The ground itself, considering the position from flank to flank, was most irregular.[5]

Apparently, several other groups of American paratroopers were attacking La Fiére from the south and from the marshlands to the west. While these American attacks were uncoordinated, they had the effect of swarming the enemy position. None of his radios were working so Dolan could only communicate with other units by voice or runner. Eventually, reinforcements arrived from several airborne units, including elements from the 507th and 508th PIRs and even the 101st Airborne Division. With American paratroopers scattered all over the area, mixed groups of paratroopers formed and were led by the ranking officer or sergeant. After a bitter fight that took nearly half the day, Dolan and these reinforcements pressed the attack and approached the farmhouse from multiple directions. The thick stone walls of the La Fiére farmhouse made an excellent defensive position for the Germans. American casualties mounted until one of Dolan's men crawled close enough to the farmhouse to fire a bazooka into the first floor. Suddenly, a German raised a white flag of surrender. When a paratrooper stepped forward to accept that surrender, another German gunned him down. As the fighting renewed, with rifle fire, machine guns, and grenades, the Americans gained the upper hand. By approximately 2:30 p.m., the Germans surrendered *en masse* and the paratroopers occupied the farmhouse. It is to the credit of these American soldiers that they took the surviving Germans alive after the false surrender, vice subjecting them to the same fate as their fallen fellow paratrooper.

Once the farmhouse was cleared, the paratroopers found the French owners cowering in the basement, frightened but alive. Dolan immediately set out for the bridge and made a quick analysis of the terrain and situation. The stone bridge crossed the Merderet River, but the Germans had flooded the area. The road thus formed a causeway for several hundred yards, with water on the north and south sides. These flooded areas stopped all vehicle movement and made any dismounted movement problematic. Dolan also noticed multiple parachutes floating above the water. By flooding the area, the Germans had created a deathtrap for the paratroopers who had jumped, heavily laden with equipment, and landed in the marshy areas during the night. It was clear to Dolan that at least a dozen Americans had drowned before they could get into the fight.

About this time, 30-year-old Major Frederick Caesar Augustus Kellam, Dolan's battalion commander, arrived with more reinforcements. Kellam, known to his troops as the "Jack of Diamonds," was a West Point graduate of the Class of 1936 and a proven commander. Kellam was born to an Army family stationed in the Philippines, but he called Texas his home and was a devout Catholic. To everyone who met him he seemed to always have a wide grin on his face and his optimism was infectious. He was regarded as an exceptional leader. He had served in the 1st Infantry Division, "The Big Red One," before volunteering for the paratroops. He was married in 1942 and his son, Michael James—whom he had yet to see but was always proud to brag about—was born in October 1943 when he was fighting in Sicily and Italy. It was during this same time that he earned his promotion to Major because of his steadfast leadership in combat. After McGinty's death, Kellam was a welcome sight, as Dolan expected that he would receive support now that his battalion commander had arrived.

Dolan reported to Kellam that his ammunition was running low, but he thought he could hold the bridge. He had some antipersonnel and antitank mines, a couple of machine guns, and two bazookas with half-a-dozen rounds each. Kellam agreed that Dolan could handle the situation. When the 82nd Airborne Assistant Division Commander, Brigadier General James Gavin, arrived, Kellam briefed him that the 505th had the bridge secured and that the Germans would not cross.

Dolan immediately moved forward and surveyed the terrain. The D-15 road ran along the stone bridge and then on a narrow causeway that stretched forward nearly half a mile to the small chapel at Cauquigny. Water covered the marshy ground north and south of the causeway, blocking any avenues of approach. The fields of fire were excellent and any German attack would have to come down the narrow causeway with little cover.

He quickly set his defense along the east side of the bridge, establishing two platoons forward and one back. He placed 3rd Platoon to the left of the bridge and 1st Platoon to the right. He set 2nd Platoon to the rear, on the higher ground, with good fields of fire on the bridge and the causeway. With the keen eye of a combat veteran who had fought desperate battles before, he made sure the crew-served weapons were sighted on specific target areas and assigned a primary direction of fire for maximum effect. Dolan ordered his men to push a disabled German truck onto the bridge to block enemy movement and ordered mines to be placed on the causeway on the western approach to the bridge.

Finally, he ordered his two bazooka teams to work their way forward of the bridge to find an optimum firing position.

Once his men were in place as he had directed, he walked among his troops, reassuring them and telling them that they would hold the bridge no matter what the enemy threw at them.

Several higher-ranking officers arrived, including General Ridgway, the 82nd Airborne division commander, who, surveying the situation, soon realized that Kellam and Dolan had things under control and moved on. A unit from the 507th PIR moved across the bridge and along the causeway to Cauquigny and established a 10-man outpost near the stone church. Sometime after the La Fiére farmhouse was taken, several 57mm antitank guns arrived to help Dolan hold off any enemy attacks across the bridge. Dolan positioned one to the east, up the D-15 road from the farmhouse, with a direct line of sight to the west side of the bridge, where the road curved off behind a stand of trees and headed to the hamlet of Cauquigny.

Around 3:30 p.m., the sound of heavy fighting erupted to the west of the bridge and causeway near Cauquigny. Soon Dolan could see Americans running pell-mell toward the east and into the marsh, only to be picked off by the pursuing Germans. A few moments later, Dolan could see German tanks and infantry heading from Cauquigny toward the La Fiére Bridge. A company of the German 1057th Grenadier Regiment of the 91st Air Landing Division and tanks from the 100th Panzer Training and Replacement Battalion (*Panzer-Ersatz und Ausbildungs-Abteilung 100*) were attacking in force.

German artillery landed on the west side of the La Fiére Bridge, signaling the German attack. Dolan's men hunkered down. He watched as the Germans herded a group of 12 to 15 disarmed and captured American paratroopers to the front of their column. Waving a submachine gun, the lead tank commander ordered the paratroopers to pick up mines from the road and throw them into the fields. The dejected American prisoners moved forward with their hands up, looking over their shoulders, as they walked down the road.

Dolan was unaware how the rest of the invasion was progressing and with the limited range of his communications gear he could not reach anyone to ask for instructions. He knew his orders were to hold this bridge and understood the "big picture," or "intent" as it is called in the Army—if La Fiére was captured by the Germans, the entire invasion would be at risk. His immediate problem was to hold off the Germans. He could see that if he commanded his men to open fire on the advancing German column that the crossfire would kill the American prisoners who were being forced to walk in front of the German attack. He also knew that if he let the Germans recapture the La Fiére Bridge, many more Americans would die. He had already lost too many good men capturing the bridge. He was not about to let the Germans take it back.

The lead German tank slowed as it came to the bend in the causeway, in direct line of sight of Dolan's defenses. The German tank commander, with his head and shoulders outside the turret and a submachine gun in his hands, again ordered the American prisoners forward.

Dolan watched as the tanks herded the American prisoners toward his minefield. He knew that he could not let the Germans clear the mines and advance on the bridge. He did not have a choice and prepared to give the order to open fire.

Then, without issuing the order, one of the machine guns that Dolan had carefully positioned on the south side of the bridge blasted away at the German tank commander. The burst killed him instantly and he crumpled in his turret. The American prisoners in front of the tank dove for cover and crawled to the south side of the causeway as the German Panzer III tank fired on them with its machine guns. Simultaneously, Dolan's bazooka teams opened fire on the lead German tank. Two rockets hit the tank and it rocked back from the detonation of the high-explosive rounds. The American 57mm antitank gun crew that Dolan emplaced on the high ground east of the farmhouse also targeted the lead tank, adding to the destruction. The Panzer III's turret stopped moving and caught fire. The surviving crewmembers tried to abandon the tank but were quickly cut down by American machine-gun fire. The tank billowed black smoke, partially obscuring the causeway. The remaining German tanks—captured French-made Renault R35s and a Hotchkiss H39—returned fire on the 57mm antitank cannon and the two bazooka teams.

The German infantry moved forward toward the burning tank and ran into more withering machine-gun fire from the Americans. A second German tank tried to push the burning Panzer III tank off the road but was rapidly hit by bazooka and 57mm antitank rounds. The tanks returned fire with machine guns and cannon, killing several gunners of the 57mm antitank gun, but other paratroopers took their place and kept up the fire. The bazooka team on the north side of the causeway ran out of ammunition and their bazooka was damaged. With German machine-gun rounds striking all around them, the bazooka team in the north abandoned their position and crawled away on their bellies to avoid the enemy fire.

With the German attack stalling, German mortars started shelling the Americans on the west side of the bridge. The bazooka team on the south side of the road shouted for more ammunition. The team in the north stopped firing and went silent. Kellam and his S3 Operations Officer, Captain Dale A. Roysdon, saw that the bazooka team had expended all their rounds and they tried to rush across the road with extra ammunition. As they did, several mortar bombs exploded, killing both of them as they were crossing the road.

With the American battalion commander and his S3 killed, the bazooka team in the south out of action, and the team in the north out of rockets, the situation was dire. The Germans only had to press on to overrun the American defense. The three surviving German tanks were plastering the 57mm cannon with machine-gun fire and gaining fire supremacy over the defenders. In a mad dash to find extra rounds for their bazooka, Private First Class Marcus Heim, the loader for the bazooka on the south side of the bridge, ran across the road where Kellam and Roysdon had been hit and reached the other bazooka team's position. He found the team gone and the bazooka damaged. Several serviceable rounds lay nearby. He carried them back to the one working bazooka. Heim later said: "This was one of the toughest days of my life. Why we were not injured or killed only the good Lord knows."

Heim loaded a round, slapped the bazooka gunner on the helmet, and the paratrooper fired. The round flew straight and true, hitting the second German tank in line. The bazooka team kept firing, switching to the third enemy tank. While this was happening, 57mm antitank fire was directed onto the last surviving German tank. The combined bazooka and the 57mm crews had ignited all four German tanks, with the resulting fires causing their internal ammunition to explode, ensuring their destruction. As the German tanks burned fiercely, the German infantry, now without tank support, halted their attack. Carrying as many of their wounded as they could, they struggled back under intense fire, taking more casualties as they retreated across the causeway to the west and to the relative safety of chapel at Cauquigny.

The Germans conducted a combined arms tank, infantry, mortar, and artillery attack against 1st Lt. Dolan's defenders at La Fiére Bridge around 3:30 p.m. on June 6, 1944. The number of tanks in the first attack is a matter of considerable controversy. Reports are often confused during and after a battle. The photo above was taken from just west of the bridge and shows the track of a destroyed tank in the immediate foreground, most likely a German Panzer Mark III tank, two captured French Renault R35 tanks in the center, and a captured French Hotchkiss H39 tank to the rear. This photo suggests that the German attack was led by a platoon of four tanks from the Panzer-Ersatz- und Ausbildungs-Abteilung 100 (100th Panzer Training and Replacement Battalion). Whether three or four tanks made the attack, Dolan's defenders decisively stopped them on the west side of the bridge using close-range bazooka and 57mm antitank cannon fire. (US Army Photo)

Dolan breathed a sigh of relief. The Germans had lost this round, but Dolan knew that they would try again soon. He surveyed the scene. He saw the dead body of his battalion commander and the S3. Both were good men and now they were gone. In fact, all the senior leaders of the 1st Battalion, 550th PIR were dead. The area around the farmhouse and the causeway were littered with fallen German and American troops. German tanks were burning on the causeway as their ammunition continued to explode.

Many of the remaining American defenders were wounded. As the German infantry withdrew, they barraged the Americans with artillery and mortar fire. Shells exploded all around Dolan's troops on the east side of the bridge. Several men were killed and many more wounded. Crawling for cover, Dolan and his men hugged the earth while the shelling continued as they awaited the next assault.

As the evening arrived, so did reinforcements and much-needed ammunition. As tired and exhausted as Dolan's defenders were, Dolan surmised that the Germans were just as ragged. The Americans were out of water and food. Dolan requested resupply and hoped for the best.

Night fell. Dolan knew that there was no better place for his company to defend. He did not have the strength to clear the enemy from the causeway and he could not fall back. He was committed to stopping the Germans at the bridge. He visited his troops, had the remaining ammunition redistributed, and told them all that they were going to hold this bridge no matter what.

Having had no rest for the last 38 hours, Able Company remained on full alert and prepared for a German night attack. Around 2 a.m., a single German tank, protected most likely by a squad of infantry, inched slowly toward the bridge in the darkness. The Germans may have wanted to retrieve one of their destroyed tanks, or possibly clear the minefield, but they did not get the chance. Sergeant Owens, a squad leader in 3rd Platoon, crawled forward to meet them with several Gammon grenades. Owens got close enough to lob two Gammons at the enemy tank. The Germans broke off the attack and returned to Cauquigny.

With the morning light at 8 a.m., June 7, the Germans tried to force the bridge for a third time. For this attempt, the Germans planned to attack in force and use everything at their disposal. An intense artillery and mortar bombardment fell on the American defenses east of the bridge. Shells burst at treetop level, raining shrapnel down on the American defenders. Many of Dolan's men were hit. Around 10 a.m., four new tanks came to lead the attack, but more cautiously this time. They stayed out of range of any American bazookas and plastered the American defenses with machine-gun and cannon fire. A full battalion of German infantry moved forward, advancing down the causeway and using the destroyed tanks from the prior day's attacks for cover.

Dolan had one ace up his sleeve. During the night, he had been reinforced with several additional 57mm antitank guns that he positioned on the high ground overlooking the bridge and causeway. Dolan had given the antitank gunners a primary direction of fire with instructions to take out any German tanks that moved into range. These antitank guns were more than a match for the obsolete French tanks of *Panzer-Ersatz und Ausbildungs-Abteilung 100*. One German tank was destroyed and, in return, an American 57mm was knocked out. Still the Germans pressed the attack. The firing on both sides was intense, casualties rose, and the ammunition was again running low.

The cry rang out among the American defenders. "Ammo! We need more ammo!"

Dolan could sense that his men were at a breaking point.

Third platoon was at the decisive point of the defense. If they broke, Dolan's line would crumble and the Germans would win the crossing.

Sergeant William Owens, a squad leader in 3rd Platoon, was firing his rifle when an enemy mortar shell hit the radioman next to him, blasting the man to pieces and killing the platoon leader, Lieutenant William Oakley.

"Sarge, we can't hold 'em," one of Owens' paratroopers said in near panic.

The Germans sensed that the Americans had reached a tipping point and pressed the assault. The situation looked grim. The Americans were running low on rifle and machine-gun ammunition, and the Germans were moving ever closer. Owens was now in charge of the critical sector of the battle and was down to only 14 paratroopers. More men urged

Owens to withdraw, telling him that they could not survive another German attack. Some of the men from other units who had been thrown in the prior evening as replacements started to leave the line. Owens sent a runner to Dolan to ask for orders.

The runner reached Dolan and explained the situation. Dolan tried shouting to Owens, but the roar of battle was too much. He wrote a short note in his notebook, tore the page off, and handed it to the trooper.

Without reading the note, the runner secured the message, took a deep breath, and began to run back. He zigzagged back to Owens, nearly getting shot on the way and diving for cover at the last minute. Panting, he passed the note to Owens.

Owens read the note and nodded. The note from Dolan read: "We stay. I don't know of a better spot than this to die."

Owens waved at Dolan, acknowledging that he understood and accepted his commander's order without argument. Owens, like Dolan, understood the gravity of the situation, as described by noted US military historian S. L. A. Marshall, who interviewed the participants after the battle: "The issue was being decided on the ground where Owens stood. If his platoon broke, the whole position was gone."[6] Owens passed the order on to his men, led by example, and inspired them to fight on. He grabbed an M1919A4 machine gun and fired it at the advancing Germans until it was out of ammunition. He then picked up a BAR (Browning Automatic Rifle) from a dead paratrooper and blasted way, reloaded, and continued firing until several magazines were gone. The German infantry moved forward, advancing by fire and maneuver, to within 40 meters of the American positions defending the bridge, continuing to use the tanks destroyed on June 6 for cover.

Dolan and the surviving paratroopers on the east side of the bridge let loose with everything they had left. The lead German tank moved forward and was finally knocked out by one of the 57mm guns. Then, another enemy tank was hit. Finally, the Germans had had enough and broke. The Germans never reached the bridge, but had gotten dangerously close. An eerie quiet ensued, with the Germans hunkered down, not far away. After a brief interval, the Germans raised a Red Cross flag and asked for a truce to recover their dead and wounded.

Dolan, knowing that his men could not hold out much longer, agreed.

During the truce, Dolan used the time to receive more ammunition and reinforce his defense. By the time the truce was over, he felt ready to repel another attack if it came. Shortly thereafter, the Germans launched another deadly mortar attack against Dolan's men, but there were no more attempts by German tanks and infantry to take the bridge. Dolan reported to his superiors that he could hold on, but that his company was spent and that another unit would be needed to push across the causeway to fully secure the approach. What was left of Able Company, 1st Battalion, 505th PIR, had held the bridge.

In the early hours of June 8, Dolan and his battle-worn men were relieved by the 507th PIR. They marched to Neuville-au-Plain, north of Sainte-Mère-Église, to rest and become part of the 82nd Airborne Division reserve.

The battle at La Fiére was, however, far from over. The Germans no longer had the strength to attack but could block US movement to the west. They still held strong positions near Cauquigny and along the western approach to the causeway. Lieutenant Colonel Timmes, whose unit was dropped on the western side of the Merderet River on D-Day, was still holding on in an orchard northwest of Cauquigny against strong German pressure. To secure the approach to Sainte-Mère-Église once and for all, and to break through to the units on the west side of the Merderet River, General Ridgway decided to force the crossing on June 9. He ordered the newly arrived companies of the 325th and 401st Glider Regiments to charge across the La Fiére Bridge. At great cost, they broke the back of the German defense and permanently secured the bridge. The historian S. L. A. Marshall wrote that the fighting at La Fiére was "the bloodiest small struggle in the experience of American arms."

For his leadership and extraordinary courage at the battle of La Fiére, 1Lt. John J. "Red Dog" Dolan was awarded the Distinguished Service Cross, the second highest military decoration for valor that an American soldier can receive. The award is given for extreme gallantry in combat, which involves risking one's life in such a manner as to set

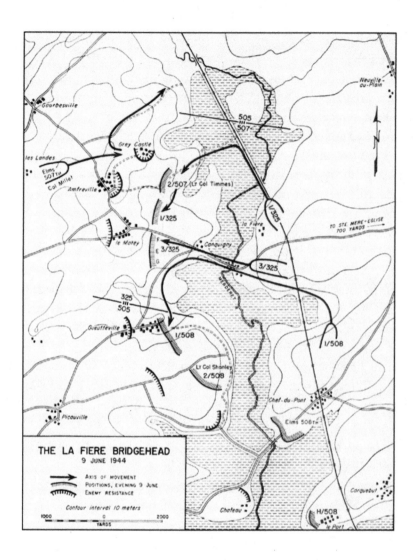

THE LA FIERE BRIDGEHEAD
9 JUNE 1944

AXIS OF MOVEMENT
POSITIONS, EVENING 9 JUNE
ENEMY RESISTANCE

Contour interval 10 meters

1000   0   2000
YARDS

the individual apart from their comrades. Dolan's Distinguished Service
Cross citation reads:

DOLAN, JOHN J.

The President of the United States takes pleasure in presenting the Distinguished
Service Cross to John J. Dolan, First Lieutenant, U.S. Army, for extraordinary
heroism in connection with military operations against an armed enemy in action
against enemy forces on 6 June 1944. First Lieutenant Dolan's intrepid actions,
personal bravery and zealous devotion to duty exemplify the highest traditions

of the military forces of the United States and reflect great credit upon himself, his unit, and the United States Army. Headquarters, 1st U.S. Airborne Army, General Orders No. 41 (1945).

★ ★ ★

Leadership Lesson

To be a good leader, first be a good follower. Leadership is not about shouting orders. Leadership requires discipline, dedication, and, most importantly, obedience. All teams require obedience. The best leaders are great followers; some of the worst leaders and tyrants are people who cannot follow anyone. No one should be allowed to give orders who cannot obey orders. Dolan was the Commander of Able Company, 1st Battalion, 505th Parachute Infantry Regiment, 82nd Airborne Division. He was a skilled veteran combat officer whom his men trusted. Since the day he entered the US Army, he was trained to be a member of a team. He followed orders, but more than that, he understood that the first prerequisite of learning how to be an effective leader is to be a good follower. We all work for someone, and in the case of 1st Lt. John "Red Dog" Dolan, his battalion commander was Major Frederick Kellam, who commanded Dolan to accomplish a critical task: "The specific mission of the Company 'A' was to seize and defend the bridge crossing the Merderet River on the road that ran East to West from Sainte-Mère-Église, with the purpose of preventing the movement of German troops down to the beachhead."[7] Dolan demonstrated obedience to those orders as an example to his men so they, in turn, would follow his orders. When Kellam was killed in action at the bridge, Dolan assumed full command to complete his assigned mission. Dolan obeyed the orders of his leaders and commanders above him because they had earned his trust in the grueling preparation and training that took place prior to D-Day. How a leader serves his commander sets the example for how the leader should be obeyed. To be a good follower, you must subordinate yourself to something greater than yourself. Dolan knew that he was working as part of a greater team and that if he was not obedient to his orders, many things could go wrong in the greater strategy of the D-Day invasion.

What type of person do you want to have on your team? Someone who is cynical, reluctant and always finding fault, or someone who is eager, trustworthy and willing to work hard? If you want the eager, willing and trustworthy person on your team, then be that kind of person and you will attract those kinds of people to your team. If you do this, when it comes time to promote someone to a position of leadership, you will be the person who is known as the one who helped the leader get things done. This is what Dolan did every day and because of this, his men trusted him and followed him. The bottom line: If you want to be a good leader, learn to be a good follower. Dolan understood this and acted accordingly. His paratroopers knew they could count on that with their lives. When their courage was faltering, and they questioned whether they could continue to hold the bridge against the Germans, he told them that there was "no better place to die." Dolan was totally committed to the mission. This emboldened his soldiers and impelled them with the courage to hang on a little longer, and that made all the difference.

Dolan also demonstrated that leaders are responsible for everything their team does or fails to do. Dolan understood the strategic importance of the bridge at La Fiére and realized his unit's role in the larger scheme of operations for the 505th PIR, the larger mission of the 82nd Airborne Division, and how all of this fit into the success or failure of the D-Day invasion. He knew that his company of 150 paratroopers had one purpose and one purpose only: seize and hold the bridge at La Fiére. The cost of failure was the possibility of the failure of his regiment, his division, and the success of the Allied beachhead. Dolan accepted responsibility for taking the bridge and holding it at all costs. He personally sighted and positioned his key weapons, supervised the emplacement of mines and obstacles, and led his force in continuous combat for two days even when his company was reduced to a fraction of its original fighting strength. When his Commanding Officer, Kellam, and the S3 operations officer, Roysdon, were killed, Dolan took command of the battalion as the senior officer present and employed all available elements of the 505th PIR to defend the bridge.

Last, Dolan demonstrated personal courage. Everyone feels fear in a crisis, particularly in combat, but leaders must quickly cycle through the fear and decide on action. Many people are frozen by fear and are unable to act. Leaders who focus and demonstrate personal courage can make decisions in a moment of crisis that inspire their teammates to keep going, even when the going is tough. This is true for anyone, be they in a boardroom or on a battlefield. During World War II, American paratroopers were conditioned to believe that they were superior soldiers and that they could accomplish any mission. This confidence was the result of years of tough training and excellent leadership. During training, the leaders were constantly with their men. The officers did what the men did, and the paratroopers and their leaders developed a close bond. Most paratroopers saw their leaders as extraordinary; this enhanced the attitude that nothing could stop them. How can you build confidence in your team by being a better follower? How can you learn from the leadership story of Lieutenant "Red Dog" Dolan to make your team more effective?

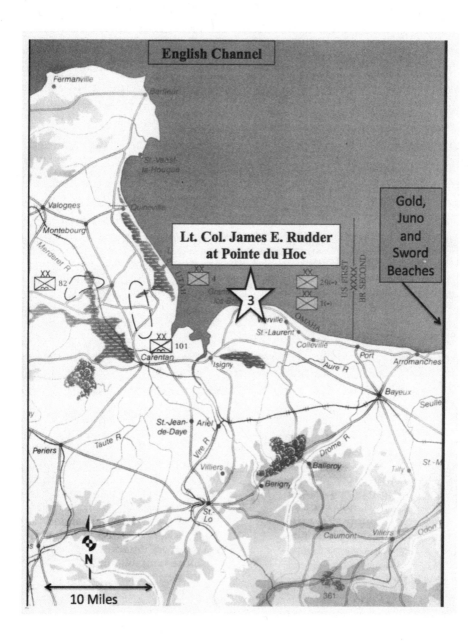

CHAPTER 3

Storming the Pointe du Hoc

Courage

*"It can't be done. Three old women with brooms could keep the
Rangers from climbing those cliffs."*
*Attributed to a naval intelligence officer from Rear Admiral John L. Hall's staff after
Lt. Col. Rudder briefed the Admiral on the plan to seize Pointe du Hoc*

"Pointe du Hoc was the lock on the door to Europe. What was needed was a key..."
Robert W. Black, author of Rangers in World War II

"I tell you, it's suicide!" the major shouted.

A dozen officers were crammed into the officers' bar of the SS *Ben-
my-Chree*, celebrating the major's newly won promotion. He had pinned
on the oak leaves of a major in the US Army on June 3, 1944. Cigarette
smoke filled the air. More drinks were poured, cigarettes passed around,
and congratulations offered, but the guest of honor grew more agitated
with each swig of liquor. He had been holding onto a dark secret for
too long. Now, with the invasion postponed and his lips loosened by
gin, he began to spill out his fears. The major pulled a sketch map
from his pocket of a German defensive position in Normandy, France.
The paper was labeled, *"Widerstandsnest* 75, the Pointe du Hoc." At the
bottom of the map, in big red letters, was stamped the classification:
"TOP-SECRET-BIGOT."

In the US government, "Top secret" is one of the highest forms
of security for information, plans and documents. The contents of a
top-secret document are to be carefully guarded and never discussed in
an open forum. "BIGOT" was the codename for a security level one

step higher, specifically designed for D-Day. If you held the "BIGOT" security classification level, it meant that you were privy to the most critical elements of the D-Day plans. "TOP-SECRET-BIGOT" information was so sensitive that several high-ranking officers, including one general officer, were relieved of duty and sent packing back to the USA for breaking the security protocols.

The other officers surrounding the major looked on with new interest as the paper was placed on the bar in front of them. Most of these men did not have a "TOP-SECRET-BIGOT" clearance, but they knew what it meant. Each of them knew that their lives, and the lives of the Rangers they were about to lead into combat, depended on the newly promoted major and the information he was about to discuss. With a bit of surprise, they looked on, wanting desperately to know the secret and to learn why their commander was so sure that their mission would end in disaster for them and their men. If the major had reservations about the mission, should they all?

The SS *Ben-my-Chree*, the ship that was transporting the Rangers destined to assault the Pointe du Hoc, was a passenger ferry launched in 1927 and operated by the Isle of Man Steam Packet Company. It had been painted naval gray and converted into a troop ship. During the British evacuation from Dunkirk in 1940, "The Ben," as its crew

The shoulder patch insignia of the elite US Army Rangers during World War II.

affectionately called it, made three trips to rescue 4,095 British and French soldiers while battling the Luftwaffe Stukas and Messerschmitts with the ship's deck machine guns. Designated as Landing Ship Infantry (LSI) to carry the Ranger Assault Group for the D-Day invasion, "The Ben" also acted as the headquarters ship of the senior officer of the 514th Assault Flotilla. The ship now carried a full contingent of combat-equipped American Rangers from the 2nd Ranger Battalion. When ordered, the Rangers would transfer into smaller British Landing Craft Assault (LCA). Each LCA could carry up to 36 Rangers to conduct the seaborne assault.

Many months of preparation and training were finally coming down to execution and the anxious soldiers and sailors of this vast Allied effort were at the starting line.

But vast is an understatement. The number of ships was tremendous: approximately 7,000 vessels, with 1,213 naval combat ships, 4,126 landing ships and landing craft, 736 ancillary craft, and 864 merchant vessels. The number of aircraft was the largest concentration of airpower yet seen in the war: as many as 13,000 aircraft supported the invasion. The planning and logistics behind all this was intricate, detailed, and all encompassing. The supplies needed to fuel, arm, feed, and fix every plane, ship, landing craft, tank, howitzer, and soldier had to be accounted for. Vast, therefore, is a word that does not reach the heights of what was about to be accomplished on D-Day.

In order to meet the D-Day invasion timetable, "The Ben" left Portsmouth on June 3, as the weather turned foul and the seas rough. At 4:30 a.m., June 4, General Eisenhower decided to postpone the attack. With radio listening silence imposed, the ships that were already at sea relayed the recall order by signal light. The mighty flotilla turned and the ships carrying seasick soldiers sailed back to their home ports. As might be expected, tensions were high on "The Ben." The Rangers, keyed up and expecting imminent combat, were given a reprieve. With the invasion was postponed for 24 hours, the Rangers could let off some steam. As a British ship and previous passenger ferry, the Ben-my-Chree had a bar that served the officers and naturally the Ranger officers made their way there to make the most of British hospitality.

"I tell you that the latest reports from the French Resistance say there are no big guns in the emplacements on the Pointe," Major Cleveland Lytle exclaimed, downing another shot of gin. "I saw these reports with my own eyes. I argued with Rudder and told him we shouldn't go in. He told me that those intelligence reports can't be confirmed. Not confirmed! And what are we risking ourselves for if the guns are not there? He said we have to go in anyway, that the Pointe is too important to leave in German hands. What are we risking our lives for it there are no guns?"

"Rudder knows what he's doing," a Ranger lieutenant countered. "He has never let us down."

"You don't know what I know," Lytle countered.

"Guns can be moved and moved back," another Ranger officer answered. "If Rudder said it's important, that's good enough for me."

"Yeah? Well, I'm not so sure," Lytle replied, gulping down another slug of gin. "I tell you, I've heard the staff officers talking about our chances and they wouldn't give you a plug nickel for our odds. I just know that we're all going to die trying to take those cliffs."

"Take it easy, Lytle," a young Ranger captain offered. "We're Rangers. We can do anything. Besides, you're hitting that bottle a bit hard. Is that your fourth shot of gin?"

"So what?" Lytle snorted. "Is Rudder climbing those cliffs with us? Hello no! Since we'll all be dead in 24 hours, why not get dead-drunk?"

Lytle kept pouring and drinking. His officers listened to him gripe, becoming more uncomfortable as the session wore on.

"We are expected to climb 100-foot sheer cliffs in the face of German defenders. Can't be done. It's simple arithmetic," Lytle offered. "And Rudder knows it, but doesn't give a damn."

As Lytle openly discussed top-secret information, the British naval officers at the bar politely asked some of the Rangers to restrain their major. The 2nd Ranger Battalion surgeon, Captain Walter E. Block, realizing that Lytle had consumed beyond his capacity, put his arm around the major and suggested they both leave. Lytle angrily threw off Block's arm and then took a wild swing at him. A struggle began. At that moment, the ship's captain arrived. The Ranger officers grabbed

Lytle in the midst of the brawl. The captain of "The Ben" ordered Lytle to be removed and restrained under house arrest. By the time "The Ben" returned to Weymouth Harbour, and the ship's captain reported the incident, the damage to Lytle's command authority had been done.

The next evening, at 7 p.m., June 4, aboard the HMS *Prince Charles*, the commander of the 2nd Ranger Battalion, Lieutenant Colonel James Earl Rudder, received the report about Lytle and shook his head in disbelief. In his headquarters at Weymouth, phones were ringing and messengers were scurrying about carrying new "TOP-SECRET-BIGOT" information to him. D-Day was postponed for only 24 hours. General Eisenhower would make the decision on whether to launch the invasion on June 6 in the next few hours. Time was pressing and the tension of the moment was fierce. As if Rudder did not have anything else to be concerned about on the eve of D-Day, now he had to deal with Lytle.

Lytle held a crucial command position. On March 26, 1944, he had assumed the duties of Executive Officer (XO), 2nd Ranger Battalion when Major Max F. Schneider was selected to command the 5th Ranger Battalion.[1] Schneider was a veteran Ranger who had fought in Africa and won a battlefield promotion to captain. In 1942, in Tunisia, North Africa, he earned a Silver Star for heroism in battle. Schneider then went on to lead Rangers in Sicily with great distinction and courage. In January 1944, Schneider was assigned to Rudder's 2nd Ranger Battalion as additional help to train the Rangers for their D-Day mission. Rudder immediately recognized Schneider's talents and made him his second in command.

When Schneider was transferred to lead the 5th Ranger Battalion, Lytle was given the job as Rudder's second-in-command. Taking over from Schneider was a tall order, but Lytle appeared to rise to the challenge. For the D-Day operation, Lytle was placed in command of Dog, Easy, and Fox companies, which were designated to climb the cliffs and seize the Pointe du Hoc. Rudder knew how vital it was to seize this key terrain and he trusted Lytle to do the job. General Omar Bradley, the commander of all US troops for the D-Day invasion, had stated during a previous briefing where Rudder was present that the Pointe du Hoc was one of the most important objectives of Operation *Overlord* and vital to the success of the landings at Omaha and Utah. The Pointe was the central high ground that offered the Germans unobstructed views of both beaches. If the Germans had guns in the six bunkers on top of the Pointe—and from reconnaissance photos, it appeared the guns were there—then the Germans would be able to hit both American beaches with deadly high-explosive shells. Intelligence reports indicated that as many as six 155mm French-made guns were mounted in the six casemates. Further west, intelligence reports indicated additional German artillery: a German battery of four 155mm howitzers at Maisy and a battery of 105mm howitzers at Géfosse-Fontenay. Even if the French Resistance reports that the guns at the Pointe du Hoc had been moved off the Pointe were correct, the position was still tactically significant. Rudder knew from hundreds of aerial photographs, some of them taken at treetop level, that the Nazis had constructed an observation and command bunker at the tip of Pointe du Hoc. This bunker enjoyed clear vistas in the direction of Omaha and Utah and could send firing coordinates to numerous German howitzer and gun batteries in range of the beaches.

To capture the Pointe, the 2nd and 5th Rangers were consolidated into a single Ranger unit commanded by Rudder. The Ranger Assault Group was divided into three forces: Force A, consisting of 250 Rangers and commanded by Major Lytle, was to seize the Pointe du Hoc. Force B, consisting of one Ranger company commanded by Captain Ralph Goranson, was tasked with seizing the Pointe-et-Raz-de-la-Percée on the west flank of Omaha Beach, Dog Green sector; and Force C, commanded by Lt. Col. Schneider.

The mission of Schneider's Force C was to reinforce Force A at the Pointe once a signal was received that the Rangers scaling the 100-foot cliffs were successful. If no signal was received by H+30, it meant that the attempt to scale the cliffs was a disaster and Schneider was to redirect his landing craft to land at Omaha Beach. Once on Omaha, Schneider's force would link up with Force B, which landed earlier, and fight their way inland to the Pointe du Hoc to complete the mission to destroy the guns.

Rudder knew that for these reasons the Pointe had to be taken and it had to be held. For many months, the Rangers had been scaling cliffs in England higher than the ones at the Pointe du Hoc. The training was intense. The Rangers were ready, but if the leadership faltered at the last minute, all could be lost.

Rudder assessed Lytle's misconduct and made a decision. He knew that removing a unit commander, especially a well-trained Ranger leader who had been with his troops throughout training, had to be handled impartially. He immediately ordered three officers—the S-2 (intelligence officer), Captain Harvey J. Cook; the S-3 (operations officer), Captain Frank H. Corder; and the Easy Company commander, Captain Richard "Dick" P. Merrill—to investigate the situation and report back to him.

The inquiry by the three captains did not take long. Cook and Corder recommended that Lytle be immediately relieved. Merrill argued to retain Lytle as he was trained for the specific mission of seizing the Pointe, but wavered when Rudder pressed him on whether Merrill believed that Lytle had the conviction to drive through to the Rangers' objective. After listening to all three officers, and knowing the stress that everyone was operating under, Rudder decided to remove Lytle from command and place him under medical supervision. Rather than relieve Lytle and order a court martial, Rudder ordered him to go to the hospital. Lytle had no choice but to comply, and was put under surveillance for security reasons. He spent the next three weeks in the hospital.

Rudder's next decision was to find a commander to lead Force A. He had very little time to decide as he knew the invasion could commence in the next few hours. He knew the magnitude of the task and understood that promoting a captain from one of the other companies (Dog, Easy or Fox Company, 2nd Rangers), would disrupt the command organization and cohesion of those units. He did not want to create cascading disruption inside Force A. He had very few options and very little time to decide. He was under orders from Major General Clarence R. Huebner, commander of the 1st Infantry Division, the famed "Big Red One," to which the Provisional Ranger Group was assigned, to remain on board the HMS *Prince Charles* during D-Day. Huebner believed that Rudder needed to stay aboard the ship, where he was expected to have the best radio communications, in order to direct the operations of the entire Provisional Ranger Group.

As Rudder saw it, there was only one course of action he could take. He would lead the attack himself and take Lytle's place. He could not command from the ship. The Pointe du Hoc was too important an objective.

Before he could make his decision a reality, he had to request permission from his senior commander. At 2 a.m., June 5, Rudder met with Huebner aboard the USS *Ancon*, a converted ocean liner that was transformed into a combined headquarters and communications command ship. Huebner was a successful leader with a reputation as a by-the-book, uncompromising, spit-and-polish disciplinarian who believed in following "the plan."[2] In Huebner's command, only strict discipline and attention to detail could overcome the friction of war. Huebner was not found of the Rangers, which were assigned to him under only temporary command and he particularly did not like last-minute decisions.

When Rudder asked to see the general, Huebner's staff was conducting a flurry of tasks that still had to be completed before the invasion was launched. The staff was not excited about Rudder interrupting the general. Prior to any military operation, there is always more to plan, more to study, and more to brief. Rudder told Huebner's staff that he must see the general and that it was most urgent. After some time, Rudder was permitted an audience. Rudder quickly explained the situation and told Huebner that he had no choice but to personally lead the attack.

Huebner replied: "I can't let you do that. I need you to oversee the entire Ranger operation. We may have Rangers spread out over a 4- or 5-mile stretch of beach. I can't risk you getting knocked off in the first round."

"I'm sorry sir," Rudder answered with determination, "but I'm going to have to disobey you. If I don't take it, it may not go."

After a bit more discussion, which remains off the record, Huebner relented. Rudder would lead the assault on the Pointe du Hoc.

Rudder now had to inform his subordinate commanders. His company commanders and Lt. Col. Schneider were scattered aboard different ships anchored in the harbor. They needed to know the change of commanders and understand why. To make it more difficult, he could not radio his subordinate leaders, as the entire invasion force was under strict radio listening silence. His only recourse was to take a small boat, sail from ship to ship accompanied by his radio operator, Technical Sergeant Francis J. Kolodziejczak, and talk to his subordinate commanders in person. More importantly, it was Rudder's belief that his men needed to see him one more time before the assault. He shook their hands and stiffened their determination. As he left the ship that Schneider was on, Rudder said: "What better way to die than to die for your country?"[3] It was late morning on June 5 before he completed this important communication task. There would be no rest for the weary; at 4:40 a.m., Eisenhower issued his irrevocable decision. The invasion was on!

The codename for the naval movement and landing operations for D-Day was Operation *Neptune*.

Operation *Neptune* was the combined Allied assault phase of Operation *Overlord*. Its mission was:

> … to carry out an operation from the United Kingdom to secure a lodgment on the Continent from which further offensive operations can be developed. This lodgment area must contain sufficient port facilities to maintain a force of 26 to 50 divisions and to enable this force to be augmented by follow-up formations at the rate of from three to five divisions a month.[4]

The naval convoys of Operation *Neptune* were divided into five forces: U (Utah Beach), O (Omaha Beach), G (Gold Beach), J (Juno Beach), and S (Sword Beach). Force O was commanded by Rear Admiral J. L. Hall, aboard his headquarters ship, the USS *Ancon*.[5] Hall was a distinguished naval officer with 31 years of active duty experience that included serving on destroyers, commanding the battleship *Arkansas*, and as commander of amphibious forces. He commanded the amphibious force that landed US troops in North Africa in 1942, and Sicily and Italy in 1943. He was renowned for his cross-training of Army artillerymen and Navy gunners so that the guns of his battleships, cruisers, and destroyers could deliver naval fire missions in direct support of the ground troops. General Eisenhower respected Hall so much that he gave him the nickname the "Viking of Assault."

The naval gunfire ships in Force O under Hall's command contained considerable firepower and included the battleships USS *Arkansas* (14-inch guns) and USS *Texas* (14-inch guns); the cruisers HMS *Glasgow* (6-inch guns); the French Navy's *Montcalm* (6-inch guns) and *Georges Leygues* (6-inch guns); and the destroyers HMS *Talybont* and HMS *Tanatside*. Force O also had 17 minesweepers and nine large troop-landing ships. The Ranger Assault Group, commanded by Rudder, were aboard the LSIs (Landing Ship Infantry) of Force O: *Ben-my-Chree* (Ranger companies Fox and Easy[-], and part of the 2nd Ranger Battalion Headquarters), *Amsterdam* (Ranger companies Dog, Easy[-], and part of the 2nd Ranger Battalion Headquarters), *Prince Charles* (Ranger companies Able, Baker, Charlie, and the remainder of the 2nd Ranger Battalion Headquarters), *Prince Leopold* (Ranger companies Able, Fox, and part of the 5th Ranger Battalion Headquarters), and finally *Prince Baudoin* (Ranger companies Charlie, Dog, Fox, and the remainder of the 5th Ranger Battalion Headquarters).

The Rangers received the word that the invasion would take place on Tuesday, June 6, shortly after the "go order" was issued by General Eisenhower's headquarters. For many of the Rangers, the tension of waiting rapidly turned to relief and then to anticipation. Most of the men, and particularly the leaders, understood the enormity of what they were about to undertake. The remainder of Monday, June 5, 1944, was spent in a burst of last-minute preparations. Hundreds of ships, boats, and landing craft sailed from port in an intricately choreographed ballet and joined the long, organized groups that would place them in their designated positions to execute Operation *Neptune*. Soldiers, crammed into crowded troopships, readied their equipment, attended religious services, gambled, wrote letters and tried to avoid the rampant seasickness as the ships tossed in heavy waves.

During the past few days Rudder had had very little sleep. There was much to do. He met with the leaders of the Ranger Force, explaining the last-minute decision that would put him in command of the Pointe du Hoc assault force. The Rangers of Dog, Easy, and Fox companies, the first assault wave on the Pointe du Hoc, were happy that Rudder would be leading them. Rudder had been with them throughout training and they trusted him. If anyone would get them through the ordeal of the next 72 hours, it would be their inspirational commander, Lieutenant Colonel James Earl Rudder.

Rudder was born in Eden, Texas, in 1910. He grew up poor but learned the value of education, training, and determination at an early age. Rudder played football in high school and after graduation was skilled enough to continue playing football at John Tarleton Agricultural College. He played there for two years before transferring to Texas A&M. Graduating from Texas A&M with a degree in education in 1932, he joined the US Army Reserves as a second lieutenant. Prior to the war, he had been a high school and college football coach. His humble upbringing and focus on the value of training teams to win helped prepare his Rangers for their D-Day mission. When he first formed the 2nd Ranger Battalion, his men were, according to combat historian and author Patrick O'Donnell, "a disaster. They couldn't do parade formation or much else. But Rudder the football coach turned them into a unit obsessed with winning. It all emanates from Rudder. He turned raw recruits into soldiers who could act on their own initiative and change the course of a battle."[6]

Allied planners knew that the Germans understood the value of the Pointe du Hoc and, even while the Germans did not know the exact location of the Allied invasion landings, the Germans were prepared for any eventuality. With typical German efficiency, the defenses of the Pointe du Hoc were carefully constructed. Casemates and bunkers with reinforced steel were built to withstand heavy bombardment. Four open positions, into which the large-caliber 155mm guns could be rapidly moved from protected positions outside of the Pointe du Hoc, were created. Two covered gun emplacements, where guns might be permanently placed, were built. Concrete ammunition caches were dug deep into the ground to provide secure, ample ammunition storage. The Germans turned the Pointe du Hoc into a formidable artillery bastion, while not forgetting to prepare the position for a possible Allied land attack. The Pointe du Hoc was reinforced with several Tobruks—bunkers with tank turrets mounted on top to provide cannon and machine-gun fire against any invaders coming by land. The defenses also included protected positions equipped with two 20mm and/or 37mm antiaircraft guns to use against Allied aircraft, while also being capable of engaging Allied ground troops. A third antiaircraft gun bunker, near the southern exit of the extensive minefields, was under construction. At least four protected MG42 machine-gun positions were set up, two facing the northeast beach and two in the south. Mazes of deep, interconnecting trenches were dug to allow the defenders and artillerymen to move, protected, from one casemate, bunker, and ammunition cache to another. The German defenses were primarily set up to protect the Pointe du Hoc from a land attack from the south, as the Germans considered the 100-foot cliffs on the northern side impossible to climb by any attacking force: the cliffs dropped off straight down to the sea. Under this assumption, the Germans established a deep belt of mines, barbed wire, and anti-glider obstacles on the most probable, southeastern approach to the Pointe du Hoc.

In the months prior to D-Day, Rudder and his leaders had created a detailed plan to secure the Pointe du Hoc. He received reliable intelligence information from air photos and detailed reports from the French Resistance. The position was formidable. Units of the German 726th Infantry Regiment, consisting of approximately 120 soldiers, defended the top. A force of approximately 200 infantrymen could rapidly reinforce the Pointe and the German counterattack would most likely be supported with mortar and artillery fires. Rudder's plan, therefore, emphasized speed, precision, and surprise. He would send his men straight up the 100-foot cliffs on the seaward side, the area from which he felt the Germans would not expect an attack. When Admiral Hall was briefed on Rudder's plan, his intelligence officer was incredulous and said, "It can't be done. Three old women with brooms could keep the Rangers from climbing those cliffs."

Rudder did not think it was impossible and neither did his Rangers. He was determined to succeed, and neither the height of the cliff nor the number of defenders would dissuade him. His final plan was purposeful and simple: The Rangers would conduct a seaward assault of the 100-foot cliffs from both the east and west, quickly climb up with ropes and ladders, gain the top, and kill all the German defenders. Then a second wave of Rangers would arrive after receiving the signal that the Pointe du Hoc was in Rudder's control to reinforce the initial assault force, and then defend until relieved. Simple.

But "simple" often results in "hard." Rudder had long ago understood that flat maps are not truly flat. If you do not consider the heights, ravines, rocks, and woods, if you fail to think about the many things that can go wrong, then you are lost. Rudder understood his men; he had lived with them, trained with them, and was one of them. He was confident his Rangers could adapt, improvise, and overcome any obstacle. They had inculcated this winning attitude in countless difficult and challenging training exercises and had learned that when the plan made on the "flat map" no longer made sense, they had to act within their commander's intent for that mission and carry on until they succeeded, even if that meant they would be the lone survivor.

There is no proof that Rudder read Clausewitz's book *On War*, but he did study warfare with energy, just like he tackled every problem in his life. From his actions prior to D-Day, there is little doubt that Rudder understood the concept of "friction" in war. In any endeavor, friction is that element that degrades your plan. As Clausewitz wrote: "Everything in war is very simple, but the simplest thing is difficult... In war, more than anywhere else, things do not turn out as we expect...," and friction is the "only concept that more or less corresponds to the factors that distinguish real war from war on paper." Without people who are trained to think for themselves, without a commander like Rudder who has coached, taught, and mentored his Rangers to think in terms of "what to do, not how to do it," even the simplest plan fails—and subsequently, the mission itself.

In the weeks before the invasion, the Pointe was designated as Army Air Force Target number 4901W/J/101 and specific bombing missions were directed to destroy the guns. In addition, every Allied aircraft that was flying back to England from missions in France that had any bombs remaining was ordered to drop them on target 4901W/J/101.

Hundreds of aircraft did this and, in total, nearly 10 kilotons (nearly the explosive power of the atomic bomb that would be dropped on Nagasaki in August 1945) fell on the Pointe. The Germans realized that they had to move the guns, and halted the permanent installation of the six French-made 155mm guns allocated to the position. They kept working, repairing, and improving the gun casemates and ammunition bunkers on the Pointe so that guns might be towed and emplaced quickly in the event of an invasion. In addition, the occupation of the Pointe as an observation post to direct artillery and mortar fire could seriously impact both Utah and Omaha beaches. The order from Allied Supreme Headquarters, therefore, was to take the Pointe, even if the guns were not there.

Rudder trained his men relentlessly, believing that a pint of sweat would save a gallon of blood. Rudder's football coaching experience was clearly evident and his men appreciated his commitment and focus. His training regime emphasized physical fitness, weapons training, cliff climbing, and realistic live-fire training ranges that took place on terrain that looked similar to the objectives that each force would have to seize. Allied intelligence officers had expended great effort to catalog every inch of the Rangers' objectives. Maps, aerial photographs, and reports from the French Resistance detailed the German defenses. Rudder and his leaders used this information to refine their plans. Intense rehearsals and additional training followed. Special ladders were borrowed from the London Fire Department. Special mortars that shot grappling hooks over 100-foot ledges were used to practice scaling steep cliffs. Although only a few Rangers of the PRAG had been in actual combat, they were as prepared and ready as any veteran outfit.

Rudder's plan to take the Pointe du Hoc was to conduct an amphibious assault on the strong German position from both the east (facing Omaha Beach) and west (facing Utah beach). Ten LCAs (landing craft assault) were to carry the assault force. Four DUKW six-wheel-drive amphibious trucks (nicknamed Ducks) and two additional LCAs carrying supplies were to follow the 10 assault LCAs. The DUKWs were specially outfitted with 100-foot ladders courtesy of the London Fire Brigade. Intelligence reports had measured the precise height of the cliffs and the fire ladders were just tall enough to reach the top of the cliff. The plan called for the first assault wave to climb the cliffs, take the top, give the signal to the second wave, and then destroy the six German guns in their bunkers.

The visibility was about 10 miles as the ships of Force O sailed from their port in England to Normandy. The wind was coming in strong from the northwest at 10 to 18 knots, causing waves averaging 3 to 4 feet in height, with occasional gusts of wind forming waves of 6 feet. The Force O ships sailed from Weymouth Harbor and approached the Normandy coast in the darkness around 3 a.m. The trip was uneventful. No German ships or planes attacked the convoy. Minesweepers that preceded Force O were able to clear the path of German anti-ship mines. Aboard their LSI transports, the Rangers continued to plan, prepare, and, if possible, rest. Relaxing aboard an LSI in the rough seas of the English Channel was problematic. Some Rangers were able to sleep through anything, but most found the trip less than restful, especially since everyone knew that this might be their last night alive. Seasickness was the most significant problem for the Rangers on board

US Army Rangers from A Company, 5th Ranger Battalion, boarding a British LCA in Weymouth Harbour during embarkation prior to D-Day, on June 1, 1944.

the LSIs *Ben-my-Chree*, *Amsterdam*, *Prince Charles*, *Prince Leopold*, and *Prince Baudoin*. In order to minimize this, Rudder ordered that the "last meal" should be light: coffee, toast, and maybe a flapjack. This foresight would pay off for many Rangers as they subsequently made the assault up the cliffs of the Pointe du Hoc.

Rudder also considered in advance how each Ranger was equipped. The soldiers of the 1st and 29th Infantry Divisions that were to land at Omaha were loaded down with a significant amount of equipment. Each one carried approximately 100 pounds of gear, including his helmet, weapon, gas mask, and enough supplies to last three days. They were woefully overloaded and many would drown, burdened by such a heavy load, as they jumped from their landing craft into the surf that was over their heads. The Rangers were more lightly equipped and carried only enough ammunition, food, and equipment for the assault. Each Ranger had the standard helmet and weapon, but instead of a pack filled with equipment, the Rangers wore a specially designed canvas assault vest. This vest had multiple pockets for ammunition, first aid kits, and rations. It helped reduce the load each Ranger carried as well as evenly distribute the weight across their bodies. This enhanced their ability to run, climb, and crawl. In addition, each Ranger wore the M-1926 Life Preserver belt that was activated by pulling a cord that initiated two compressed air cylinders. The M-1926 could be quickly discarded once the Rangers were ashore. The Rangers were outfitted with an M5 gas mask and, on each Ranger's upper right arm, a British-made gas detector sleeve that was designed to turn pink if the Germans employed chemical weapons. Most Rangers carried the M1 Garand rifle, two grenades, and a combat knife. Some carried Thompson submachine guns or an M1 carbine if they were assigned to also carry heavier equipment, such as components of the two 81mm mortars that were part of Force A. For extra firepower, each Ranger company had a minimum of four Browning Automatic Rifles (BARs) and two light 60mm mortars. Ten thermite grenades, to be used for demolition, were distributed within each company.[7]

The loading of troops and equipment from the LSIs to landing craft in the dark, early morning hours of D–Day was a complex and dangerous operation. Hundreds of ships and landing craft were packed with combat-laden troops in choppy waters. After their light meal, the less burdened Rangers, all expert climbers from their intense, pre-D-Day training, easily climbed down the cargo netting into their LCAs without mishap. Once loaded, the LCAs circled in holding patterns, waiting for the other transports to join them and for the day to dawn. One coast guardsman, Marvin J. Perrett, who was coxswain for a landing craft on D-Day, described sailing a landing craft banging against the surging waves off the Normandy coast as "like driving a bulldozer in the water."

As the assault force formed, the sky began to turn gray. On signal, the LCAs of Ranger Force A headed for the Pointe du Hoc. Rudder was in LCA 888, the lead craft of the assault force. He understood that all leadership is by example. In the dim light, as his LCA pitched in the rough waters, Rudder could see the eight troop LCAs, each carrying 21–22 Rangers, two additional LCAs carrying supplies, and an LCT with four DUKWs. Each LCA had special mortars that would shoot grapnel-tipped rockets, attached to coiled climbing ropes, up the 100-foot sheer cliff sides of the Pointe du Hoc.

"Each LCA was fitted with three pairs of rocket mounts, at bow, amidships, and stern, wired so that they could be fired in series of pairs from one control point at the stern..." a report on the 2nd Ranger assault of Pointe du Hoc later chronicled. "Ropes were carried by one pair of rockets, affixed to the rocket's base by a connecting wire... The rockets were headed by grapnels. The rope or ladder for each rocket was coiled in a box directly behind the rocket mount. Each craft carried, in addition to the six mounted rockets, a pair of small, hand-projector-type rockets attached to plain ropes. These could be easily carried ashore if necessary."[8]

In addition, each LCA carried an extension ladder that could be removed from the craft and manually carried, in sections, and assembled against the side of the cliffs. These ladders were especially important to bring up supplies. Lastly, the DUKWs carried the specially fabricated London Fire Brigade ladders that could extend from the narrow, rocky beach under the Pointe's walls and reach the clifftop. On each ladder, twin Vickers K machine guns (also called the VGO or Vickers Gas Operated Gun) were fastened to the top rung to provide the first Ranger up the ladder with a means to sweep the surface of the Pointe du Hoc with machine-gun fire to suppress the German defenders.

At 5:50 a.m., the Allied naval bombardment began. As Rudder's landing craft passed the USS *Texas*, the roar of the battleship's big guns was deafening. The USS *Texas*, nicknamed the "Big T," along with its sister ships, pounded the Pointe du Hoc with a continuous barrage. From 11 kilometers away, the 10, 14-inch/45-caliber guns, and 21, 5-inch/51-caliber guns of the "Big T" were particularly effective in blasting the top of the Pointe du Hoc. One shot tore away part of the cliff, so that fragments fell down onto the narrow beach, essentially creating a 60-foot ramp on the eastern face of the cliff. Collapsing a portion of the cliff was not a planned effect of the naval gunfire, but it clearly would assist the Rangers once they landed. At 6:10 a.m., 18 B-26 medium bombers from the 9th Air Force made a final airstrike on the Pointe du Hoc. The naval gunfire continued for another 16 minutes, when the naval force shifted their fire to support the Omaha Beach landings. As the Rangers sailed in rough seas toward their objective, the previous, eerie silence was soon filled by the sound of hundreds of aircraft flying overhead.

The LCAs of Rudder's Force A followed a small guide-boat which led them nearly 12 miles across the stormy English Channel. The sea swells became a significant problem, as the box-like landing craft bounced around on their final approach to the shoreline. Waves swept over the sides of the LCAs and the Rangers were forced to bail water with buckets and helmets. LCA 860, carrying Captain Harold K. Slater and 20 men of Company D, swamped in the rough waves. All 20 men were thrown overboard but were eventually picked up by naval rescue craft. Another supply landing craft, LCA 914, was swamped and sunk. The remaining nine LCAs continued on, following the guide-boat through surging waves and shifting winds. They became engulfed in smoke designed to protect the ships and landing force from observation by German shore batteries. As the landing craft broke through the smoke, Rudder immediately realized that they had drifted off course. He was not at the Pointe du Hoc. His Force A was facing the Pointe-et-Raz-de-la-Percée on the west flank of Omaha Beach. It was now 6:39 a.m. and they were four miles from their objective.

Rudder faced a crushing dilemma. The mission seemed doomed. He could not ask for instructions, as everyone was under strict orders not to make any radio calls during the assault for fear of alerting the Germans. He was already past the time that his force was to land at the Pointe du Hoc. He knew that this delay meant that he would not be able to signal the reinforcements under Force C to follow him. Absent a visual signal from Rudder, Schneider's 5th Ranger Battalion, with the three companies of the 2nd Ranger Battalion of Force C, would shift to Omaha Beach. Rudder had to make a decision.

He had two choices. He could land at Omaha, fight through the beach defenses and attempt to maneuver his Rangers overland, and assault the Pointe du Hoc at its strongest defense, the landward side; or he could take his LCAs in Force A and sail parallel to the coast, in daylight with perfect visibility, and face the possibility of withering German fire all along the route. In addition, Rudder realized that the naval gunfire had shifted according to plan, and this would give the German defenders on top of the Pointe du Hoc at least 40 minutes to recover and prepare their defense. The element of surprise was lost.

Fear is a reaction; courage is a decision. Rudder was determined to succeed and decided on courage. He did not hesitate, panic or freeze, but acted immediately. He ordered the LCAs to follow him as he sailed west, a few hundred yards from the shore and parallel to the coast. He was singularly focused on reaching his planned landing zone. The German defenses along the way opened up on the line of LCAs. Machine-gun and rifle fire smacked against the landing crafts' armor. The Rangers blasted back with their Vickers K machine guns and BARs. Three Rangers were wounded by plunging fire. Soldiers ducked against the walls of the LCAs for protection, as it was useless to fire back as they bounced across the waves heading toward their objective. As they ran this gauntlet of fire, a German 20mm gun hit one of the DUKWs, sinking it and killing five of the nine Rangers on board. The Germans were now firing mortars at Rudder's LCAs as they continued on their parallel path along the shoreline.

Having recovered from the naval and air bombardment, the Germans of the 726th Infantry Regiment, on top of the Pointe du Hoc, saw the advancing landing craft and opened up with machine-gun fire. Some Rangers fired back with machine guns and BARs. Rudder stood up and looked over the ramp of the LCA as his column of landing craft approached from the east. He realized that he would not be able to assault the cliffs simultaneously from the east and the west. Again, he was faced with a critical, time-sensitive decision. He reckoned that if he tried to send part of his Force A to the western side of the cliffs, the men in the landing craft could be slaughtered by German fire as they sailed in front of the Pointe du Hoc. He made his decision; he communicated to the other LCAs by hand-and-arm signals that the entire force would land on the east side.

At 7:10 a.m, Rudder's landing craft hit the shallow, rocky beach in front of the 100-foot cliffs. His LCA was the first to reach the Pointe du Hoc. As the ramp dropped, Rudder and the men in LCA 888 ran for the cliffs. LCA 861 was next, followed by LCAs 862, 884, and 887. LCAs 668 and 858—originally set to land on the west side—hit the east side as well. LCA 883 was the last to land. All nine surviving LCAs were now tightly jammed on the narrow beach as they rushed to unload their troops. The special grappling hook mortars on the front of the LCAs fired, but since most of the ropes were soaked from the surging waves, many of the rockets did not carry to the top of the cliffs and fell uselessly back onto the beach. A few of the grapnels, however, reached the top. The Germans immediately began to blast the Rangers with machine-gun fire, dropping grenades from the top of the cliff. As the ramps on the LCAs dropped onto the narrow beach, 15 Rangers were killed from the enemy fire. Other Rangers fell into holes with neck-deep water. Rudder ran toward the cliffs, was knocked down, but quickly recovered and made it to the base.

The face of the cliff offered some protection from enemy fire, but not from the falling grenades. A pair of Rangers exposed themselves to return fire on the Germans. A few Germans fell, but more Rangers were hit as well. Once the LCAs had delivered their troops, the coxswains revved their crafts' engines in reverse, leaving the beach to return to their mother ship. As the LCAs pulled away, the Rangers knew there was no possibility of retreat.

As the LCAs withdrew, the three surviving DUKWs arrived and raised their ladders, but the beach was so covered with rocks, rubble, and shell holes, they could not get close enough for their ladders to touch the upper cliff edge. One DUKW extended its ladder, and Sergeant William Stivison, dangling from the top, fired the twin Vickers K machine guns at the enemy on the crest. The ladder swayed back and forth as German tracers flew all around him, but he miraculously managed to continue firing without falling or being hit. If his actions had not been deadly serious, it would almost have been funny watching him sway back and forther at the top of the ladder. Finally, the waves pushed the DUKW against the shore. The DUKW operator retracted the ladder with Stivison still barely holding on.

Nothing was going according to plan. The Rangers at the bottom of the cliff immediately started to climb. There was no hesitation. To stay on the beach was to die, as German fire swept their ranks and grenades exploded all around them. "My whole psyche that day was like I was in a football game," said First Sergeant Leonard Lomell, from Dog Company, 2nd Ranger Battalion. He continued his account:

> I remembered my instructions, and we charged hard and low and fast. That was our secret, and we stayed together. The 2nd Platoon stayed together as a team on D-Day. We got in, and our ramp went down and all hell broke loose. The boat leader goes off the front straightaway. I stepped off the ramp, and I was the first one shot. The bullet went through what little fat I had on my right side. It didn't hit any organs, but it spun me around and burned like the dickens. There was a shell crater there underwater. I went down in water over my head with the spare rope, the hand launcher and my submachine gun. Keeping in mind that the idea was to get to the top as fast as we could, I got myself together and went up the cliff.[9]

Rudder made it to the cliff and found a small cave. He established his headquarters and a medical aid station. Surprisingly, he also met two American paratroopers, Pvt. Leonard Goodgall and Sgt. Raymond Crouch, of I Company, 506th Parachute Infantry Regiment, 101st Airborne Division. They were the only survivors of a C-47 that crashed into the sea during the mass parachute jump in the early hours of D-Day. They had followed the coast in the dark until they found the small cave under the Pointe du Hoc. Rudder "told them to stay with him; days would pass before they saw their parent unit again."[10]

The remaining Rangers at the bottom of the cliff, except a few from the headquarters team and the medical personnel, started to climb. According to Lomell:

> Foremost in our minds was the challenge of getting up that cliff, which was wet from rain and clay and very slippery. The Germans were shooting down. They were cutting ropes. They were trying to kill us. I'd already been shot. Were we going to make it to the top? Were we going to get shot? These are the things we were thinking about. I think we were too cocky to be too fearful or frightened. I never thought I was going to get killed. These guys were positive thinkers. I don't think they thought much about getting killed. They thought if they got an even chance in a fight they would win as they always had.[11]

The Rangers climbed with whatever they had, using the few ropes with grappling hooks that had caught on the top of the cliff, or were tangled in the German barbed wire that ringed the crest above. Some Rangers ascended hand over hand, free-climbing, reaching for hand and toeholds as they scaled the cliff, carrying their weapons and equipment.

Rangers were shot, many fell from the cliff, but the others pressed on. The Germans continued to drop hand grenades, and even 20mm shells, off the side of the cliff in an effort to stop the advancing Rangers. Rudder was climbing up the cliff when a German shell exploded nearby, throwing him back down. He quickly recovered and, undaunted, started climbing again.

A few hundred yards off the Pointe du Hoc coastline, the destroyers HMS *Talybont* and USS *Satterlee* navigated in dangerously close, nearly running aground, in order to rake the German positions on the crest with machine guns and cannons. The fire from these two destroyers bought the Rangers time and kept the Germans ducking as Rudder's men climbed the cliff. Within five minutes of landing, the first Rangers reached the top. Other Rangers threw ropes down to their comrades, as the rest continued to follow. Rangers at the top attacked the German defenders with rifles, BARs, and grenades, killing the enemy they encountered and clearing the crest. Each Ranger team had assigned objectives and they pressed on to their objectives, not waiting for orders.

"Ranger tactics stressed rapid movement by small groups. From the first man up the rope, the aggressive spirit of the Ranger was demonstrated… An estimated twenty separate parties of Rangers quickly assembled at the top of the cliff and headed toward their objectives."[12] The top of the Pointe du Hoc was covered with huge craters from previous aerial and naval bombardments. Many of the German bunkers were severely damaged. The Rangers moved from one shell crater to the next, avoiding the withering machine-gun and small-arms fire of the defenders as they inched their way toward bunkers, throwing grenades or exploding them with satchel charges. The Rangers discovered that each bunker they captured was empty of artillery guns. By 7:40 a.m., the Rangers had taken all the designated 155mm gun casemates on the top of the Pointe du Hoc but the guns were not there. The Rangers realized that the intense Allied bombing prior to D-Day must have caused the Germans to safeguard their guns by positioning them away from the Pointe, but they might be nearby. The Rangers had to be sure that the guns were neutralized. Small groups of Rangers began patrolling to the south to find the guns.

At 7:45 a.m., Rudder established his command post in a shell crater on the top of the Pointe du Hoc. He sent the code words "Praise the Lord," signaling that the objective had been seized. He did not receive a confirmation that his message was received by his higher headquarters. Most of his long-range SCR-284 and SCR-300 radios were inoperative, either soaked with seawater or shot full of holes. Thus, Rudder was unable to make radio contact with anyone with the exception of a few short-range conversations using walkie-talkies carried by his own men. Germans still fired on the Rangers, but Rudder realized his men held the most significant positions on the Pointe. One German position—a protected antiaircraft gun Tobruk fortification at the southwestern edge of the Pointe du Hoc defensive area—was proving very difficult to capture. Several Rangers who attempted to destroy it were killed. Rudder was hit by a sniper's bullet. The 8mm Mauser round penetrated his calf, but he fought on. While the Rangers were trying to take out this Tobruk, an errant shell from a British ship exploded against the side of a bunker, killing a Ranger captain and wounding several Rangers with spalling cement fragments. Fortunately, Rudder's second wound was not serious and he chose to ignore addressing it. Instead, he ordered his men to keep the Germans inside the antiaircraft position pinned down while he worked on getting naval guns to bear on the target. In the interim, the Germans continued shelling the Pointe du Hoc with mortar and artillery fire.

Ranger casualties mounted. In Dog Company, only 20 of the original 65 Rangers that landed were still able to fight. As his men continued to battle German snipers, fight off squad-sized counterattacks, and dodge artillery shells, Rudder was faced with another crucial decision. The friction of war had completely disrupted the plan. He knew that he would not receive reinforcements. He could not communicate with the rest of the Allied forces. He did not know if the landings at Omaha Beach were succeeding. He could not withdraw, and he did not have enough ammunition and supplies to hold against a determined German counterattack for very long. He made his call: push ahead with all his might, be steadfast, and persevere. His men immediately set out on small-unit patrols to search for the missing German artillery pieces. Other Rangers moved to the southwest to secure their next objective, the D-514 road, to prevent German reinforcements from attacking the Pointe du Hoc or Omaha. On the Pointe du Hoc itself, Rudder organized a few headquarters personnel and wounded Rangers to defend the perimeter against the inevitable German counterattack.

The Rangers moved through the German minefields and established a blocking position along the D-514 road to prevent enemy troops from attacking east toward Omaha. Once that position was established, two Rangers, First Sergeant Leonard Lomell and Staff Sergeant Jack Kuhn, noticed some tracks that ran south. Moving with speed and stealth, deep inside enemy territory, Lomell and Kuhn discovered an unbelievable target: a battery of 155mm howitzers positioned on line and heavily camouflaged under the trees. They were poised to shoot, and totally unguarded. Crawling up to the guns, they observed a German officer briefing a group of enemy artillerymen about a hundred yards away from the guns' position.

Lomell explained what happened next:

When we got to the gun position and looked over, I saw some Germans being talked to. They were gathering there, putting on their jackets. It was 8 o'clock in the morning or thereabouts. I guess they were organizing themselves. Their positions were textbook ready. There was nothing to indicate that the guns had been fired. There were no ejected shells. If you know what an artillery position looks like, they're never that perfect after they're fired. The entire battery, five big coastal guns, was there at the ready. All the shells were stacked, and there was no debris—no empty shells or powder bags. If you've ever been in an artillery outfit after it's been engaged, it's a mess cleaning up after it. This position was in perfect order. I believe the reason they couldn't fire was because E Company had taken out their observation post at the Pointe first thing. That was where their concrete observation bunker was. They had no directions to fire, nor any firing orders. Their lines of communication had been cut off. I don't think those Germans knew there were any Rangers or American soldiers within a mile of them. They were so nonchalant about walking around, acting as if there was no enemy about because we were so quiet. They weren't in a hurry to do anything. Some have said: "We don't believe it. No good artilleryman ever left his position unguarded." Well, all I know is, that morning there weren't any guards in their gun position. We didn't draw any fire at any time while near their guns.[13]

As quickly as they could, with Kuhn providing cover in case any enemy appeared, Lomell disabled the five guns one-by-one, some by destroying the sights and a few by using thermite grenades which burned through metal but did not explode like a fragmentation grenade. "I put one thermite grenade in each of the first two guns' visible moveable gears," Lomell reported. "Then I took my Tommy gun, wrapped it in my field jacket and smashed the sights on all five guns [for unknown reasons the sixth gun was missing]."[14] With the noise of the battle of Normandy occurring all around them, the two Rangers destroyed the artillery pieces without alerting the German gunners. Lomell and Kuhn then rapidly departed back to the roadblock. Just a few moments later, a four-man Ranger patrol led by Sgt. Frank Rupinski arrived at the same site and destroyed the sixth gun and an artillery ammunition cache.

With the guns destroyed and the coastal highway blocked, Rudder's Rangers had accomplished their D-Day objective. In battle, however, the enemy always gets a vote. The Germans counterattacked the Rangers with a vengeance. With artillery fire falling all day on the Pointe du Hoc, and German snipers popping out from hiding places along the line of trenches and bunkers, the Rangers remained decisively engaged. Most importantly, since Rudder could not communicate with anyone outside of his own men at the Pointe du Hoc, there were no reinforcements or resupply. The original plan had called for eight Ranger companies to defend the Pointe du Hoc from German counterattacks, but Able and Baker companies, 2nd Ranger Battalion, and the entire 5th Ranger Battalion, had shifted to Omaha Beach and were fighting to break through the fortified German defenses around the Vierville Draw. Rudder's Rangers were on their own and could not expect support. To solve the reinforcement and resupply problem, and to evacuate his ever-growing number of wounded, Rudder had to find a way to communicate with the rest of the Allied forces.

Rudder's communications officer, 1st Lt. James W. "Ike" Eikner, had foreseen communication problems and had trained his men to use

Heavily laden US Army Rangers of the 2nd Ranger Battalion move under the cover of the cliffs at the Pointe du Hoc, Normandy, France, on Tuesday, June 6, 1944. The third man in the file is carrying a .30-caliber, water-cooled Browning machine gun while others carry machine-gun ammunition. (US National Archives photo)

international Morse code. He had also secured a World War I vintage tripod-mounted EE-84 signal lamp. By using blinker light and Morse code, Eikner and his men were able to maintain contact and adjust naval gunfire. Rudder then sent signals to the portions of the naval fleet that could observe and fire on the Pointe du Hoc. Specifically, Rudder asked for air support. When several P-47 Thunderbolt fighters flew over the Pointe, they acted as though they were going to attack the Rangers. Rudder had brought an American flag ashore, quickly unfolded it, and placed it on the seaward slope of his command post. "The P-47 pilots waggled his wings in recognition, then accurately struck the target."[15] Eikner signaled to the ships: "Located Pointe-du-Hoc—mission accomplished—need ammunition and reinforcement—many casualties." He then requested that they send in boats to bring in supplies and remove the wounded, but the German fire was too intense and the boats could not make it to the shore. No one could get in, or out of, the Pointe du Hoc. With the tough fighting that was raging on Omaha Beach, there were no reserves to spare. The Rangers would have to hold out until the 5th Rangers and the remaining companies of the 2nd Rangers could fight their way from Omaha.

The Germans counterattacked, hoping to dislodge the stubborn Rangers, only to be repulsed in one attack after another. While the Rangers killed numerous enemy soldiers, the snipers seemed to be everywhere and with the Rangers continued to take casualties. The situation seemed to be going from desperate to disastrous. But each time it appeared to those around Rudder that the Rangers might be overrun, Rudder found a way to get them to hold on. First Lieutenant Elmer "Dutch" Vermeer, the 2nd Ranger Battalion's Engineer Officer, reported to author Stephen Ambrose after the war: "The biggest thing that saved our day was seeing Colonel Rudder controlling the operation... It still makes me cringe to recall the pain he must have endured trying to operate with a wound through the leg and the concussive force he must have felt from the close hit by the yellow-colored shell [a US Navy marking round had exploded closeby and nearly killed Rudder]. He was the strength of the whole operation."[16]

One bright ray of hope flared on the evening of D-Day, just before sunset, when a force of 22 Rangers, led by Lieutenant "Ace" Parker, who had fought off Omaha Beach and infiltrated through German lines, linked up with the Rangers at the Pointe du Hoc. In the chaos of the fighting on Omaha, Parker's unit was separated and he moved forward of the rest of the 5th Ranger Battalion without knowing it.

> He assumed that they had moved on to Pointe du Hoc, when in truth, they were still fighting for control of the bluffs overlooking Omaha. Parker set out for the 5th Rangers objective, having several firefights all the way. At one point, this tiny band of Rangers acquired forty German prisoners, which Parker had to free in order to avoid him and his men being captured themselves. Two hours before the sunset on June 6th, 2100 hours, Parker's platoon arrived at Pointe du Hoc and Rudder's CP on the cliff face.[17]

Rudder was happy to see Parker, but the news that Parker was on his own, and not the vanguard of a relief force, was ominous.

Lieutenant Colonel James Earl Rudder on the Pointe du Hoc during the battle. (US Army photo)

The Germans fought ferociously to retake the Pointe du Hoc. At the roadblock, the Rangers came under continuous attack. Rudder's Rangers would defend an ever-decreasing perimeter for the next two days, without reinforcement and with very little resupply. He was reduced to about 140 soldiers from his original 225 men. Many of those were wounded, but still fighting.

As night fell on D-Day, Rudder knew the Germans would try to overwhelm his defenses under the cover of darkness, when he could not receive any naval gunfire or air support. From midnight to 3:30 a.m., the Rangers defended against several heavy counterattacks from the German 914th Grenadier Regiment of the 352nd Infantry Division. Some of Rudder's men were overrun and some were captured. The Rangers withdrew from the blocking position along the D-514 road and returned to consolidate their defenses at the fortifications of the Pointe du Hoc. Running low on men, weapons, and ammunition, Rudder pulled in his defensive line. His Rangers used captured German rifles and machine guns to fight off the enemy attacks. At one point during the most ferocious German attack, a lucky Ranger mortar strike hit a German artillery ammunition cache and set it on fire. The resulting bright light silhouetted the enemy attackers and the Rangers mowed them down. The Rangers ceded ground during the night. Their defensive perimeter tightened until it was a thin line along the edge of the cliff, only 450 yards wide and 180 yards deep. Rudder was determined not to give up. He prepared for his last stand. The Germans, however, had taken heavy casualties in their three attempts to retake the Pointe du Hoc at night, and could not mount another assault.

As the sun rose on June 7, the Rangers redistributed ammunition, food, and water, moved forward to better positions, tended to their wounded, and prepared to hold out against more anticipated German attacks. They were nearly out of ammunition. For the rest of the day, the Germans harassed the Rangers by attacking in small groups but did not launch any large-scale, coordinated assaults during the day. Rudder kept the enemy at bay with naval gunfire support. In the afternoon, a single platoon of Rangers arrived by landing craft to reinforce Rudder and evacuate his wounded. The new arrivals told Rudder that the 5th Rangers, with the remainder of the 2nd Ranger Battalion, were fighting their way from Omaha Beach toward the Pointe du Hoc. All Rudder had to do was hold on a little longer. The Rangers were now defending primarily with captured weapons and bayonets as they prepared for another night cut off from American lines. Around 10 p.m., patrols from Schneider's Ranger Force made it to Rudder's dwindling defensive perimeter. They relayed to Rudder that help was only hours away and that he must hold on. Rudder intended to do just that.

There was sporadic firing throughout the night. The Germans attacked in small parties, but they were spent and unable to muster the strength to launch another major assault. When dawn broke on June 8, a force approached Rudder's final defensive position. Rudder could see tanks headed his way and assumed the worse. Firing erupted from both sides until the Rangers on the Pointe du Hoc realized that the forces approaching them were American, not German. The tanks supporting the advancing 5th Ranger Force were M4A3 Duplex Drive (DD) tanks

Rudder's Rangers defend the ever-shrinking perimeter of the Pointe du Hoc on June 7, 1944. Nearly driven into the sea, the Rangers held on tenaciously, never considering surrender or defeat. The Ranger at the top right is manning an M1919A4 .30-caliber machine gun. Empty ammunition cans at his feet testify to the fury of the fighting. (US Army photo)

of the 743rd Tank Battalion. The Rangers had never seen DD tanks with their swimming skirts down and thus did not identify them as American. Since the Rangers defending the Pointe du Hoc were using German weapons, and firing German tracer bullets, the relief force and their supporting DD tanks were equally confused. After a short time, the firing stopped and the situation was resolved. Before noon on June 8, 1944, Rudder's defenders linked up with their much anticipated and welcomed relief force.

Throughout the difficult times on D-Day, and until they were relieved two days later on June 8, Rudder's leadership held the Ranger force together. He transformed disaster into victory more than once during the Pointe du Hoc operation. According to author Thomas M. Hatfield:

> He had to cope with the unknown. He and his men were cut off, isolated. They had no communication... They didn't know the outcome of the invasion. Yet Rudder was steadfast without knowing when relief was coming. He remained calm, a dedicated leader. Some of his men told me they were better soldiers with him than at other times. That's because he was consistent, whatever the circumstances. He was always the same, authentic leader—and with him, his men knew the mission came first.[18]

Of the 225 Rangers that landed on the Pointe du Hoc on D-Day, only about 90 could be considered fit to fight on June 8. For his action as Commander of the Provisional Ranger Assault Group, Lt. Col. James E. Rudder was awarded the Distinguished Service Cross. His citation reads:

> The President of the United States of America, authorized by Act of Congress, July 9, 1918, takes pleasure in presenting the Distinguished Service Cross to Lieutenant Colonel (Infantry) James Earl Rudder (ASN: 0-294916), United States Army, for extraordinary heroism in connection with military operations against an armed enemy while serving with the 2nd Ranger Infantry Battalion, in action against enemy forces on 6 June 1944, at Normandy, France. Lieutenant Colonel Rudder, commanding Force "A" of the Rangers, landed on the beach with his unit, which was immediately subjected to heavy rifle, machine gun, mortar and artillery fire. Devastating fire was also directed from the cliffs overlooking the beach. Completely disregarding his own safety, Lieutenant Colonel Rudder immediately scaled the cliffs in order to better direct the attack. By his determined leadership and dauntlessness he inspired his men so that they successfully withstood three enemy counterattacks. Though wounded again he

still refused to be evacuated. Lieutenant Colonel Rudder's heroic leadership, personal bravery and zealous devotion to duty exemplify the highest traditions of the military forces of the United States and reflect great credit upon himself and the United States Army.

General Orders: Headquarters, First US Army, General Orders No. 28 (June 20, 1944)

★ ★ ★

Leadership Lesson

Fear is a reaction. Courage is a decision. Courage is the backbone of leadership. No leader can advance in any endeavour without courage. Many Rangers who served with Lt. Col. James Earl Rudder during World War II believed that he did not know what fear was. Rudder strongly disagreed. As he expressed years after the war, he was as afraid as anyone else, sometimes even more so as he knew the big picture and had reason be fearful. He understood, however, that fear was a normal human reaction. He knew fear was "good" as it generated awareness of danger. Totally fearless people don't last long. Rudder also knew that he had to cycle through the fear as fast as possible and arrive at that mental state where he could make a decision. This is not easy and requires focus. Fear can be gripping. Fear can paralyze. The key is to focus on action. To focus on action in the midst of fear takes a strong mind. Leaders must understand this, move rapidly though the fear, gain situational awareness, and decide. The first step of any leader is to decide to be courageous, whether that be facing down the division commander when you tell him, "I'll have to disobey that order," as Rudder did with Gen. Huebner, or if you are facing the CEO to report that a project is off schedule. Easier said than done; it is all a matter of the degree of danger and your level of experience, but there are ways to prepare to be better at handling fear. Training that involves making decisions under stressful situations can reinforce confidence and can enable a leader to learn how to push through the fear and decide on courage. Once the leader decides on courage, communication and leadership by example become the vital forces of motivation. To win, leaders must motivate and impel teams to action. To do this, leaders must communicate by action and word. Of these two, action is the most powerful. Colorful speeches may be great for the cinema, but in the real world, leaders inspire primarily by example. Saying "Follow me" and moving forward means so much more than "Go ahead, I'll be watching you and staying safely behind." What can you learn from Lt. Col. Rudder's leadership at the Pointe du Hoc? How can you learn from Rudder's story to enhance your team's performance, and bring out the best in your people?

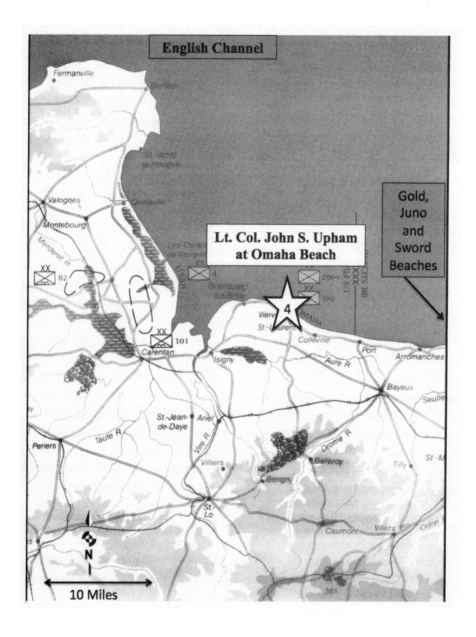

English Channel

Gold, Juno and Sword Beaches

Lt. Col. John S. Upham at Omaha Beach

10 Miles

CHAPTER 4

Tanks on Omaha Beach

Adaptability

"This war is not, however, a war of masses of men hurling masses of shells at each other. It is by devising new weapons, and above all, by scientific leadership, that we shall best cope with the enemy's superior strength."
From a memorandum by the Prime Minister, Winston Churchill, for the War Cabinet on September 3, 1940

Off the coast of Normandy, France, June 6, 1944: Lieutenant Colonel John S. Upham, Jr., the commander of the 743rd Tank Battalion, stood in his M3A1 halftrack command vehicle at the front of the landing craft, his right hand firmly grasping the side of the vehicle to steady himself. Cold, angry waves smashed against the side of the flat-bottomed Landing Craft Tank (LCT) as the craft tossed across the dark, foreboding waters of the Baie de la Seine, the part of the English Channel that borders the coast of Normandy. The rough waves showed no mercy to the ship's crew and passengers. Everyone but the most veteran seaman was seasick, with most having already vomited their breakfast.

Although the weather was marginally acceptable for General Eisenhower to "green light" the invasion, the conditions were far from ideal, and the rough seas immediately began to disrupt the carefully timed amphibious landing plan. Visibility was up to 10 miles, but the sky was overcast with clouds over the beachhead. The wind was forceful, at 10 to 18 knots and, coming from the northwest, pushed the ships and landing craft off their designated courses. The waves were 3 to 4 feet, with surges up to 6 feet, and with breakers on the beach reaching up to 4 feet high.

Upham's radio operator, Corporal James Robins, leaned over the side of the halftrack and puked on the slick, water-drenched floor of the LCT.

"Sorry, Colonel," the young corporal coughed as he tried to regain his composure.

Upham merely nodded as if to say, "It's okay." The gesture was worth more than any words. Upham was also feeling queasy and, except for a cup of coffee, was glad he had skipped breakfast. He was determined not to be sick in front of his men. As the gray morning sky began to lighten, Upham could see through the chilly morning mist the ships of the huge invasion fleet, the greatest armada ever assembled, all around him. It was an amazing sight. He felt like a small cog in a great machine that was about to make history. He was right.

This insignia is the shoulder patch of the 743rd Tank Battalion. Lieutenant J. P. Wharton of the Tank Corps of the American Expeditionary Force (AEF) created the three-colored triangle in 1918. The colors of the triangle each represent the three combat arms of the US Army: blue for infantry; red for artillery; and yellow for cavalry. This was a color representation of the doctrine of "Combined Arms," in which tanks would play a significant role. A triangle in heraldic terms has always been associated with armor as it represents the head of a spear. This was adopted with the belief that armor would be the spearhead for future armies in the US Army's combined arms tactical doctrine. The number 743 designates the unit as one of the Army's independent tank battalions. The 743rd landed on Omaha Beach with 32 tanks on June 6, 1944, during the first wave and played a significant role in breaking through the German defenses.

Omaha Beach, located between the Port-en-Bessin and the Vire River, was about 8 kilometers wide, a bit more than the distance of an 18-hole golf course. The Germans had occupied the area since 1940 and were experts at creating strong defensive lines formed from multiple firing positions, positioned and sighted with interlocking fields of fire. Tons of concrete had been poured into the defenses of the Atlantic Wall. These pockets of resistance or "resistance nests" (called *Widerstandsnester*, shortened to the military abbreviation "WN") were formidable. On Omaha, these positions were manned by five companies of German troops in 15 WNs, numbered WN-60 in the east to WN-74 in the west. The bunkers that made up the WNs were positioned to maximize the cover of the terrain and make any direct sighting by enemy ships difficult. Most importantly, the cannon and machine guns of the WNs were sighted to shoot left and right, in enfilade and crossfire down the beach, and not straight ahead. This clever tactical disposition made the beach defenses even more deadly, as every obstacle was covered by machine-gun and mortar fire.

To stop the Allied invasion, the Germans needed to fix the landing forces in predesignated kill zones and create a devil's matrix of anti-invasion obstacles and barbed wire to make movement off the beach for troops and vehicles impossible. At least 200 metal Belgian Gates were dug into the sand at the low-tide line. Each gate had mines tied to the top and primed to explode upon contact with an incoming landing craft. Behind these obstacles, the Germans had driven a forest of logs into the sand that extended 6 or 7 feet above ground level. Some were tipped with Teller Mines, an antitank mine that contained a powerful explosive that could blast boats, tanks, and men apart. Next came a line of steel tetrahedron-shaped hedgehogs, looking a bit like large steel jacks, to block the movement of armored vehicles from crossing the beach. Further inland on the beach, the Germans had laid an extensive belt of antipersonnel mines. Dense minefields were also placed to block the exits off the beach and to protect the front and rear of the WNs. In short, the Allies had an extremely complex and deadly barrier to breach.

To soften these defenses, Allied planners had prepared an intense 40-minute naval and 30-minute aerial bombardment of Omaha Beach.

The big guns of one battleship, two cruisers, and six destroyers, and the rockets of nine Landing Craft Tank-Rocket ships, LCT(R)s, would engulf the Germans in a fury of fire. Nearly five hundred B-24 Liberator heavy bombers of the US Army 8th Air Force would drop over 13,000 bombs on the Germans defending Omaha. They would concentrate on 11 key targets: the Pointe et Raz de la Percée; the "Fortified House"; the Vierville Draw, designated D-1; the Hamel au Pretre; the Les Moulins Draw West (D-3); the Les Moulins Draw East (D-3); the St Laurent Draw West (E-1); the St Laurent Draw East (E-1); the Colleville Draw (E-3) West; the Colleville Draw East (E-3); and the Cabourg Draw (F-1). Each of these targets was to be hit by one B-24 heavy bomber group comprised of six squadrons, with six planes per squadron. The aerial bombardment was scheduled between H-25 and H-5 (from 25 minutes

The Duplex Drive (DD) tank shown above was one of the top-secret Allied weapons of D-Day. The 743rd Tank Battalion was specially equipped with 32 DD Sherman tanks with the mission to swim to shore and land on the western side of Omaha Beach at Dog Green, Dog White, Dog Red, and Easy Green before the first wave of assault infantry arrived. (Imperial War Museum photo)

to 5 minutes) before H-Hour—the time that the first wave would land on Omaha Beach.

This level of firepower was anticipated to decimate the German defenses. Allied planners predicted that any German forces would be killed or stunned by the sheer brutality of firepower from the combined aerial and naval bombardment.

As the LCT headed toward the beach, Upham thought about the journey his battalion had embarked upon to reach this point, off the coast of Normandy, to serve as the spearhead for the 29th Division on Omaha.

He had trained his battalion and its leaders thoroughly.[1] He knew that Hitler's Atlantic Wall would be a hard nut to crack. He trusted that Allied leaders had sought every advantage possible to reduce friendly casualties and that his tanks were a vital part of that plan. The Operation *Overlord* planners had thoroughly and painstakingly studied how to assault Omaha successfully and overcome the German defenses. Although the tanks could be landed directly on the beach by LCTs, the landing craft were also big, slow targets for the German coastal guns. With each LCT

In this photo, taken on the morning of D-Day, the USS Augusta (CL/CA-31), a Northampton-class cruiser of the United States Navy, served as a headquarters ship for General Omar Bradley, the commander of First Army. LCVPs of the 2nd Battalion, 18th Infantry Regiment, 1st Infantry Division, are seen heading toward Omaha Beach. (US Navy Photo NARA 80-G-45720)

loaded with four tanks, they might be hit and sink before the tanks could unload. To ensure they arrived on the beach, the idea was discussed that the tanks needed to be unloaded from their LCTs outside of the range of most of the German guns and then swim to shore under their own power. From this idea, the concept of a swimming tank was born.

The British demonstrated the Duplex Drive "DD" swimming tank to US planners in November 1943, and the Americans quickly adopted the DD tank for the invasion of Normandy.[2] The Americans rapidly converted existing M4A1 Sherman tanks to the DD design and equipped the 70th, 741st, and 743rd Tank Battalions with the Sherman DD. These units trained to perfect the tactics, techniques, and procedures of employing the DD tank for beach assault operations. The 70th would land on Utah Beach. The 741st and the 743rd would land on Omaha Beach.

In the months prior to the invasion, these three tank battalions trained their tank crewmen non-stop to master the top-secret DD tanks. The crews learned how to prepare the waterproofing prior to the launch and to quickly raise the screens that were supported by 36 rubber tubes inflated by compressed air. A well-trained crew could erect the screen in 15 minutes. They then practiced launching the DD tanks from LCTs, engaging the duplex drive, and swimming the tanks ashore under their own power on the surface of the water. Once ashore, the crews rapidly dropped the collapsible canvas screen from inside the tank, with the crew remaining under armor, and then continued the attack as normal tanks. The canvas skirts that allowed the tank to float, however, covered the bow machine gun, so the tank had to operate with one machine gun less than the standard Sherman.[3]

During this training, the executive officer of the 743rd Tank Battalion, Major William Duncan, was selected to run the US DD Tank School at Camp MacDevon, located at the English coastal resort town of Torcross near the Slapton Sands. This beach area was used as a dress-rehearsal for the Normandy assault due to its similarity with the Normandy beaches. Upham, with the help of Duncan and the school at Torcross, learned the strengths and weaknesses of the DD tanks while rehearsing with the tank crews from January to May 1944.

The major question in Upham's mind was whether the DD tanks would perform under dire conditions in combat. Upham considered the DD tank a brilliant, bold, and innovative concept that was tested in training but untested in combat. In training, the DD tanks had only been employed in relatively calm waters, and even then, accidents occurred. If the DD tanks were not perfectly waterproofed, if the struts buckled or the canvas tore, then the tank sank like a rock. Several soldiers had drowned in swim training exercises. The DDs, therefore, became unpopular and some of the men nicknamed them "Donald Ducks," after the silly Disney cartoon character.

On April 27, 1944 at Slapton Sands, a large dress rehearsal was conducted for the force that would land at Utah Beach. The rehearsal was code-named "Exercise Tiger" and it turned into a debacle. During the training, 70th Tank Battalion experienced a sinking, in which the crewmen of a DD tank were unable to abandon the sinking tank in time and drowned. Exercise Tiger was an unmitigated failure in nearly every sense. Soldiers were killed in the landing exercise due to miscommunication involving friendly naval gunfire. Worse still, nine German torpedo-laden S-Boats (German: *Schnellboot* or *S-Boot*, meaning "fast boat"), similar to American PT boats, attacked a convoy of Allied ships during the exercise, sank two large troop ships (LSTs), damaged three more, and killed 749 US servicemen (198 sailors and 551 soldiers). Due to the impending launch of Operation *Overlord*, everything about the disaster during Exercise Tiger was kept top secret and the casualty figures were not released until August 1944.

After the appalling results of Exercise Tiger, several briefings were given to high-ranking Allied leaders. One of these presentations was to Prime Minister Churchill on the role of DD tanks in the invasion. The Prime Minister asked Upham if he had confidence that the DDs could swim to shore. Upham showed tremendous personal courage when he respectfully told the Prime Minister that he knew, and his soldiers knew, that the DD tank was not seaworthy and that the majority of the battalion would become casualties if the tanks were launched in rough seas or too far from the beach. Nevertheless, the DDs would swim to the shore as planned.

Allied strategists decided that any invasion had to be conducted at low tide. At low tide, it was approximately 250 meters from the exposed water line to the nearest cover—a line of sand and rocks called the "shingle." The area from low tide to the shingle was covered in a deep belt of anti-invasion and antitank obstacles. To blow through these obstacles, a specially trained Army-Navy Special Engineer Task Force was assigned to land on the beach right before the tanks. They would cut lanes with high explosives through the German obstacle belt blocking the five draws, codenamed west to east D-1, D-3, E-1, E-3, and F-1, and the tanks and infantry would pour through.

As these lanes were being cut, the tanks would land, drive through the breaches created by the engineers, and knock out the German defenses with direct tank cannon and machine-gun fire. The infantry would then follow. The tanks would subsequently shift their fires to destroy enemy bunkers, gun emplacements, and machine-gun nests and provide fire support to the infantry as they penetrated the German defensive line. With the tanks in close support, the infantry would move through the breaks in the German defenses and overwhelm the Germans manning positions on the high ground. Upham's ultimate goal, come hell or high water, was to land tanks onto the beach before the infantry arrived.

The western portion of Omaha was subdivided into smaller beachheads, from west to east, code-named Dog Green, Dog White, Dog Red, and Easy Green. The 743rd was to spearhead the assault, with the DDs of Charlie Company swimming 16 DD tanks to shore on Dog White, and Baker Company swimming 16 DD tanks to Dog Green. The rest of the battalion's tanks were loaded aboard special armored LCT(A)s (the "A" for "Armored"). Since the LCTs would launch the DD tanks 3,000 yards or more from shore, they did not need the extra armor required for a close-in assault landing.

That was the plan.

Upham was an experienced Army leader. He knew that plans were merely a basis for changes and seldom survived first contact with the enemy. As a direct result of his experience in training, Upham and Lt. Col. Robert N. Skaggs—the commanding officer of the 741st Tank Battalion that was to launch on the eastern side of Omaha—discussed

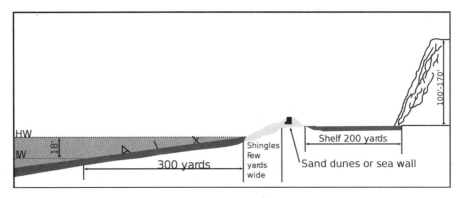

This is a cutaway diagram of Omaha Beach, depicting the distance to the shingle, the shelf, and the commanding heights. The only way off the beach was through three valleys or draws at five points along the beach, codenamed west to east D-1, D-3, E-1, E-3, and F-1. The Germans blocked these draws with obstacles and covered them with artillery, mortar, antitank cannon, machine guns, and small-arms fire. (Wikimedia Commons)

the possibility that if the sea was too rough, the DD tanks might not be able to swim to the beach. In that case, they believed the Navy should take the tanks directly onto the beach.

It was a unique idea with much promise but was not yet battle-tested.

Upham's tank battalion, the 743rd, was an independent tank battalion. Independent tank battalions were not assigned to US Army armored divisions, but were instead attached to infantry divisions to support the infantry's ability to fight German armor and execute combined-arms operations. The integration of the effects of infantry, tank, and artillery units, if properly orchestrated, could create a striking power greater than the sum of its individual parts. The 743rd was organized as a standard medium tank battalion and consisted of a headquarters and headquarters company (HHC), service company, three medium tank companies (A, B, and C companies), and a light tank company (Company D). The three medium tank companies were equipped with Sherman tanks and the light tank company with M5 Stuart tanks. The battalion's radio codename was "Verify."

Two of the 743rd's DD tank companies, Baker and Charlie companies, were equipped with DD tanks. Each company had 16 DDs, and these tanks were expected to be the tip of the Allied spear on Omaha. Another battalion that would land at Omaha Beach, the 741st Tank Battalion, was similarly equipped and trained. The plan called for two tank battalions to launch their 32 DD tanks, for a combined total of 64 DD tanks, to swim to the beach. During training exercises, they practiced swimming as far away as 3,000 yards to the beach.

Four DD tanks were loaded on each LCT. When the launch order was given, the LCTs would lower their ramps and the DDs would plunge into the water, appearing like a "tank in a canvas bucket." Rear-mounted propellers would propel the tank to the shore at a speed of 6 knots (about 7mph). Following behind the LCTs would come smaller Landing Craft, Infantry (LCI), which carried Navy Beach Units and Army combat engineers. These LCIs would move forward of the slower-swimming DDs and arrive on the beach a few minutes ahead of the tanks. The DD tanks of the 743rd and 741st tank battalions would subsequently land and spread out along the length of Omaha Beach. From these positions, they would provide critical support to protect the Army engineers and the Navy demolition teams as they blew gaps in the German beach defenses to clear the way for the follow-on tank and infantry assault.

The 743rd was to land in the west at Dog Green, Dog White, Dog Red, and Easy Green beaches. The 741st would occupy the rest of Omaha to the east. Able Company, 743rd Tank Battalion, commanded by Captain Vodra Phillips, with 16 Sherman tanks and eight Sherman tank-dozers, was to land on Easy Green, Dog Red, Dog White, and Dog Green sectors of Omaha at H-5 (6:25 a.m.). Companies Baker and Charlie, commanded by Captains Charles Ehmka and Ned Elder, consisting of 16 DD tanks each, were to land on Dog Green and Dog White sectors of Omaha Beach at H-10 (6:20 a.m).

At 5:55 a.m., the tremendous, pre-H-Hour Allied aerial bombardment and naval gunfire shelling would pulverize the German beach defenses. If all went as planned, the Germans would be surprised and stunned by the overwhelming firepower and the swift combined-arms assault of engineers, tanks, and infantry. The infantry would then move forward to seize the exits from the beach while the engineers cleared obstacles from these egress points. The combined force would then advance through the exits and secure the important Vierville–Colleville coastal road.

Upham looked at his watch and worried. The plan was already changing. For reasons he did not know, the Navy had set the line of departure for the DD tanks at 6,000 yards from the beach, much farther out than they had practiced in training. Those training exercises had been conducted in better weather with calmer seas. The sea swell that was smashing against his LCT was 3 to 6 feet. Many of the LCTs and smaller landing craft were taking on water, and their overtaxed bilge pumps could not keep up with the surging waves. Several LCIs swamped and many of the soldiers in those landing craft drowned, pulled down by their heavy packs, weapons, and equipment. Upham looked at the waves and the water pouring over his LCT. Getting to the shore in these rough seas would be a terrible test of equipment and men. He pondered the critical question: Would the DD tank canvas flotation device hold up under these conditions?

Corporal Robins yelled for Upham to come to the radio. "Sir, the Navy says it's too dangerous to bring the LCTs any closer. They're asking Captain Elder if he wants to launch the DDs."

Upham knew his men, his equipment, and his mission. He especially knew Elder and was confident that the young captain understood the limitations of his DD tanks. Upham had learned from detailed study, experience, and pre-invasion training that his DD tanks could operate in waves up to 1 foot high. The waves smashing against his LCT were at least 6 feet high. Upham realized that the DD tank canvas shrouding would most likely fold like a wet napkin against such powerful waves. If that happened, then his tanks would become 36-ton anchors. He shook his head in disbelief. He knew Elder understood these limitations as well. The question was one of obeying preconceived orders that were clearly laid out in the "plan," or adapting to the situation and using their judgment to make a decision that would still meet the intent and accomplish the mission. "No," Upham muttered aloud. "Elder will not launch the DDs in these rough seas."

A few days earlier, Upham had coordinated the landing of his tanks with US Navy Lieutenant Dean Rockwell. Rockwell was the group commander of 12 LCTs that would take Upham's battalion to Omaha. In their discussions, they decided that, due to the strict radio listening silence that would be imposed during the approach to the beach, it would be up to the discretion of the senior company commander, Elder, located with his DD tanks and on the LCT heading to the beach, to decide whether to launch or not.

Upham had trained Elder and his tankers intensively for the D-Day mission and had total confidence in Elder's decision-making skills. He trusted Elder to make the right decision on the spot. Upham delegated the authority and responsibility to Elder to make the decision as needed. Upham knew that there was no other way. This decision could not be micromanaged by anyone but the leader at the point of decision.

He moved to the halftrack, clambered up the side, and grabbed the headset. He radioed the company commanders of the two DD companies, Baker and Charlie, and told them not to launch their DDs, but to wait until he could convince the Navy to bring the LCTs straight onto Omaha, even though the LCTs were not armored for a direct assault onto a beach.

Upham looked at his watch again: it was 5:35 a.m. The word came over the intercom that the DD tanks of the 741st were launching on discretion of the commander, Lt. Col. Skaggs. Upham said a silent prayer and listened to the reports as the commander of the 741st ordered his DDs into the water as planned, rough seas notwithstanding. Holding his breath, he waited for the report on his tanks. Would Elder follow the plan or make the correct decision not to launch his DD tanks into these rough seas?

The next report brought Upham a great sigh of relief. Elder decided he could not launch. He asked for the LCTs to take his tanks straight onto the beach. When Upham heard this, he knew that Elder's decision would save many lives.

In true Navy style, Rockwell, in charge of the LCT flotilla and on LCT 535, made the heroic decision to disobey orders and break radio listening silence. The DD tanks of the 743rd would not be lost swimming in these rough seas. Rockwell ordered the LCTs carrying the DD tanks to join with the other LCTs loaded with the remainder of the 743rd's tanks and carry them directly to the beach. Once all the LCTs were collected, Rockwell dashed toward Omaha while the tanks fired at the shore from the decks of their landing crafts.

As soon as Rockwell's LCTs hit the sand, the ramps went down and the 32 tanks of the 743rd churned onto Dog Green Beach just opposite the D-1 Vierville Draw on Omaha, just 30 seconds before H-Hour (6:30 a.m.). The Germans opened up with everything they had and several tanks were immediately hit. Rockwell would later recall: "As soon as we landed our tanks we pulled the famous naval maneuver, known through naval history as 'getting the hell out of there.'" The most effective German fire was coming from WN-72, carefully positioned in defilade on the western edge of Omaha Beach and able to enfilade most of the landing area with antitank fire. Not able to observe where the enemy fire was coming from, the 743rd tanks were unable to target WN-72.

Upham watched as all this was happening. The smoke and haze from the beach obscured much of his view, but he could see that the rough sea and a list of unforeseen errors were affecting the plan. The timing was off, and this would affect every follow-on wave of reinforcements. The detailed landing schedule was slamming headfirst into the inevitable friction of war.

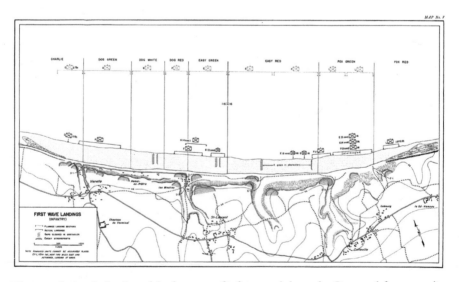

This map depicts the landing of the first wave of infantry and shows the German defenses guarding the vital draws D-1 at Vierville, D-3 at Les Moulins, and E1, E3, and F1 in the east. The 743rd Tank Battalion landed 32 tanks on the western side of Omaha Beach along Dog Green, Dog White, and some on Dog Red beaches. (US Army map)

At this point, all Upham could do was wait and watch. He used his binoculars to scan the waves to his left and sadly observed the gallant 741st attempting to execute as they had trained and swim to the beach. Some of their DD tanks sank immediately. The rest of the 741st DDs were foundering. One by one, Upham saw the DD tanks of the 741st Tank Battalion sink in the rough, icy waters off Omaha Beach. He was helpless to assist. He said a silent prayer for those tankers as their vehicles dropped below the waves and out of sight. Since the landing craft coxswains had been issued orders to ignore men in the water and carry on to the beach, many of these hapless tank crews were sure to drown.

In all, 27 of the 32 DD tanks from the 741st Tank Battalion were lost in the rough and unforgiving English Channel on D-Day.

Upham watched as the LCTs carrying his DD tanks turned toward the beach, surging forward and bucking as they hit the waves. The sounds of explosions rumbled to the south. Upham knew that the Army Air Corps was pummeling the German defenses. Suddenly, Navy battleships, cruisers, and destroyers began to fire in the direction of Omaha. The battleship *Arkansas* fired its big, 14-inch guns at the high cliff at Pointe-de-la-Percée, the western edge of Omaha. At the same time, the battleship *Texas* trained its 14-inch guns on the cliff Pointe du Hoc. Dozens of other ships joined in the shelling, including the launching of thousands of 76mm RP-3 rockets from the LCT(R)s.

Upham watched as the salvos hurtled overhead, striking targets unseen. Sometimes flames would shoot up from the strike of the shells. He could hear the blasts and feel the concussions of the explosions. It was a tremendous display of firepower. Would it do the trick? Would the bombing and naval gunfire reduce, daze, and disrupt the German defenders?

The ferocious naval shelling lasted 35 minutes.

A sudden quiet filled the air as the air bombardment and naval gunfire ceased. The assault waves of LCTs, followed by LCIs and LCVPs (Landing Craft Vehicles and Personnel), were now moving toward the beach. The Navy ceased their fire in order to avoid hitting friendly forces. The bombers continued to drop their lethal loads further inland. The beach was shrouded in mist and smoke. Six LCT(A)s carrying Able Company were now heading toward the beach. The more heavily armored LCT(A)s carried three tanks each and had special planking to allow the Sherman tanks to drive off swiftly once the ramp dropped onto the beach. Upham observed a massive, ragged line of landing craft bravely heaving through the rough sea toward the beach, waves splashing against their sides. Upham's LCT hung back, as planned, while the LCTs bearing the DD tanks of Baker Company moved to Dog Green and Charlie Company moved to Dog White.

As his LCT bobbed up and down in the waves, Upham trained his binoculars as best he could onto Omaha Beach. The beach landing area was arrayed with a thick and undisturbed belt of antitank and anti-boat obstacles. The intense air bombardment and naval shelling had not hit the beach defenses. Somehow, the Army Air Corps and the Navy had overshot their targets and the German defenses were left untouched.

The first LCT carrying 743rd tanks hit the beach at 6:29 a.m. and its ramp slammed down. A DD tank lurched forward, dipped its front to the surf, and plowed ahead through the waves, firing as it surged forward. At that same moment, the Germans opened up with every weapon in range and sent a withering wave of fire onto the beach from a dozen bunkers and emplacements on the flanks and high ground ringing Omaha.

With radio listening silence now lifted, Upham was under orders to command his battalion by radio from the LCT, a thousand yards from the shoreline. As the LCTs landed tanks onto the beach, the leaders of the 743rd heard the calm, crisp voice of their commander directing them onto the beach. Upham saw one of his LCTs, number 607, hit by German artillery fire just off the beach. Other LCTs were disembarking their tanks directly onto the beach.

Rows of beach obstacles covered the shoreline in front of the tanks. The landing craft carrying the US Navy and Army Engineer Gap Assault Teams hit the beach a few minutes after the tanks landed. Each vessel carried a team of 44 men and explosives for demolition operations. Machine-gun fire tore into them as soon as the ramps dropped. Some men fell while others jumped straight ahead, struggled through the surf, and tried to do the vital work of blowing up beach obstacles while under vicious fire. The Germans focused their machine-gun and mortar fire on the engineer teams as a priority target. Casualties among these brave engineer teams were heavy, with entire squads killed or wounded. Mortar and artillery shells fell as the supporting tanks inched forward from the water's edge, as best they could without getting hung up on an obstacle or tripping a Teller antitank mine. The DDs fired on possible targets on the high ground overlooking the beach, but the exact location of the enemy fire was nearly impossible to pinpoint. Additional engineer teams landed, taking the place of those who had already fallen, and valiantly set to work to detonate paths through the obstacles, but many were cut down mercilessly by German fire. Without the benefit of the naval and aerial bombardment to disrupt the enemy, the Navy and Army engineers became sacrificial lambs on the altar of desperation. Only a few obstacles were detonated and no paths were cut to get the tanks off the beach.

The plan was falling apart. When plans fail, leaders must step forward.

Upham struggled to talk to his company commanders on the battalion SCR510 radio, but communications were sporadic and quickly went silent. Through the smoke of the battle, he saw a couple of LCTs landing tanks near Dog White Beach. *That must be Able Company*, he thought. He tried to get Able on the radio without success. Frustrated, he watched as the first wave of infantry landed. Enemy machine guns sliced into the Americans even before many could exit their landing craft. German artillery and mortar shells slammed into the beach, sending men and equipment flying into the air. Through the smoke and flames, Upham could see that several of his tanks were firing from the water's edge at enemy positions. Obstacles and a seawall blocked their movement forward. He could see at least two tanks burning on the beach. He could not see anyone moving forward.

Upham pounded his fist against the side of the halftrack. He could not get through to his commanders by radio. He watched, feeling useless, as his tanks were being knocked out. More landing craft brought fresh assault infantry onto the beach, but the men seemed to vanish as the landing craft dropped their ramps. Several landing craft exploded in furious balls of flame that sent metal and bodies skyward. The beachhead was piling up with more men and equipment. Explosions erupted everywhere. He could see that the losses were staggering and wondered if anyone was alive on the beach. He did not know how many of his tanks were in the fight. He did know that he was not commanding anything from his LCT. He needed to do something, but what?

At that moment, everything was going wrong for the 743rd Tank Battalion, except one thing: leadership. Upham knew that he had to get onto the beach and lead. He climbed out of the back of his halftrack and pulled himself by the hand-rail over to the Navy coxswain. "I can't command my tanks from here. Bring this damn boat onto the beach."

The Navy coxswain obeyed. The LCT rushed toward the beach.

"Thirty seconds!" the coxswain shouted using a loud-hailer megaphone. "When the ramp drops, clear this boat!"

Before the LCT made it to the beach it hit a sandbar. The coxswain tried to back up the boat. Upham did not wait for the ramp to go down but dove over the side of the LCT. He waded through the icy waves as bullets zipped by and made his way to the nearest tank.

Upham survived a hail of fire and ducked behind a tank that was in water up to its road wheels. He pulled himself up and onto the back deck of the tank and banged on the hatch until the tank commander peeked out. Upham pointed at a German machine-gun bunker to the right flank that was clobbering the men on the beach. The tank commander had not seen the enemy position before, but now he understood. He moved his turret to the right and fired three rounds, eventually getting one right into the firing aperture of the bunker and knocking it out. Upham ordered him to fire at other targets on the bluff, specifically the German gun emplacements to the west, on the Point-de-la-Percée, which fired enfilade onto Omaha. Upham then jumped off the tank, and ran from obstacle to obstacle until he arrived at the next tank. Again, he climbed up on the back deck, banged on the turret, and gave instructions to that tank commander. He proceeded under constant fire to run from tank to tank, shouting orders and pointing out more targets.

With the beach swept by German machine-gun fire, infantry casualties soared. Survivors from the first wave sought cover behind the tanks. The tanks could not move forward due to the obstacles and the clumps of men using the obstacles for cover. Wounded men drown as the tide rose. With dead and wounded troops covering the beach, and no cleared paths through the obstacle belt, the tanks became stationary firing platforms in the rising tide and primary targets for German antitank guns. Other soldiers tried to hide from the fire by staying low in the water, but this offered little concealment and no cover. With death, chaos, and fire all around, only a few men were moving forward. Dazed and confused, with most of their officers and sergeants dead or wounded, only a few of the assault infantry of the 29th Infantry Division were shooting at the Germans.

Upham was in the middle of the killing zone. The air buzzed with bullets. Machine-gun slugs sparked against the metal side of a burning tank and Upham dove for cover. The initial wave of infantry had been decimated and most of their leaders killed. The dazed survivors of the first wave sought cover wherever they could. Upham crawled through the sand to another tank, seemingly oblivious to the Nazi fire. In this fashion, he directed the fire of the tanks of his battalion and inspired his men.

The beach was now congested with destroyed and burning vehicles of all types. With the gaps in the obstacle belt still not blown, the vehicles were unable to negotiate through the obstacles and over the shingle that lined the beach shore. The noise was deafening as German machine guns raked the beach. Men were wounded, dying or in shock all around him.

Upham continued to move from tank to tank and point out targets. The tanks fired concrete-piercing rounds at German bunkers and pill-boxes with some success. The explosion of these rounds against the concrete of the German bunkers billowed a plume of grayish smoke. As he climbed onto the back deck of a fifth tank, Upham was hit in the shoulder and fell to the sand. Getting up, he ducked behind the tank, quickly plugged his wound with a field dressing, and carried on. Unwilling to give up command to seek medical attention, Upham continued to personally direct his tanks' fires on the Germans.

Suddenly, the tanks received much needed help. A "silent cooperation" quickly developed between the Navy Destroyer USS *Carmick* (DD-493) and Upham's tanks on the beach. As the tanks struck an enemy bunker with concrete-piercing shells, observers on the *Carmick* watched the strike of the tank rounds. The *Carmick*'s gunnery officer realized that the tanks on the western portion of Omaha Beach were striking German positions, effectively marking the enemy's location. In the smoke and haze of the battle, it was difficult for the *Carmick* to identify exactly where the enemy was, but the gunnery officer quickly recognized the strike of the tank rounds and redirected the *Carmick*'s fires. The *Carmick* moved as close to the beach as possible and its big guns were soon knocking out German positions.

Upham recognized the situation and adapted. He ordered the tank commander to switch from firing concrete-piercing shells to firing white phosphorus (WP) shells. Every tank in the 743rd carried a dozen 75mm WP shells. Upham recognized that WP was excellent for marking targets. This made identification much easier for the Navy's destroyers. With the tanks marking the targets, the *Carmick*'s 5-inch guns hammered the German bunkers. Other Navy destroyers soon joined the effort. Without any radio communication between them, the individual tanks and the Navy's destroyers began to eliminate the German gun emplacements. Neither the tankers nor the *Carmick*'s crew had practiced this kind of targeting cooperation before, but in the heat of battle, they quickly learned how to adapt, improvise, and overcome.[4]

As he continued to direct the fire of his tanks on foot, Upham was hit a second time. The strike of the bullet knocked him down, but he quickly applied another bandage to slow the bleeding. He struggled back to his feet and kept on commanding his battalion.

While the tanks and the *Carmick* were targeting the German gun emplacements, three companies of the 2nd Ranger Battalion landed on Dog White Beach and were met with intense German fire, sustaining many casualties. Lieutenant Colonel Max Schneider's 5th Rangers landed 1,000 yards east on Dog Red. Conditions there were less deadly than at Dog White, and the Rangers made it to the shingle with few casualties. The destruction of German gun emplacements by the tankers and the Navy provided valuable protection for the surviving first waves of the newly arrived Rangers and the survivors of the first few waves of the 29th Infantry Division.

The relatively fresh Rangers soon met Brig. Gen. Norman Cota, the assistant division commander of the 29th Infantry Division. Cota, with an unlit cigar in his mouth and carrying nothing more than a .45 pistol, was rallying his men and looking for a way off the beach. Most of the initial assault units of the 29th were shattered, but the Rangers offered him a unit that was relatively intact and his best option on a very bad day. Leading by example for everyone to see, Cota met with Schneider. "You men are Rangers; I know you won't let me down. Lead the way off this beach!"[5]

The Rangers quickly moved out, blew through the barbed wire with Bangalore torpedoes, and climbed the bluffs. The tanks of the 743rd continued their supporting fire and the *Carmick* kept blasting away at the German gun emplacements. With the Rangers and 116th Infantry, 29th Infantry Division, moving up the bluffs, the battle at Omaha seemed to be tipping in favor of the Americans. At this point, Upham found a medic and let him treat his wounds. The tanks had made a difference. The commander of the 2nd Battalion, 116th Infantry, noted that the tanks of the 743rd had "saved the day. They shot the hell out of the Germans and got the hell shot out of them."

In spite of these heroic efforts, the task at hand was still to get the tanks off the beach, but the German beach defenses had not been breached. These obstacles and the high bluffs opposing Omaha denied the tanks the ability to drive off the beach except at the beach exits. As the destroyers and cruisers knocked out the last of the German antitank guns, Upham's tanks had to sit and wait until special engineer demolition teams could breach the concrete wall blocking the exit.

In the afternoon, after the Rangers and infantry cleared the bluffs, the tanks of the 743rd inched toward the D1, Vierville Draw. Fresh Army combat engineers landed and worked feverishly to blast a way through the draw for the tanks. By the early evening of D-Day, the beachhead was reinforced by the landing of the 745th Tank Battalion. With only three tanks of the 741st, and 38 operational tanks from the 743rd, the reinforcements from the 745th were very welcome. Every leader on Omaha expected the Germans to counterattack. The more firepower that was able to get ashore, the greater the chance that any counterattack would be defeated.

The Germans, however, did not attack. Surprised, confused, and waiting for orders rather than acting as the situation required, the German defenders fought in place. They could not muster the strength to mount a meaningful counterattack on Omaha Beach. By evening, the greatest danger to the desperate Americans, who were clinging to a very small area of beach, had passed. The 743rd Tank Battalion lost

16 tanks destroyed or disabled. Finally, around 10:30 p.m. on D-Day, June 6, 1944, the 743rd pushed 38 tanks through the Vierville, D1 Draw. The American forces started moving inland. Eventually, Able Company, 743rd Tank Battalion, would accompany the 5th Rangers and fight through German lines to relieve the heroic Rangers of Lt. Col. James E. Rudder's 2nd Ranger Battalion on the Pointe du Hoc on June 8.

Upham, however, would be evacuated the evening of D-Day and leave the battalion forever. Twice wounded, and suffering a great loss of blood, he survived the trip to England and began a long medical recovery. He never commanded the 743rd Tank Battalion again, but would remain a lasting, inspirational memory to the men he led so gallantly on D-Day.

The Distinguished Service Cross, the Navy Cross, or the Medal of Honor was awarded to 235 soldiers, sailors, and airmen for extraordinary heroism on D-Day. The soldiers of the 743rd Tank Battalion earned nine Distinguished Service Crosses (DSC), an amazing ratio that attests to their part in winning the beachhead. The DSC is the second highest military award that is given to a member of the United States Army for extreme gallantry and risk of life in actual combat with an armed enemy force. In addition to nine DSCs, the 743rd was awarded the Presidential Unit Citation for their courageous performance on D-Day. The common belief is that there was no tank support for the infantry on Omaha Beach on D-Day. The legacy of the 743rd Tank Battalion, and leaders like Upham, prove that that belief is patently false.

Lieutenant Colonel John S. Upham, Jr., US Military Academy at West Point, Class of 1928, was one of the men awarded the DSC for his actions on D-Day. The citation for this award reads:

LIEUTENANT COLONEL JOHN SOUTHWORTH, UPHAM, JR.
Unit: Commanding Officer, 743rd Tank Battalion attached to the 1st Infantry Division, US Army
Awarded for: Operation Overlord
Action: Lieutenant Colonel John S. Upham, Jr., O-17178, 743rd Tank Battalion, United States Army, for extraordinary heroism in action against the enemy on 6 June 1944, in France. Early on D-Day, when his tank battalion was landing in the assault, Lieutenant Colonel Upham was directing operations by radio from a craft several hundred yards offshore. The unloading of tanks and men became

743rd Tank Battalion, US Army Distinctive Unit Insignia. (US Army image)

increasingly difficult as, under the devastating enemy fire, tanks were knocked out and the wreckage impeded movement across the beach. Realizing the gravity of the situation, he went over the side of his landing craft and waded ashore in the face of the enemy fire. He proceeded to the tanks, personally guided them across the fire-swept beach, and directed their fight to open the beach exit. Though seriously wounded twice, he disdained to seek medical attention but continuously remained exposed to the enemy fire and coordinated the fire and movement of his tanks. It was only after his battalion had seized its objective that he was evacuated for his wounds. The extraordinary heroism, the personal bravery, and the determined leadership displayed by Lieutenant Colonel Upham reflects great credit upon himself and is in keeping with the highest traditions of the Armed Forces. Headquarters, First US Army, General Orders No. 68 (14 October 1944).

Leadership matters and the leadership of Lieutenant Colonel Upham made a dramatic difference on June 6, 1944. He retired as a lieutenant general (US Army), where, according to his West Point memorial, "he and his wife Harriette lived in Alexandria, Virginia, surrounded by their loving children and five grandchildren. Graced with a dry wit, a pun for every occasion, and an incomparable imagination, he charmed his family as he imparted the enduring values of service to Nation." He died in 1993.

★ ★ ★

Leadership Lesson

Leaders must adapt, improvise, and overcome. When the plan no longer makes sense, the only antidote to inertia and defeat is leadership. Leadership overcomes the inevitable friction that acts against any plan. At Omaha Beach, Lt. Col. John S. Upham quickly understood that his leadership was needed on the beach where he could communicate with his tank crews. He could have followed orders and safely stayed on his landing craft, trying to direct the battle by radio from afar. Upham was made of sterner stuff and realized that he had to be at the point of the action where he could understand the challenges and lead his soldiers.

All plans are made up of both variables and constants, and most of the variables work against the plan. Leaders must know when the plan must change and learn to adapt, improvise, and overcome in all situations. Plans usually offer one way to get a task accomplished, and often, if you can control enough of the parameters that can influence the plan, a good plan will work. Most likely, however, the friction of operations will cause the plan to start to unravel. When that happens, leaders must step in, inspire, and direct their team to adapt the plan, improvise as needed, and overcome the friction. In business, in leading a family, and in war, it is the same. The leader's role is to rapidly assess the situation when the plan is failing, devise a new way to accomplish the intent of the original plan, and overcome.

Gen. Eisenhower once said that "Plans are nothing. Planning is everything." Eisenhower recognized that plans change, but understood that the planning effort that helped prepare the minds of the planners was critical. It's not the final plan but the learning that occurs during the development of the plan that is important. Upham understood this and took action when he realized the original plan was no longer sufficient. No matter what your occupation, your team can learn from Eisenhower's admonition. What can you learn about overcoming adaptability from Lt. Col. Upham? How can you take your organization to the next level by teaching your team leaders how to adapt, improvise and overcome rapidly changing circumstances?

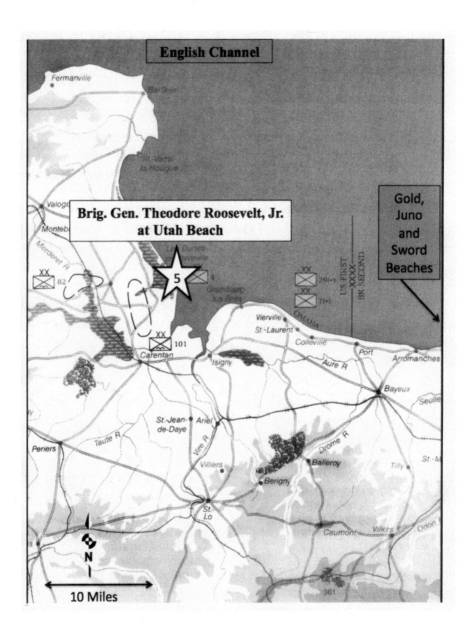

English Channel

Gold,
Juno
and
Sword
Beaches

Brig. Gen. Theodore Roosevelt, Jr.
at Utah Beach

10 Miles

CHAPTER 5

Decision at Utah Beach

Point of Decision

"Do what you can, with what you have, where you are."
Theodore Roosevelt, 26th President of the United States and
father of Brig. Gen. Theodore Roosevelt, Jr.

"Leaders must be seen to be up front, up to date, up to
their job and up early in the morning."
Marcus Joseph Sieff, Baron Sieff of Brimpton OBE
(July 2, 1913–February 23, 2001

He was not supposed to be there, but ever since he was assigned to the 4th Infantry Division, he had argued that this was exactly where he needed to be. His commanding officer, Major General Raymond Oscar Barton, disagreed. First, Barton had pointed out that he was just shy of his 57th birthday and "too damned old" to lead an infantry assault. Second, his wounds from World War I, in which he barely survived a gas attack and was shot in the right leg, forced him to hobble around with a cane. Third, he was too important to the unit to lose in the chaos and confusion of the first minutes of the invasion. Fourth, the first wave of the assault was called the suicide wave, a term that needed no further explanation. It was a good thing, Roosevelt thought, that Barton did not know about his arthritis and his weak heart.

An empty Landing Craft, Vehicle, Personnel (LCVP) bobbed in the cold dark water below, positioned against the side of the USS *Barnett* (APA-5) Attack Transport, a reconfigured passenger steamer. Brigadier General Theodore Roosevelt, Jr., the son of the famous "Rough Rider" of the Spanish American War and 26th President of the United States, "Teddy" Roosevelt, looked out at the dark, misty morning as the *Barnett* swayed in the rough waves of the English Channel. Carefully, with the help of his aide de camp, First Lieutenant Marcus Stevenson, he climbed down the cargo net to the LCVP, the efficient acronym of the military that designated a boxy, flat-bottomed, 36-foot-long and 10-foot-wide Higgins boat.

"Stevie, you still have our map?" Roosevelt asked.

"Yes sir," Lieutenant Stevenson replied. "Right here with me, when you need it sir."

Roosevelt smiled. Stevenson was a good officer. Reliable. Eager. Reminded him of his younger brother, Quentin.

"I don't know how you talked the old man into going in with the first wave," Stevenson added as they touched down on the steel floor of the LCVP. "But I'm glad you did."

Roosevelt nodded and thought about his last meeting with his commander, Major General "Tubby" Barton. Barton was a superb leader, considered by many as one of the best division commanders in the US Army, but he was reluctant to see Roosevelt assigned to the first wave and was sure his assistant division commander would be killed. Roosevelt did his best to convince Barton that the troops expected him to be there. He had been with them throughout the tough days of training and had spent many miserably cold nights in LCVPs, practicing movement to a "hostile" beach. Now that the show was on for real, he had to be with the men. "They'll figure that if a general is with them it can't be that rough," Roosevelt said. "It will steady them to know I'm with them, to see me plodding along with my cane." Barton argued that his death would be a tragedy for the 4th Infantry Division as well as the entire nation, but Roosevelt was persistent and finally put his request in writing:

> The force and skill with which the first elements hit the beach and proceed may determine the ultimate success of the operation… With troops engaged for the first time, the behavior pattern of all is apt to be set by those first engagements. [It is] considered that accurate information of the existing situation should be available for each succeeding element as it lands. You should have when you get to shore an overall picture in which you can place confidence. I believe I can contribute materially on all of the above by going in with the assault companies.

Furthermore, I personally know both officers and men of these advance units and believe that it will steady them to know that I am with them.[1]

Barton finally, and reluctantly, agreed to the request. He never expected Roosevelt to survive the landing. Roosevelt knew the odds as he stoically held onto the wall of the LCVP. He knew it was one hell of a gamble. He also knew that he had no other choice. If his father, President Theodore Roosevelt, were still alive, he would have approved of his son's decision to lead from the front, in the first wave, and would have urged him on. His father might have added: "In any moment of decision, the best thing you can do is the right thing, the next best thing is the wrong thing, and the worst thing you can do is nothing." Roosevelt, Jr., knew this was the right decision. He had to be here.

Shoulder patch of the 4th Infantry Division that landed on Utah Beach on June 6, 1944. (US Army image)

His close friends knew Theodore Roosevelt, Jr., as "Ted." Many thought he was the spitting image of his father. Like President Roosevelt, Ted graduated from Harvard. When the United States entered World War I, Ted was 30 years old and in good physical condition. The newly formed American Expeditionary Force (AEF) needed officers. He and his three brothers, Kermit, Archibald and Quentin, joined the call to arms. After some preliminary training, Ted earned a reserve commission as a major in the 26th Infantry Regiment in 1917. Kermit, who was yearning for action, joined the British Army as an Honorary Captain in 1917 and saw action against the Turks in Mesopotamia (present-day Iraq), being awarded the Military Cross, a British decoration awarded for "exemplary gallantry." He then transferred to the US Army in May 1918 and served as a captain, commanding Battery C, 7th Artillery of the 1st Infantry Division. Archibald joined the US Army in 1917 and was assigned to the same regiment as his brother Ted. Quentin, the youngest of the lion's brood, entered the newly formed Army Air Corps.

The 26th Infantry was sent overseas as part of the 1st Infantry Division, nicknamed the "Big Red One". He was promoted to lieutenant colonel and led his infantry battalion in the American victory at Cantigny in May 1918, but was wounded in a gas attack. He was decorated for his bravery. The citation reads: "At Cantigny, although gassed in the lungs and gassed in the eyes to kindness [he] refused to be evacuated [and] retained command of this battalion through heavy bombardment." He was awarded the Silver Star and the French *Croix de Guerre*.

Ted healed and went back to the front. During the battle of Soissons in 1918, he led his battalion into action at Ploisy and was wounded in the leg by German machine-gun fire. The bullet entered above his right knee and exited the back of his leg. In spite of his wound, he refused to leave his unit until the battle was decided. According to the 1st Division Commander, Major General Charles P. Summerall, Roosevelt was recognized as the best battalion commander in the Big Red One Division for his actions at Soissons.

While in the hospital in Paris, Ted learned of his younger brother Quentin's death in aerial combat with the German air force. Ted's other brother, Archibald, was wounded in the leg in March and was sent home in September. Ted stayed in the hospital in France for a short time recuperating, until November when he was notified that the 26th Regiment was in need of a new regimental commander. The division commander told Ted that if he was able and could get to the front, the regiment was his to command. Ted swore to his commander that he was fit to fight and, although the hospital would not discharge him, he disregarded their concerns and quickly returned to the front line. Limping from his wound and using a cane, he led the 26th Infantry Regiment during the last few weeks of the critical Meuse-Argonne offensive. Commanding the 26th made him the first reserve officer in US Army history to command a regular Army regiment in combat. While Ted was leading the 26th, his brother Kermit continued to command his artillery battery. Although one brother had been killed and another wounded and sent home, the remaining two sons of Teddy Roosevelt remained in the fight.

The Meuse-Argonne offensive was the largest operation in US military history, involving over 1.2 million soldiers. The fierce fighting resulted in over 122,000 American casualties, the bloodiest battle in US history. The battle was fought over a period of 47 grueling and bloody days, from September 26 until November 11, 1918. The Allied armies succeeded in breaking the German line, forcing the Germans to accept an armistice and bringing an end to World War I. For his heroism, Ted was awarded the Purple Heart, the Distinguished Service Medal, and the Distinguished Service Cross. France awarded him the *Chevalier Légion d'honneur* (Legion of Honor).

After World War I, Ted returned to America and was instrumental in the founding of the American Legion to recognize the heroism and sacrifice of the men who had served in the Great War. He then applied his leadership abilities to government service. Many influential members of the Republican Party saw the young war hero as a potential future US president. To prepare to walk in the footsteps of his father, Ted served in the New York State Assembly, and then as Assistant Secretary of the Navy (1921–25). Feeling that he was ready for the next step, he ran for New York Governor in 1924, but was narrowly defeated. Undaunted, he served as Governor of Puerto Rico (1929–32) and then as Governor-General of the Philippines (1932–33). Upon his return to the US, he was involved in business as the vice president of Doubleday, Doran & Company Publishing, and later as an executive with American Express. In 1936, he was encouraged by many Republicans to campaign for the White House against his cousin, President Franklin D. Roosevelt, but declined. In 1940, Ted could see that war was imminent. He took a military refresher course and entered the Army once more, this time with the rank of colonel. Ted returned to active duty in April 1941 as the commander of the unit he had fought with in World War I, the 26th Infantry Regiment, 1st Infantry Division. He was promoted to brigadier general in 1941, just before the Japanese attack on Pearl Harbor.

With the Japanese attack on December 7, 1941, the United States entered World War II. The situation across the globe looked bleak for America. Britain was barely hanging on against a terrible German air blitz, Russia was on the brink of being overrun by German tanks, and in one horrendous swoop, Japan had conquered much of the Pacific. In true Roosevelt fashion, all three surviving sons of the 26th President answered the call to arms and entered the military, as well as seven grandsons. Archibald Roosevelt sent a letter to his cousin, Franklin D. Roosevelt, in which he wrote: "The whole clan turned out to a man." For the Roosevelts, America was worth fighting for and, if required, dying for. They were all determined to do their part.

Roosevelt led his old unit, the 26th Infantry Regiment, during Operation *Torch*, the invasion of North Africa in 1942. He was subsequently selected to be the Assistant Division Commander of the 1st Infantry Division in 1943. Major General Terry Allen, a tough fighter with a very direct leadership style, commanded the Big Red One. Allen and Roosevelt got along famously, but their commander, General Omar Bradley, who commanded II Corps, believed both leaders were insubordinate, unconventional, and unpredictable. Together, Allen and Roosevelt led the Big Red One and helped defeat the German forces in Sicily during Operation *Husky* (July 9–August 17, 1943). As the Sicilian campaign ended, however, General Bradley relieved both Allen and Roosevelt for having a cavalier attitude toward discipline and being "too friendly with the troops."[2] Undaunted, Roosevelt asked to be reassigned to serve with a French unit that included Italian volunteers who had recently fought for the Axis. He led those troops with such distinction that he was awarded his second French Legion of Honor, complementing the one he received for his heroic actions in World War I.

On D–Day however, he felt that his past success meant very little as he lowered himself into the landing craft. He stood silently, wet and cold, bracing himself as the LCVP bounced on the waves. In the LCVP, Roosevelt was just one of the troops and would share in their fate. The craft was loaded with many seasick young infantry assault troops from the 4th Infantry Division, all huddled shoulder to shoulder. The landing craft pushed away from the mother ship as the sky began to turn from dark to gray. Roosevelt could see the vast armada of ships all around

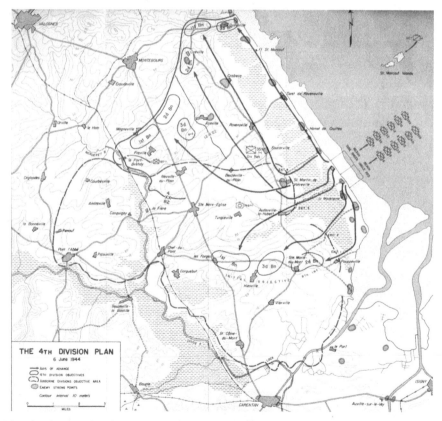

The plan for the 4th Infantry Division to seize Utah Beach on D-Day. (US Army CMH map)

him and hundreds of landing craft, like the one he was in, circling at designated collection points to await their time to head to the beach.

He checked his watch. The carefully timed and intricately planned invasion to seize beachheads in Normandy would soon begin. The plan called for expert timing and exact location placement. One wave of landing craft would follow another, and then a third, until the beachhead was won. Once the beach was secured, hundreds more landing craft were scheduled to land at precisely designated areas, to bring in reinforcements, vehicles, ammunition, and supplies. Nothing had been left to chance. Sticking to the invasion plan was paramount. To succeed, his superiors had told him, the plan must be executed precisely as designed.

The sea was dotted with vessels of every size and shape. Roosevelt watched the heavy seas gush over the hull and blunt bow of the LCVP, inundating the troops onboard. The water filled the bottom of the landing craft and the men started to bail out the water with their helmets. The sea swells pushed the tiny LCVP about the surface of the water like a shoebox in the surf, but somehow the landing craft managed to maintain formation with the others. Nearby, other LCVPs struggled to keep in column and circled in their designated waiting areas.

After what seemed like an eternity of circling and waiting, the first wave of LCVPs turned toward the beach. Behind the first wave of landing craft were dozens more. The plan was to quickly land large masses of men, tanks, and equipment to pre-planned beachheads to build up sufficient forces to defend against the expected German counterattack. The second wave was scheduled to land five minutes after the first. Each wave followed a precise landing schedule and timetable that placed men and equipment exactly where the plan called for them to land. The survival of the invaders, and the success of the invasion, counted on sticking to the plan. General Omar Bradley, the commander who had relieved Roosevelt in Sicily, was the commander of the American invasion force at Omaha and Utah beaches. Having been relieved of command in Sicily for being considered insubordinate, Roosevelt clearly understood the consequences of disobeying orders.

Thirty anxious men from the 8th Infantry Regiment stood with Roosevelt in the landing craft. Many of these young men were shivering, wet to the skin, seasick, and already tired from hours of preparation and anticipation. As the choppy sea broke again over the square bow of the LCVP, Roosevelt could see that the tensions of the men were running high. The men knew the Germans were waiting for them in prepared defenses on the beach. They also knew that for some, as soon as the ramp to the landing craft swung down, death would be waiting.

"Sir, do you think you have all your equipment?" A soldier asked the general.

Roosevelt gave a wide grin and answered: "I've got my pistol, one ammunition clip with six rounds in it, and my walking cane. That's all I expect to need."

The soldiers close enough to hear the remark, laughed.

"Sir, don't you think you ought to wear your helmet?" a young sergeant asked.

"Son, it's okay. I've never really liked them," Roosevelt replied with a wide, toothy grin. "Besides, the men know me better without it."

The sergeant chuckled and shook his head in disbelief.

Roosevelt checked his wristwatch again. It was 6:20 a.m. The guns from hundreds of ships, ranging from battleships to destroyers, were firing at the beach. *Maybe the Navy's guns would sweep the Germans from the landing zone*, he thought. One ship in particular, the USS *Nevada* (BB-36), an American battleship that was a survivor of the Japanese attack on Pearl Harbor, blasted away at the enemy shore with 10 huge 14-inch guns. As the massive shells whistled and arced overhead, their deadly payload hurtling toward the Germans, Roosevelt sensed that the shelling reassured his men. They were not in this alone.

As the naval gunfire lifted and shifted farther inland, Roosevelt's landing craft closed on the beach. He peeked over the top of the ramp and watched a flight of three American B-26 Marauder medium bombers attack the beachhead. Amazingly, these aircraft flew very low, soaring just above the enemy positions. They dropped a string of 250-pound bombs while simultaneously strafing the area with their machine guns. Green tracers from German antiaircraft machine guns shot into the air, but the B-26s ignored the enemy fire as they accurately pounded the German defenses with their bombs. Roosevelt could see the white

The USS Nevada *fires on German occupied France on D-Day, June 6, 1944. (US Navy photo)*

invasion stripes on their fuselages and the wings as the Marauders rolled skyward after depositing their bombs onto the enemy.

These Marauders were from the 386th Bombardment Group. The 386th was considered one of the most accurate bombing groups in the Army Air Force in the European Theater of Operations (ETO). Their willingness to dip below the cloud cover, brave the German antiaircraft fire, and drop their bombs precisely on target, just minutes before the assault infantry landed at Utah Beach, made all the difference. At Omaha Beach, the bigger B-24 heavy bombers had stayed above the clouds and dropped their loads using instruments. As a result, at Omaha, few if any of the bombs hit the German defenses. At Utah, only medium bombers were employed. The crews of the B-26s that hit the German positions at Utah were determined to knock out their targets, even if they had to fly at treetop level.

Roosevelt smiled and nodded his head in agreement with what he saw. *God bless the Army Air Corps*, he thought. The Marauders were really working over the German positions. His late brother Quentin would be proud.

"Get ready!" the Coast Guard coxswain steering the LCVP shouted. "God be with you!"

"Remember, you are the Fighting Fourth Division! When we stop, move quickly off the boat," Captain Leonard T. "Moose" Schroeder, Jr., the 25-year-old commander of the 219 men of Company F, 2nd Battalion, 8th Infantry Regiment, 4th Infantry Division, shouted. "No stopping. No hesitation."

Several men crossed themselves. Others stood silently, ready for the inevitable fate of the next few moments.

At 6:28 a.m., the LCVP suddenly ground against the sand. The craft stopped and the heavy metal ramp fell. Roosevelt could see the beach in front of him. Smoke smoldered from several German bunkers up ahead, courtesy of the high-explosive bombs from the Marauders. Next to Roosevelt was Captain Schroeder. There was no hesitation. The two men jumped out at nearly the same time, but history records Schroeder as the first man on Utah. Despite a heart condition and arthritis, Roosevelt waded through the water and onto Utah Beach.

The assault infantry quickly rushed forward and moved around the beach obstacles to the protective cover of the seawall. Roosevelt hobbled with his cane as best he could, following the younger men. Many of the Germans were dazed by the close-in bombing by the B-26s, but a few of the enemy could still function and started shooting at the invaders. Schroeder was hit twice in the left arm as he ran for the seawall, but he continued to command. Five of his soldiers were killed and a dozen wounded, but many other Americans charged forward. German mortar fire exploded at the water's edge. Geysers of water shot up into the air. Men sought cover behind the steel obstacles. Roosevelt moved forward, a cane in one hand and a pistol in the other, and struggled to gain his footing on the sandy beach. Riflemen ran past him and flopped on the ground. Some fired their rifles toward the suspected enemy. Others hesitated. Roosevelt urged all of them forward.

Like his father, Colonel Theodore Roosevelt at the battle of San Juan Hill, this was Ted's "crowded hour."

A few short bursts of German machine-gun fire sprayed the sand and several men fell to the ground. The assault infantry pushed forward past dozens of beach obstacles and ran to the cover of a seawall a hundred yards away. Roosevelt walked, painfully, step-by-step, ducking behind a steel beach obstacle, and took in the scene. After several minutes, he reached the wall and joined a group of soldiers who looked at him, incredulous, waiting for orders.

"Let's go boys. We can't stay here," he ordered. "Up and over."

The men obeyed. The first squad climbed over the wall, quickly followed by another group. Roosevelt led them forward. More shots were fired. German soldiers, shell-shocked and dazed, were captured. Roosevelt moved back and forth from the seawall to the beach and positioned squads, then platoons, and finally companies to protect the beachhead to repel any German counterattack.

As more troops collected at the seawall, a Duplex Drive (DD) amphibious tank from the 70th Tank Battalion swam ashore and moved onto the sand. Other DD tanks followed, swimming to shore with their big canvas skirts providing buoyancy to make the 32-ton tanks float. Roosevelt ducked behind the seawall, with Stevenson at his side, just as German machine-gun fire ripped across the top, showering them with sand.

"Someone needs to take out those sonsabuzzards," Roosevelt offered with a business-like calm.

A dozen American riflemen popped up from their positions and assaulted the final German position. Roosevelt heard the sound of grenades. The German machine gun went silent. In a few more minutes, all of the German defenses directly overlooking the landing area were captured.

So far, so good, Roosevelt thought, as only a few men had been killed or wounded. He saw more tanks arriving, followed by another wave of LCVPs carrying infantry. As more men pushed forward, Roosevelt noticed that something did not look right. He decided to personally scout the area. With cane in hand, he walked over the seawall and

Soldiers from the 4th Infantry Division jump from their landing craft and head onto Utah Beach in the early hours of D-Day. (US Army photo)

scanned the terrain. He suddenly realized that he was at the exact right place and time to make the critical decision of the day.

"Stevie, give me the map," Roosevelt ordered.

Stevenson opened his map case and laid it in front of the general.

Looking at the map, Roosevelt saw the error. According to the plan, they should have hit Uncle Red Beach opposite Exit 3. The 1st Battalion was supposed to land directly opposite the strongpoint at Les-Dunes-de-Varreville; however, they had landed opposite Exit 2, approximately 2,000 yards south of the planned beachhead. As Roosevelt was studying the map and cross-referencing it with the terrain, a thin young officer, wearing the gold oak leaves insignia of a major, moved up to him. He also had a map of the landing zone in his hand and a concerned look on his face.

"Major, report," Roosevelt ordered.

"Sir, as you know, the first wave is mostly at the seawall. We're lucky, so far, only a few casualties. The amphibious tanks are late, but at least they're landing. The good news is that there is no sign of any German counterattack... so far," the major replied. "But there is a problem. The bad news is... from the best I can tell, we landed at the wrong beach."

Roosevelt nodded. "I came to that same conclusion a few moments ago, Major. The current must have pushed our landing craft south."

"Yes sir, but if this is the wrong beach, we could be in big trouble," the major announced. "Since there are only a few exits, we may not be able to get off this beach. The Germans have flooded the low areas... And what if the follow-on waves and support go to the right beach? If you call the landing craft back now, they may be able to pick us up and then take us to the right beach."

Roosevelt turned to his aide. "Stevie, assemble the command group here and I'll issue orders immediately... And find me a radio."

"Right away, sir!" Stevenson replied and then took off running in the direction of the troops. He quickly found a soldier carrying a big square FM radio pack on his back. Stevenson then ran along the seawall telling all the officers he could find where to meet with Roosevelt.

Roosevelt looked at the map and surveyed the ground again. He knew the plan required everyone to be at the right place. The major may be right. If he could radio the Navy, they might be able to send the landing craft back to reload and then reposition the first wave onto the correct beach.

Lieutenant Stevenson moved down the line, notifying Colonel James Van Fleet, the commander of the 8th Infantry Regiment, and other officers where to meet with Roosevelt. In short order, the command group assembled around Roosevelt behind the seawall.

"Van, we're not where we were supposed to be!" Roosevelt shouted as Van Fleet ran to meet him.

"How do you know, General?" Van Fleet offered, nearly out of breath.

Roosevelt pointed to a red brick building that was the southern border of the 8th Regiment's zone. "Our beach is to the right."[3]

Van Fleet quickly understood the predicament. "Should we try to shift our entire landing force more than a mile down the beach, and follow the original plan? Or should we proceed across the causeways immediately opposite where we had landed?"

Roosevelt paused and then looked at the radio operator that Stevenson had brought with him.

"Can you get in touch with division headquarters on that thing?" Roosevelt asked the soldier packing the radio.

The radioman quickly nodded. "Yes sir!"

"Inform division headquarters that we've landed at the wrong beach, about 2,000 meters southeast of the planned landing site," Roosevelt announced. "But that doesn't matter now. We have a secure beachhead. Tell them we'll start the war from here."

An artillery officer crouching next to Roosevelt looked up. "But, sir, what about the next wave and the reinforcements?"

"The rest of the invasion will have to follow us wherever we are," Roosevelt said with determination. He pointed with his cane in the direction of Exit 2. "Move your men off the beach, colonel. The Airborne was dropped last night somewhere behind the beach. We need to link up with them."

"Yes sir," the colonel answered.

Roosevelt turned to the major. "Did you happen to see a beach control party along the seawall?"

"Yes sir, General, just off to our left."

"Direct them to signal all subsequent waves to be redirected here," Roosevelt ordered.

The men moved out. The Beach Control Party signaled the next wave of landing craft and directed them where to land. More amphibious tanks swam to shore, dropped their canvas curtains, and churned through the sand past the obstacles and up to the seawall. Back at the water's edge, engineer demolition squads landed and went to work destroying the exposed obstacles while the infantry pushed farther inland. Soon, a bulldozer tank landed to help clear paths through the beach obstacles. The invasion of Utah Beach was redirected as Roosevelt had ordered and the American lodgment was soon secure.

Fifteen hours after Roosevelt's landing craft hit the beach, the 4th Infantry Division was able to land nearly 20,000 men and 1,700 vehicles. The Fighting Fourth was moving inland along the three causeways that led off Utah. By the afternoon of D-Day, 4th Infantry Division forces had linked up with paratroopers from the 101st Airborne Division that had been parachuted just after midnight, several hours before the seaborne landings. Later, as evening fell, the casualty reports for Utah Beach came in. Roosevelt was amazed. The 4th Infantry Division's casualties were very light, only 197 men. Compared with the bloodletting on Omaha Beach, this was truly a miracle.

General Theodore "Ted" Roosevelt Jr.'s actions on D-Day at Utah Beach are an example of a decisive decision, by a courageous and calm commander, during the confusion and chaos of combat. Roosevelt positioned himself to be at the right time and place to make one of the most important decisions of D-Day. He was subsequently awarded the Medal of Honor. Roosevelt's citation reads:

> For gallantry and intrepidity at the risk of his life above and beyond the call of duty on 6 June 1944, in France. After 2 verbal requests to accompany the leading assault elements in the Normandy invasion had been denied, Brig. Gen. Roosevelt's written request for this mission was approved and he landed with the first wave of the forces assaulting the enemy-held beaches. He repeatedly led groups from the beach, over the seawall and established them inland. His valor, courage, and presence in the very front of the attack and his complete unconcern at being under heavy fire inspired the troops to heights of enthusiasm and self-sacrifice. Although the enemy had the beach under constant direct fire, Brig. Gen. Roosevelt moved from one locality to another, rallying men around him, directed and personally led them against the enemy. Under his seasoned, precise, calm, and unfaltering leadership, assault troops reduced beach strong points and rapidly moved inland with minimum casualties. He thus contributed substantially to the successful establishment of the beachhead in France.

When General Omar Bradley, the commander of the United States First Army in Normandy, was asked about the bravest act he had ever known, he responded, "Ted Roosevelt on Utah Beach." On July 12, 1944, a little over one month after the landing at Utah, Brigadier General Roosevelt died of a heart attack near Sainte-Mère-Église. He is buried at the

Brigadier General "Ted" Roosevelt in his jeep, "Rough Rider," in Normandy, weeks after landing on Utah Beach on D-Day. (US Army photo)

American Cemetery at Colleville-sur-Mer in Normandy, alongside his troops. He is interred next to his brother, Quentin, the American aviator killed in action during World War I. There are 33 other pairs of brothers buried together at the American Cemetery in Normandy among the total of 9,387 Americans who died in the Normandy campaign.

★ ★ ★

Leadership Lesson

Leaders must place themselves at the optimum place and time to make accurate and timely decisions—or, as leadership expert John Maxwell says: "The wrong action at the right time is a mistake. The right action at the right time results in success." In the military, being at the right time and right place is called the point of decision. The key for every leader is to determine where the point or points of decision are and anticipate them.

At Utah Beach on June 6, 1944, Brigadier General Theodore Roosevelt, Jr., knew that he had to be at the point of decision. He was in the first wave for a very specific reason: only by being in the first wave could he appreciate the complex environment that required rapid and accurate decision-making. He understood his higher commander's intent (Task, Purpose, and End State): establish a beachhead in Normandy in the Utah Beach area and form a safe lodgment for follow-on forces. Roosevelt positioned himself at the right time and place to be able to change the plan rapidly to accomplish this intent. The skilled leader learns from study and experience when and where to be when critical decisions must be made. Being able to read a situation and see the next steps is called foresight.

To gain foresight takes practice. The first step is to understand what decisions will need to be made and then understand where the leader should be to best make those decisions. Leaders can learn to project their thoughts forward in time and space by wargaming their plans against an opponent who acts as the devil's advocate. If you don't play devil's advocate to test the strength of your plan, reality will do it for you.

The US Army has formalized the role of "devil's advocate" into its decision making and created a concept called "red teaming." To confront the problems inherent in group decision-making, a "red team" plays the role of the opposition to test the plan. Red teaming is simply the practice of looking at a situation from the perspective of the enemy or competition. For an infantry platoon leader, for instance, the platoon sergeant could act as the red team. For a business CEO, any member of the team with knowledge of the project and experience in the business can act as the red team. Red teaming is investigative, anticipatory, and educational. It does not provide solutions, but raises situational awareness and allows leaders to better anticipate where and when to be to make informed decisions by thoroughly wargaming the plan. The wargame can be very simple, consisting merely of a list of key events that are expected to occur and with each side playing the expected plan against the most likely and most dangerous opposing reaction. During this wargame, the leader can learn where to be in time and space in anticipate key decision points.

Timing is often the difference between winning and losing. Being at the right place can provide the leader with better awareness and empower decision-making. Being at the right time and the right place, at the point of decision, is the best recipe for victory. Roosevelt's statement, "We are going to start the war from right here," is a metaphor that explains decision-making for all walks of life, not just for combat situations. If the best decisions come from leaders who have a clear view of the situation and are where the action is, then Brig. Gen. Theodore Roosevelt, Jr., was a master of the art of determining and being at the point of decision on D-Day. How can you learn about being at the point of decision from Brig. Gen. Roosevelt's actions on D-Day? Would "red teaming" help your organization to test plans and be better prepared for changing circumstances?

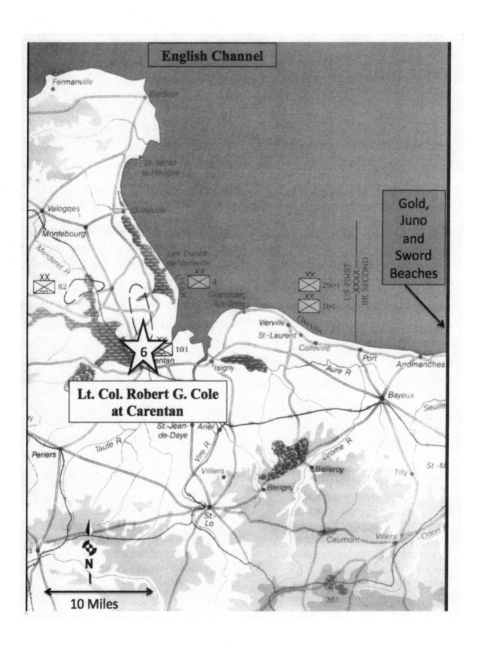

CHAPTER 6

Before the Sun Rises

Example

"I doubt that there has ever been a finer fighting unit in the Army of the United States. It never tasted defeat nor was it ever given an easy assignment. At least three of its engagements are historically noteworthy examples of heroically successful achievements against great odds."
Brigadier General (Ret.) S. L. A. Marshall, in describing the 3rd Battalion, 502nd Parachute Infantry Regiment, in his study Men Against Fire

"Always do everything you ask of those you command."
– General George S. Patton

On the outskirts of Saint-Côme-du-Mont, Normandy, France, June 10, 1944: It had been only four days since D-Day; four days of hard fighting since he and the soldiers of his battalion had parachuted into the darkness over Normandy. Only four days of fear and death… less than 96 hours ago, but now those four days seemed like a lifetime ago. He started with about 573 men on D-Day and now he could only muster about 400.

"The Germans destroyed the second bridge, the one over the Douve River," a grimy, battle-weary lieutenant reported.

"Yeah," the battalion commander, Lt. Col. Robert G. Cole, replied. "Looks like we are going to have to do this the hard way."

A sound of a German 88mm Flak 36 cannon sounded in the distance; two seconds later an 88mm shell exploded to the side of the causeway near the second bridge. The explosion sent a geyser of water and mud into the air.

"Lieutenant Gehauf, give your men a short rest and then get 'em ready to go. We'll be moving soon," Cole announced.

Lieutenant Ralph. B. Gehauf, the battalion intelligence officer (S2) saluted and moved off. Cole squatted behind a hedgerow and scanned the ground to the south with a pair of binoculars. It was late and the day was waning. He studied the narrow causeway, which looked peaceful enough now, except for the occasional German 88mm shell sent hurtling toward the Americans from Carentan. In daylight, the Germans could observe anything that moved on the causeway and could then bring accurate fire onto the target. Attacking down the causeway in daylight was out of the question. At the end of the causeway was a wide-open field. Cole scanned this carefully, trying to pick out the German positions that would turn that field into a kill zone. The Germans held positions that could fire on anyone crossing the field to the west and the south. Beyond the field was the town of Carentan.

He took out the metal canteen from its cover on the left side of his web belt, unscrewed the cap, and took a drink. The water tasted awful, but it was all he had. His men had been living off the rations they carried when they jumped into Normandy on June 6. Water was replenished from the many streams, stagnant pools, and flooded areas. Drop in an iodine tablet, swirl it around, and you had bad-tasting but relatively safe drinking water.

Cole returned the canteen to its pouch and raised his binoculars again, taking in the terrain and the enemy's positions. His orders were to cross the causeway and its four bridges, then clear and hold enough ground at the entrance of the town to allow follow-on battalions to pass through his unit and secure the rest of Carentan. His regimental commander, Colonel George Mosley, had been wounded and evacuated. The Regimental Executive Officer (XO), Lieutenant Colonel John Michaelis, was now in charge. Michaelis had made it crystal clear how important it was to gain a foothold in the town. A railroad and four major roads converged in Carentan to make it one of the strategic points in Normandy. The link-up between US forces at Utah and Omaha beaches depended upon securing the Carentan road network.

Cole knew this would not be an easy task. The Germans had fought stubbornly for the village of Saint-Côme-du-Mont, causing his paratroopers, nicknamed the "Widowmakers," considerable trouble and

General Dwight D. Eisenhower, the Supreme Allied Commander, speaking with Lt. Col. Robert G. Cole, the commander of 3rd Battalion, 502nd Parachute Infantry Regiment (PIR), the Widowmakers, on June 5, 1944. Cole's face is blackened in preparation for combat. He wears a white scarf that identified the 3rd Battalion on D-Day. Colonel George Van Horn Moseley, Jr., wearing the helmet in the middle of this photo, is the commander of the 502nd Parachute Infantry Regiment, 101st Airborne Division. A few hours after this photo was taken, 13,100 American and 7,900 British paratroopers parachuted into Normandy to spearhead the D-Day invasion.

heavy casualties. These Germans were not like the *Osttruppen* they had been fighting since D-Day. The Osttruppen were German prisoners of war turned into soldiers. They came mostly from Eastern European countries of the Soviet Union, and were pressed into switching sides and fighting for the German Army, tasked with defending bunkers and static positions. The Osttruppen were of dubious fighting quality and many had surrendered as soon as they could escape or kill their German leaders.[1]

The German troops the Screaming Eagles had fought and pushed out of Saint-Côme-du-Mont, after a very tough fight, were primarily from an elite *Fallschirmjäger* (German paratrooper) regiment led by a courageous and brilliant regimental commander, Major Friedrich August Freiherr von der Heydte. These German paratroopers had fought savagely, but the Widowmakers and other units of the 101st Airborne Division had driven them out of Saint-Côme-du-Mont and south to Carentan. Now, von der Heydte and the men of the 6th Fallschirmjäger Regiment were digging-in near the exit of the causeway. If the fighting at Saint-Côme-du-Mont was any indication, the German paratroopers would fight fiercely to stop the Americans from entering Carentan.

To win the hard-fought skirmish at Saint-Côme-du-Mont, the American paratroopers had the help of some tanks from the 70th Tank Battalion that had landed at Utah Beach. One of these tanks, an M5 Stuart light tank, had been hit by a German hand-held antitank weapon called a *Panzerfaust*. The Panzerfaust's 149mm grenade-like warhead created a large hole in the armor of the tank and produced massive spalling inside the armored vehicle. The Stuart tank had burned most of the day and the tank commander had been killed in the turret and cooked to a char. The grizzly sight of the lifeless tank commander, who was still in the turret of his dead tank, caused the paratroopers to name the intersection "Dead Man's Corner." The tanks that had helped in the fighting for Saint-Côme-du-Mont had been pulled away to support other units. Cole and his Widowmakers were left largely on their own for the attack down the causeway from Dead Man's Corner to Carentan.

Cole looked back at the destroyed tank. *An ominous place to start an attack*, he thought. The odds were fierce. The causeway was a mile-long, single roadway. The areas on both sides of the causeway were flooded. The Germans were in prepared positions on the other side of the causeway and could observe his moves from positions on higher ground in the town. There was no air support to aid his attack and the tanks had been withdrawn to fight elsewhere. His mortars were nearly useless, as they didn't have the range, accuracy or stocks of ammunition required to knock out the German positions. His paratroopers were expected to carry everything they would need for a two- to three-day fight, and then be pulled out. Paratroopers, he'd been told, were a strategic asset and were too valuable to be used like regular infantry, but there was no one else. Carentan had to be taken.

The shoulder patch of the 101st Airborne Division, the Screaming Eagles. (US Army image)

On D-Day, the Americans had landed at Utah Beach in the west and Omaha Beach in the east. The British and Canadians landed at Gold (British), Juno (Canadian), and Sword (British) beaches, east of Omaha Beach. All of these beaches were linked except for Omaha and Utah. As noted, Carentan was a critical road junction and the key to joining the American forces of VII Corps at Utah Beach with the American V Corps at Omaha Beach. If the Germans continued to hold Carentan, they would block the only road that would join these two American Corps and could deny the Americans the ability to unify their front. If the Germans could mount a counterattack, especially a tank attack, they might be able to defeat the beachhead at Utah and then box in the Allies on the other four beaches. This had happened before at the battle of Anzio, Italy, on January 22, 1944. At Anzio the Allies planned a surprise amphibious landing and rapid breakout that would lead to the surrender of Rome. The Germans, initially surprised, recovered rapidly and fought tenaciously. The landing at Anzio, planned as a brilliant amphibious surprise attack, had turned into a 136-day slugfest with heavy Allied casualties. The Allied planners did not want this repeated in Normandy.

Carentan, therefore, had to be taken as rapidly as possible. The five beachheads had to be joined. More troops, equipment, and supplies were landing at the beaches every day. The Allies needed space to maneuver and a solid front for operations. With the majority of the 4th Infantry Division that had landed at Utah Beach heading west to capture the vital port of Cherbourg, the job of taking Carentan was assigned to the 101st Airborne Division. Cole's 3rd Battalion, 502nd Parachute Infantry Regiment, was given the mission to lead that attack.

Tomorrow morning, he was promised, a battery of 105mm and 75mm howitzers would be supplied and in position to support his attack. It was possible that his attack might also be supported by the larger caliber 155mm howitzers of the 4th Infantry Division. Cole knew that 75s were not as effective as the bigger 105mm howitzers that normally supported regular infantry units. The 105mm howitzers were much better at pounding enemy positions prior to a deliberate frontal attack, and that is what the 3rd Battalion was about to conduct—a frontal attack right into the teeth of the Germans.

Cole was bone-weary, but he didn't show his fatigue in front of the men. He wiped his face with his grimy right hand and then shouted for his company commanders and his executive officer to assemble for orders. His S2's report—that the Germans had destroyed the second bridge across the causeway—was significant and would slow his movement south along the causeway. The American engineers who were trying to create a makeshift crossing were pinned down by German fire and unable to make any progress. Lieutenant Gehauf had found the other three bridges intact, but covered by German fire the entire way, and at least one German 88mm cannon was positioned in Carentan to fire high-explosive shells along the length of the causeway. In addition, a Belgian Gate—a large, heavy steel gate fence about 10 feet wide and 7 feet high—blocked the southern end of the causeway. Gehauf's patrol was able to shove the gate open slightly, so that one man at a time could get through, but the Belgian Gate would further impede the 3rd Battalion's attack.

The sun was sinking and soon it would be dark. Without tank, artillery or air support, Cole's best option was to use the cover of darkness to help conceal the attack. Night attacks are always difficult to control; Cole knew his men were exhausted and recognized that inertia was setting in. The men had little energy to do anything. When inertia sets in, in combat, Cole knew that men would die. The only antidote to inertia is leadership. Cole knew he must decide his next move, issue orders, and give his men time to organize and prepare. He also needed to inspire or cajole his Widowmakers to reach down and muster one more ounce of courage for another tough fight.

His officers and a few senior noncommissioned officers began to assemble quietly, behind the hedgerow, protected from enemy fire, ready to receive his orders. Cole gathered them around him as they arrived. He laid his map out on the ground and pointed to the causeway with a twig.

"We move just after dark," Cole told his orders group confidently, putting forward his best command presence to stiffen his officers' resolve. "Our objective is to secure and hold enough ground on the south side of the causeway to allow follow-on battalions to enter and secure Carentan. No matter what else happens, my intent is to push the Germans away from the causeway so they can't interfere with the other battalions that must use the causeway to attack into Carentan. We are to kick the door open and hold the entrance. The follow-on battalions will take the town."

The officers grouped around Cole studied the map and wrote in their notebooks. In spite of their fatigue, each of them had confidence in their commander. His command presence—that ability to gain the respect of others by conveying confidence, focus, and self-assuredness—buoyed their lagging spirits. They knew that Cole was not the kind of leader who would ever lead from behind. If Cole said it would work, then it would.

Lieutenant Colonel Robert "Bob" G. Cole was a native Texan, born March 19, 1915 at Fort Sam Houston. He came from a career military family and always wanted to be an officer in the US Army. He graduated from West Point in 1939, was commissioned as an infantry officer, and volunteered for the paratroops in 1941. Before the war, he had served in the 15th Infantry Regiment with General Eisenhower, who recognized Cole as an up-and-coming officer who led from the front and never let his men down. On May 29, 1943 he took command of the 3rd Battalion, 502nd Parachute Infantry Regiment, 101st Airborne Division.

"We'll have no artillery support until daylight tomorrow morning, so we'll cross the causeway at night and use the darkness to attack across the open ground toward the farmhouse to the west," Cole continued, trying to be as clear and confident as possible. "Our patrol identified the heaviest concentration of Krauts at the farmhouse and along the hedgerows that flank the farmhouse. Once we are across the causeway we use the darkness to conceal our attack of the German line centered at the farmhouse. We'll have to hit them hard and fast, secure the area, then form a defense and wait for reinforcements."

"Any questions?" Cole asked.

"How are we going to get across the blown bridge?" his XO, Major John P. Stopka, asked. "The second one?"

Cole was silent for a moment. Stopka was a tough fighter and an excellent executive officer. Stopka was the kind of soldier who seldom complained, usually asked the right questions, and always found a way to get the mission accomplished. He had fought on D-Day with particular skill, single handedly attacking German positions and personally killing many Germans. His fearlessness had earned him the nickname "The Mad Major."

"I'm sure you will figure that out," Cole replied. "Find a way or make one."

Stopka nodded.

"We'll attack with I Company in the lead, followed by G, H, and the Headquarters Company," Cole ordered. Any more questions?"

The officers shook their heads. The deadly task that lay before them was brutally clear. They had to force their way down a single-lane road for nearly a mile under constant German observation and fire, with no tanks, artillery or air support and only the cover of darkness to protect them, but they just could not say no—ever—to Robert Cole. If anyone could lead them into hell and back, they all knew, it was Cole.

The officers and sergeants left the orders group and quickly issued verbal orders and prepared their men. Just after dark the Widowmakers moved out. They had only made it to the first bridge when German machine guns and snipers opened fire. Blue and green tracers crisscrossed the air. Everyone ducked, but there was no real cover. Crouching, they moved forward. In spite of the darkness, there was just enough light to see shadows moving along the causeway. The Germans shot up flares. Everyone froze and lowered to the ground. More tracers flew overhead, and slugs from an MG42 machine gun hit the dirt near Cole. Several more men were wounded. The wounded that could crawl were quickly bandaged and crawled back on their own to the relative safety of Saint-Côme-du-Mont and the temporary aid station established in the house at the intersection.

As they moved to the second bridge, Major Stopka organized some paratroopers and the engineers to hang ropes and fencing to span the gap. Then, one at a time, the paratroopers crossed the makeshift bridge. All this took time, too much time. The causeway lit up with more machine-gun tracers and several Americans fell to the ground, killed or wounded. More wounded were evacuated to Saint-Côme-du-Mont. Once the majority of the battalion was across the second bridge, the German fire intensified and the paratroopers ducked lower and started crawling forward.

The attack was now slowed to the pace of a crawl. Communications was nearly impossible as the radios failed, probably because Signal Operating Instructions (SOI) with codes and frequencies had changed or had not been coordinated. Company commanders resorted to messengers who had to crawl back and forth to communicate with their platoons. Casualties mounted. There was very little cover along the causeway. The Widowmakers inched forward across the deadly ground, and when they arrived at the third bridge the Germans shot up more flares. Tracers filled the air.

Cole observed that some of the German fire was coming from the inundated areas on both sides of the causeway. *The Germans must have boats in the water,* he thought. The only protection was to fire at the enemy. Hiding or lying silent would only result in more casualties. Cole shouted for his men to fire at the enemy by watching for the flashes of their rifles. A few Widowmakers responded, but not enough. More men were wounded and evacuated. Other men dragged some to the second bridge. Every time this happened it took two men out of the fight.

The Germans continued a steady rate of fire, but very few of Cole's men fired back for fear of giving away their position with the flash of their weapons. Cole was red-hot furious. He could not get his men to return fire. Many of his men were gripped in fear and inertia. When Cole ordered the soldiers near him to fire, they did so. But the moment he passed on, they quit shooting. He walked up and down the line, yelling, "God damn it! Start shooting!" But it did little good. They fired only while he watched them or while some other officer stood over them.[2]

Cole realized that the movement across the causeway, under the intense fire of the Germans, was taking too long, but there was no option but to push forward. During the night a German aircraft flew overhead and dropped flares over the causeway, lighting up the area in a stark whitish glow that slowed progress even further. Later, a German Ju-87 Stuka dive-bomber strafed and bombed the causeway, killing 30 men.

Cole knew his men could not hide in this killing zone. He had to move them to the south side of the causeway before the sun rose. He urged his men forward, kicked them if he had to, but got them moving. Cole walked up and down the causeway, disregarding the German fire and, with curses and the power of his fearlessness, impelled his men to keep moving forward. More Americans were killed or wounded as they inched toward the final bridge. Finally, Cole and the lead elements crossed the fourth bridge, passing through the Belgian Gate one man at a time. Once they squirmed through the gate, the men took up hasty defensive positions, waiting as the rest of the battalion assembled for the

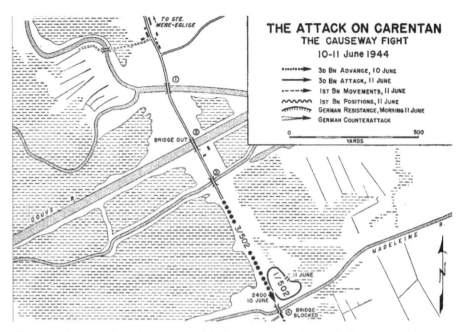

Cole started the attack under the cover of darkness on June 10, 1944. German machine guns, snipers, mortars, 88mm cannon, and a rare night attack by German Ju-87 Stuka dive-bombers caused considerable casualties to Cole's battalion. (Adapted from US Army Map 16, p80, from Utah Beach to Cherbourg, 6–27 June 1944, Center for Military History, Washington, D.C. 1990)

push across the open ground. The men kept coming, the Germans kept sniping, but the opportunity to use the cover of darkness to launch an attack was lost. The majority of the battalion finally assembled along the defensive line to the south of the fourth bridge just as dawn was breaking.

Things seemed to be rapidly going from bad to worse. Cole checked his watch. The night was over and the sky had turned from black to gray. In a few minutes it would be dawn and he would lose the only advantage he had. He had already lost at least a third of his battalion just getting across the causeway. He wasn't sure how many men he had left. Now he was facing open ground, opposing Germans defending from prepared positions, and the sun was about to rise.

Cole scanned the horizon and saw the farmhouse to the right front of his position. Flames from a German MG42 machine gun sputtered from the first-floor window of the farmhouse. Nearby the farmhouse was an apple orchard with the telltale flashes of German rifle fire.

"Do you have communications with the artillery on that thing?" Cole shouted to a forward artillery observer, Captain Julian Rosemund, from the 377th Parachute Field Artillery Battalion, who was wearing a large backpack radio.

"Yes sir," Rosemund replied.

"Hell, that's the first good news I've heard in a long time," Cole cursed. He waved for the man to move toward him. "Get the hell over here!"

The captain crawled forward to Cole.

"Get some shellfire on the farmhouse and those hedgerows," Cole ordered. Rosemund radioed the artillery but the artillery battery couldn't get permission to fire.

Lying on the ground to avoid enemy fire, Cole pulled the captain close to him and grabbed the radio transmitter. "Goddamn it! We need artillery, and we can't wait for any general."

Cole's intervention convinced the artillery—a battalion of 75mm howitzers positioned near Saint-Côme-du-Mont—to provide the support. Artillery fire was soon falling on the farmhouse, the hedgerows, and the orchard near the farmhouse. In spite of this shelling, the fire from the German lines continued.

The executive officer crawled over to the commander. "Those 75s aren't having much effect on them. We've taken a lot of casualties… too many. When the sun comes up, we'll be sitting ducks. The damn Krauts will kill us all."

"Yeah… I know," Cole replied.

"As I see it, we have two options," Major Stopka offered. "Pull back the way we came, or stay here and dig in and take our chances."

The sun was rising. Cole knew he had to decide.

German mortar fire fell along the causeway and exploded among the Americans who were desperately digging in with shovels and bayonets. German machine-gun fire raked the ground. The Americans hugged the ground, looking for whatever cover they could find.

"If we go back they'll slaughter us. There is no cover on the causeway," Cole announced.

The major nodded.

"And if we stay here," Cole said, shaking his head, "the Krauts will kill us all. We'll be fish in a barrel."

"Well, I think I know where this is going," Major Stopka replied, "but we don't have much of a battalion left."

"These goose-stepping Heinies think they know how to fight a war," Cole said. "We're about to learn 'em a lesson!"

Major Stopka looked up Cole with a grin. "Do you intend to do what I think you are going to do?"

"Yeah," Cole said as he looked sternly into the major's eyes. "We're going to order artillery smoke," Cole announced to Stopka, and pointed to a farmhouse to his right, "and then make a bayonet charge on the house."

"That looks like the center of the Kraut defense," Stopka replied, nodding.

Cole spit. "Yeah... Tell the men to fix bayonets... Anyone who can still walk and carry a rifle. Once the smoke hits near the farmhouse, I'll let the smoke build a bit, then H Company will charge across that open ground and take out the Krauts at the farm. I'll lead. G Company will attack south at the same time. We all charge when I blow my whistle. Pass the word."

"Okay," Stopka said with a grin. "Okay."

Cole reached for the radio again. "I want smoke on the farmhouse and the apple orchard, RIGHT NOW. And as much as you can give me!"

It was approximately 6:15 a.m. Cole handed the radio transmitter back to the radiotelephone operator. The next salvo of artillery shells burst in gray clouds of smoke, right on target, just in front of the farmhouse. Slowly the smoke built up into a fog, providing a slight veil over the open ground near the farmhouse, and drifted to the south. It wasn't perfect, but it would have to do.

Cole stood up, waved his .45-caliber M1911 pistol in his right hand in the air and shouted: "FIX BAYONETS! If it moves, shoot it. If it speaks German, shoot it twice!"

The men around their battalion commander seemed dazed.

The paratroopers looked at each other, trying to comprehend what they were about to do, hoping beyond hope that the orders were not what they thought they were—a frontal assault into prepared enemy defenses. The open ground in front of them was a killing field and their commander was now ordering them to cross that deadly space.

German sniper fired continued. A short burst from a German MG42 machine gun blasted away. The surviving men of Cole's battalion took whatever cover they could find. Cole looked at the German positions. He saw the sun rising. He knew his situation was grim. Cole stood up, so all his men could see him, and yelled: "FIX BAYONETS!"

Major Stopka ran across the line of paratroopers who lay prone on the ground seeking whatever cover they could find.

Cole walked up and down the line as bullets hit the ground near him. He seemed oblivious to the German fire.

The men, incredulous at the order, looked at each other. Was the old man serious? The word passed along the line. *Bayonets?* The men grabbed their bayonets form their scabbards and clicked them onto their rifles.

A moment passed. The artillery stopped.

Cole blew the whistle—a long, loud blast.

"Let's go! Charge!" Cole yelled, waving his pistol. He rushed forward at a full run, hollering as he sprinted toward the farm. At least a dozen men followed, but no more.

Major Stopka and the rest of the battalion remained in their positions, as if they were unsure of what was happening.

Cole and the dozen men charged forward, alone. Several men running near him were hit and fell to the ground.

The major stood up and blew a whistle. "Come on. What are you waiting for? Are you going to let him attack alone? Move forward!"

The men waiting behind cover looked up, ashamed. The entire battalion then rose, as if one man, and charged. They ran at full speed, trying to catch up with their commander, yelling and screaming as they ran.

Cole saw the men getting up, running toward him. They were all bunched up, too close together and an easy target. He cursed at his men to spread out and keep moving, while meanwhile firing his pistol and yelling, "I don't know what I'm shooting at, but I gotta keep on!" Some of his paratroopers, hearing Cole's comment, broke into laughter in spite of the German bullets whizzing by them.

It was a wild, chaotic, unbelievable charge. German fire took its toll on the Americans, machine guns ripped their ranks, many paratroopers fell, but the Americans kept coming. The Germans held their ground at first, shooting as fast as they could fire, but the Americans cleared the open ground too quickly for the Germans to repulse the attack. The fighting now became close, hand-to-hand, no-quarters combat. The wild-eyed American paratroopers, looking like banshees from hell, shot and bayoneted the German defenders. They killed the German defenders in and around the farmhouse to a man and then quickly set up a defense. The paratroopers were exhausted from fighting all night and spent from making such a tremendous charge, but they hung on.

The Germans counterattacked again, as they were prone to do, but the Americans stopped them from regaining any ground. Somehow, the paratroopers, low on ammunition and using captured German weapons when they ran out of bullets for their own weapons, held off these attacks. Cole's men had opened a breach in the German lines that allowed more men from the 101st Airborne to move down the causeway and join Cole's positions. By noon, the 1st Battalion, 502nd Parachute Infantry, reinforced Cole's Widowmakers. Cole's men were holding but were physically spent and nearly out of ammunition. At the same time the Germans had taken heavy casualties, were nearing their own point of exhaustion, and were also almost out of ammunition. With no way to retake the ground against a surging tide of American paratroopers, the Germans pulled back. The Americans were now in Carentan to stay.

In two more days the 101st Airborne would clear all the Germans from Carentan. On June 13, 1944, the weary paratroopers of the

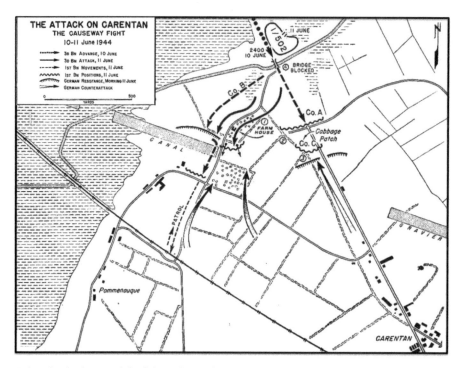

Cole ordered what was left of the 3rd Battalion, 502nd Parachute Infantry Regiment, to charge the farmhouse and the German positions along the nearby hedgerows. After Cole's battalion took the enemy positions, he was then reinforced by A, B, and C companies of the 1st Battalion, 502nd Parachute Infantry Regiment, as shown in the map above. The farmhouse was owned by a family named Ingouf and therefore is known as the Ingouf farmhouse. (Adapted from US Army Map 16, p80, from Utah Beach to Cherbourg, June 6–27, 1944, Center for Military History, Washington, D.C. 1990)

101st Airborne were holding the line along Hill 30 when the Germans launched a powerful counterattack led by the 17th SS Panzergrenadier Division (Waffen SS) and reinforced with what was left of Major von der Heydte's 6th Fallschirmjäger Regiment. Panzergrenadiers were Germany's version of armored or mechanized infantry and these soldiers were the best-equipped and most highly trained in the Wehrmacht. The 17th SS didn't have any real tanks, but they had 37 *Sturmgeschütz IV* (StuG IV) assault guns and other tracked vehicles and halftracks. The StuG IV was a "turretless tank" with a four-man crew and carried a powerful 75mm gun for direct-fire support for infantry and was more than a match for dismounted paratroopers.

The 17th Panzergrenadier Division rushed forward with their StuGs in the lead, followed by Panzergrenadier infantry without much of a reconnaissance. The StuGs pounded the thin defensive line of the stunned American paratroopers. Quickly reacting to the threat, the Americans fought back from their foxholes with bazookas, grenades, machine guns, and rifles and kept the German assault guns at bay for a while. Then, one of the units in the defensive line, F Company, 506th PIR, broke and ran, causing a dangerous gap in the American defense. The commander of F Company was relieved on the spot by his battalion commander, but the hole in the line was wide open. Just when it looked like the Germans were about to exploit this breach, and just in the nick of time, the advance elements of the US Army's 2nd Armored Division—60 Sherman tanks strong from Combat Command A—arrived from Omaha Beach and slammed into the unprotected flank of the 17th SS. The attacking American tanks knocked the Germans sideways and stopped the attack cold. The tanks and the paratroopers of the 502nd PIR continued to attack the Germans and pushed the defensive line out one mile farther west. The 17th SS took heavy casualties and were forced to withdraw, realizing that Carentan was no longer within their reach.

Always colorful in their descriptions of combat, the paratroopers called the battle with the 17th SS, which took place near the Manoir de Donville—or Hill 30 as designated on US tactical maps—as the "Battle of Bloody Gulch." With this victory, all five Allied beaches were linked and cleared of Germans. The first major step in the Allied invasion of Europe had been achieved, largely because of the bravery of men like the paratroopers of the 3rd Battalion, 502nd Parachute Infantry Regiment, of the 101st Airborne Division.

That step, however, came at a high cost. Of the roughly 400 soldiers that Cole led in the attack down the causeway, only 132 remained fit for duty on June 13. That is a casualty rate of nearly 67 percent.

For his courage during the attack on Carentan and the fighting at the farmhouse that followed, Major Stopka was awarded the

Distinguished Service Cross. For his heroic actions at Carentan, which would become known to history as "Cole's Charge," Lt. Col. Robert G. Cole was awarded the Medal of Honor. Unfortunately, he would not live to receive the medal, as he was killed in Holland on September 19, 1944, bravely leading his paratroopers in battle during Operation *Market Garden*. Major Stopka took command of the battalion and was killed in January 1945 during the Battle of the Bulge. Leadership often bore a heavy price in the 101st Airborne during World War II.

The Medal of Honor citation for Lieutenant Colonel Robert G. Cole reads:

> For gallantry and intrepidity at the risk of his own life, above and beyond the call of duty on 11 June 1944, in France. Lt. Col. Cole was personally leading his battalion in forcing the last 4 bridges on the road to Carentan when his entire unit was suddenly pinned to the ground by intense and withering enemy rifle, machinegun, mortar, and artillery fire placed upon them from well-prepared and heavily fortified positions within 150 yards of the foremost elements. After the devastating and unceasing enemy fire had for over 1 hour prevented any move and inflicted numerous casualties, Lt. Col. Cole, observing this almost hopeless situation, courageously issued orders to assault the enemy positions with fixed bayonets. With utter disregard for his own safety and completely ignoring the enemy fire, he rose to his feet in front of his battalion and with drawn pistol shouted to his men to follow him in the assault. Catching up a fallen man's rifle and bayonet, he charged on and led the remnants of his battalion across the bullet-swept open ground and into the enemy position. His heroic and valiant action in so inspiring his men resulted in the complete establishment of our bridgehead across the Douve River. The cool fearlessness, personal bravery, and outstanding leadership displayed by Lieutenant Colonel Cole reflect great credit upon himself and are worthy of the highest praise in the military service.

Later, after Cole was killed in combat in Holland, General Eisenhower sent a tender letter to Cole's widow on March 8, 1945. Before the war, Eisenhower had served with Cole in the 15th Infantry and got to know Cole personally. In his letter Eisenhower wrote:

> I do not wish to bring afresh to your mind memories of your tragic loss. I admired and liked him so much that I feel impelled to send you some expression

of my sympathy and regret. He was one of our ablest and certainly one of our most gallant officers. He had earned among his associates a universal respect and liking and, of course, I had an additional interest in him because of our old association the 15th Infantry.

Today, Cole rests in peace with 8,300 of his fellow American soldiers at the Netherlands American Cemetery in Holland.

★ ★ ★

Leadership Lesson

All leadership is by example. Leaders influence others through action. When you are a leader, every member of your team watches what you do. If the leader is cowardly, dishonest, or undependable, the team will reflect those failings. If the leader is courageous, honest, and dependable, then it is more likely that the leader will gain the trust of the team. To earn your teammate's trust, as a leader, you must say what you mean, *do* what you say, and then lead by example.

And what is trust? Trust is a relationship of consistent and coherent action observed. It is not what you say; it is what people see you consistently do. You must work hard to earn the trust of those you lead, and you must be aware that you can lose that trust easily if you do not act trustworthy at all times. If you are consistently honest, people will believe what you say. If you act consistently in a certain way, people will learn to depend on that fact. Erratic leaders do not gain trust. If your actions are coherent with the values and goals of the team or organization to which you belong, your team will recognize that you are acting correctly and are worthy of their trust.

Trust is the core of leadership. Trust is not about compelling people to do something; it is about impelling them to act because they wish to follow your leadership, your example. Compel means to force. Impel means to propel through persuasion and trust. Trust has always been the essential ingredient to empower leaders. Trust must be earned through a relationship that displays consistent and coherent action observed. Lead by example and you can earn people's trust.

Leaders must share the same danger, hardship, and discomfort as they expect their team members to bear. If you want your teammates to act in a particular way, set the example by acting that way. If you want them to arrive on time, *be* on time. If you want them to be courteous to customers and clients, *be* courteous to them. Provide clear instructions. Hold people accountable. Share their conditions. If you want them to listen, listen intently to them. Your actions will speak louder than any words and will create an example for others to emulate.

Lieutenant Colonel Robert G. Cole led by example. He took the decisive decision to attack, rather than withdraw or dig in, even though the odds looked grim. He led by example, physically moving into extreme danger and inspiring his soldiers to follow. Under the stress of combat he compelled and impelled his paratroopers to fight on. Other leaders might have tried to pull out, but not Cole. He knew what was at stake. Cole understood that his options were limited. He could not plea bargain with the Germans. He couldn't quit because the situation was too tough. He had to act and he couldn't expect his men to make that charge if he led from behind.

Cole had earned the trust of his men. They knew that if he said "Charge!" it was because it was the only way to win and survive. They also knew he would lead the way. The 3rd Battalion's attack decisively broke the German defenses and allowed the American 101st Airborne Division to gain a vital foothold in Carentan. Although his casualties were heavy, they might have been *total* if Cole had hesitated, stayed in position, or tried to move back across the causeway to friendly lines. Had he hesitated, or decided to withdraw or dig in, his battalion would have been wiped out and the Germans would have denied Carentan to the Americans. Cole's decision made all the difference and by leading by example, he saved the situation and his men.

You most likely will never face such a dramatic and dire situation as Cole did at Carentan, but you can learn volumes from his act of leadership. There is no doubt that if you lead—in your family, your school, your sports team, your business, or in the military—you will be expected by those you lead to set the example for everyone to follow. Your loyalty, interpersonal skills, attitude, focus, discipline, and work ethic are always on display. Your team members will watch *everything* you do. If you want your teammates to act a certain way, you must model that behavior for them, every day. If you tell everyone to work late to accomplish a vital task, but leave early thinking no one will notice, you had better think again, as they will notice. How can anyone trust a leader who talks about one thing, but does another? To lead by example means that you say what you mean and you *do* what you say. Your correct words must be followed by correct action. How can you use Lt. Col. Cole's story to learn how to lead by example? What can you learn from Lt. Col. Cole's actions at Carentan to help inspire your emerging leaders to earn the trust of their teammates?

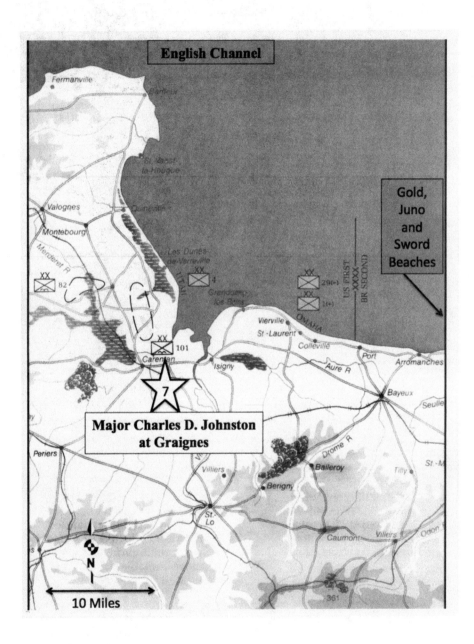

CHAPTER 7

The Alamo of Normandy

Intent

*"We landed fifteen to twenty miles from where we were supposed
to and I landed in the water up to my shoulders."*
1Lt. Frank Naughton, 507th Parachute Infantry Regiment,
82nd Airborne Division, describing his night jump on D-Day

*"We lost a lot of troopers because they got tangled up in their parachute risers and
drowned... We saw in the distance, on the horizon, a cross and a steeple so we
figured that had to be the high ground and so we made our way towards that
and dawn was just breaking as we entered the village of Graignes."*
Sgt. John Hinchliff, Headquarters Company,
507th Parachute Infantry Regiment, 82nd Airborne Division,
recounting his first few hours in Normandy on D-Day

Normandy, France, just before noon, June 6, 1944: The distant sound
of explosions and machine-gun fire echoed in the cool morning air. A
19-year-old American paratrooper struggled through the cold water of
a murky marsh. He was soaked, cold, tired, and hungry. Still, he carried
on and did his best to keep his M1 rifle above the waterline, hoping
that it would fire if he came face-to-face with a German. Behind him,
three men followed.

The great Allied invasion of Nazi-occupied France was unfolding.
American paratroopers of the 82nd "All American" Airborne Division
and the 101st "Screaming Eagles" Airborne Division had flown from
airfields in England to parachute into Normandy in the early hours of
June 6. The Allied air armada that carried thousands of US paratroopers
was greeted that night by a low ceiling of dense clouds. Many of the

US paratroopers, loaded with the equipment they will need to fight for several days without resupply, prepare to jump from a C-47 Skytrain Aircraft. On D-Day, many paratroopers of the 3rd Battalion 507th PIR, 82nd Airborne Division, were miss-dropped far behind German lines. (US Army photo)

twin-engined C-47s were scattered by the clouds and were forced to fly lower to navigate to their designated drop zones. As they flew over the Cotentin Peninsula the Germans greeted them with intense antiaircraft fire. Confusion reigned as the aircraft maneuvered to avoid the deadly flak. Aircraft lost formation and some veered off course. Finding the drop zones became difficult, if not impossible, for some of the pilots. A few aircraft were hit and, in a blazing display of fire, crashed to the ground before the paratroopers could exit the aircraft. Others dropped their paratroopers as best they could. Some paratroopers jumped as low as 500 feet, with barely enough altitude for their chutes to open. Some chutes didn't open. Paratroopers were scattered all over the countryside. Small groups of paratroopers banded together to try to find their way to their objectives. Many landed in areas that had been deliberately flooded by the Germans to obstruct parachute landings. Dozens of paratroopers drowned or were gunned down by Germans before they could get out of their parachutes. Many of the men who survived, alone and struggling in water up to their necks, felt that the invasion must be a disaster.

"Hold it," the second man in column ordered. "That looks like a church steeple up ahead. See, there!"

The private stopped and scanned the terrain. "Yes, sir, Major. I think it is."

"Let's get out of this damn swamp," Major Charles D. Johnston announced. If nothing else, he thought, they could take cover there, hide, and possibly find out where they had landed. "Move toward the church."

The private led the column of paratroopers through the deep water. It took some time, but finally they reached dry ground. The strain of carrying a heavy pack, weapons, and ammunition through water up to their chests all night and half the day had worn the men out. When the paratroopers reached solid land they lay down on their backs and rested for a moment as the water drained from their heavy packs and water-soaked boots.

"Any idea where we are sir?" Henshaw asked.

"Son, all I know… is that we're in Normandy… near a church that's older than my great-grandmother." Major Johnston shook his head in disgust and then looked at his wrist compass to get a bearing. An explosion reverberated in the distance, followed by the faint staccato sound of machine-gun fire. "That shooting is coming from the north. From the sound of that firing, the fighting is miles north of us."

"Damn C-47s missed the drop zone," another paratrooper in their small group complained. "I'm lucky I didn't drown when I landed. I must have landed in 10 feet of water. My chute pulled me down. Had to cut my way out."

Johnston nodded. He had seen the bodies of several dead paratroopers in the swamp. These poor souls had drown without even having had a chance to fight.

The shoulder patch of the 82nd Airborne Division. (US Army image)

The sun was high in the sky.

"Sir, someone is coming our way," Private Henshaw announced as he rolled onto his belly and aimed his rifle at the figure approaching them.

The other paratroopers readied for action. Johnston flicked off the safety on his M1 Thompson submachine gun.

"Vous êtes en sécurité," an older man in a long black habit said with a wide smile on his face. The kind-looking man waved his hands and beckoned them to come forward. *"Venez avec moi."*

"What if it's a trap?" one of the paratroopers whispered.

"Quiet. Stay here," Johnston ordered. He then stood up and walked toward the man and quickly saw that he was a priest. Johnston lowered his weapon but was ready to fire in a moment.

"Vous êtes Américain?" the priest asked.

"Oui Américain," Johnston replied, "but, Padre, that's about all the French I know."

The priest smiled. "I... English, not so well. Come." The priest then pointed to the entrance of the church and waved.

Johnston signaled to the three men waiting on the edge of the marsh. "Let's go. Into the church."

The priest and the paratroopers scurried into the church. When they were inside, the priest closed the door and beamed another wide smile.

"*Beaucoup*... ah... many *Américains*," the priest offered. "Welcome to France."

Johnston chuckled. This was not what he expected. He quickly looked around and was amazed to see at least 60 paratroopers crowded into the church. He recognized many from the headquarters company of the 3rd Battalion, 507th PIR. Others were not even from the 82nd Airborne Division, but wore the Screaming Eagle patch of the 101st Airborne. Many of the paratroopers were so exhausted that they were asleep, lying in the pews. Many, however, were awake—drying their clothing, smoking, chatting with each other as they ate K-rations, or cleaning weapons.

"*Capitaine!*" the priest shouted to a man at the other end of the church.

The captain turned, then nodded and moved toward Johnston. The captain had an M1 carbine slung over his shoulder and carried a map in his left hand.

"Man, am I glad to see you, Major," the captain said as he offered his hand to Johnston. The two men shook hands.

"Brummitt, it's good to see you too," Johnston replied. "Know where the heck we are?"

"The priest told me this village is called Graignes," Captain Leroy D. Brummitt, the 3rd Battalion Operations Officer (S3), said as he unfolded the map and placed his finger on their location. "As best I can tell, we are here, about 8 miles southeast of Carentan on the only high ground in the middle of a huge swamp."

"That would put us about 15 miles from our drop zone," Johnston said, shaking his head in disbelief. "We're much farther behind German lines than I thought."

"Do you know how things are going with the invasion? The main landings should be happening right about now," Brummitt said, looking at his wristwatch. "I saw a mess of flashes earlier this morning. Probably the Navy and Air Force bombing the beaches. I'd sure hate to miss the big show."

Johnston shook his head. "Hell, I didn't even know where we were until just now. I spent all night in that damn marsh, trying to keep from drowning. Do you have any radios that work?"

"No, sir. The one radio we have is waterlogged. Even if we could manage to get the thing working, I don't think it could transmit that far."

"Yeah," Johnston answered. "What's our strength?"

"Last count, we have nearly 90 men, most from our headquarters company. There are stragglers coming in all the time as they find the high ground to get out of the swamp," Brummitt replied. "I've stationed some of the men in the nearby homes and barns in this village to provide security… And we're in pretty good shape for weapons and rifle ammunition. I've seen a couple of machine guns with ammo and three mortars with plenty of mortar shells."

"Any sign of the enemy?" Johnston asked.

Brummitt pulled out a cigarette and lit it with a silver-colored zippo lighter. He offered a smoke to Johnston. Johnston shook his head.

"There was some shooting about an hour ago," Brummitt reported, taking a puff of tobacco. "One of our guys fired at a two-man German patrol. The Germans ran off to the north. It came from along the road that leads north to Carentan."

"Carentan," Johnston said, as if he was trying to figure out a mystery. Johnston looked at his watch: 12:10 p.m. "You remember what they said about Carentan in our briefings?"

"Yes sir—most important town in our area of operations," Brummitt replied. "But our immediate mission is to find the battalion … and get back to the 82d. Right?"

"Let's go up in the steeple and take a look at the ground first," Johnston said. He slung his M1 Thompson submachine gun over his shoulder and headed for the steps to the steeple with the captain in tow. Together, they climbed up the winding stairs to the belfry. Once they reached the top Johnston took out a pair of binoculars and scanned the area.

A rooster crowed nearby. A series of loud explosions resonated from the north.

"Pheww, will you listen to that," Brummitt said as he looked out from the steeple. "I guess the fighting is up there."

"Yeah," Johnston answered.

"Maybe we should be heading that way," Brummitt offered, "toward the fight."

Johnston didn't reply. He continued to scan the village and the approaches to the area that ran through the swamp. The village of Graignes consisted of about 200 widely separated buildings. Many of these were sturdy Norman stone houses and barns. Johnston took the map from Brummitt and oriented it to the terrain. The village was the only high ground for miles around. Everywhere to the north and west was flooded. *This was why so many paratroopers naturally migrated to the village*, he thought. There was one main road that went north (now the D89 road) and it went right by the village. The village dominated the only route to Carentan. Because of the flooding, the terrain was very restricted. If that road was blocked, no military unit could move north.

His mission, however, was miles north, at Saint-Mère-Église. Missing the drop zone had not negated those orders.

Johnston quickly analyzed the possibilities.

He could assemble all the men he could find in the village and head northwest to Carentan. They would have to move in small groups and might have to fight along the way, but if they left later tonight, there was a chance that some of them could slip by the Germans by staying off the roads and traveling in the marsh. It would be slow going, but if these small groups could get to Carentan, they might be able to link up with other American units. He knew that the plan called for the Americans to secure Carentan as soon as possible, as the town controlled a vital road junction to link the American forces in the west at Utah Beach with the Americans in the east at Omaha Beach, but he didn't know if the Americans were in Carentan.

The problem was, he didn't know where the Germans were either. Small groups of paratroopers, moving at night through the swamp, might just fall into the hands of the enemy.

A second course of action, he soon realized, was to organize a defense of the village and hold this ground. He could continue to gather as many troops and as much equipment as possible and defend the village and block the enemy from using the road to Carentan. With nearly a hundred troops and ample ammunition, he might be able to hold long enough for friendly forces to link up with his defenders.

He surveyed the terrain. Graignes was good ground to defend. He saw that the village of Graignes was decisive terrain. If he could turn the houses of the village into small fortresses, he could stop any Germans from using the road to Carentan. He had been thoroughly briefed in the months prior to D-Day that the specific mission of the 82nd Airborne Division was to block approaches into the vicinity of the amphibious landing at Utah Beach and to establish crossings over the Douve River at Carentan to assist the US V Corps in merging the two American beachheads. Carentan was the key to the second part of the mission. If he could not move his force from Graignes as a unit to achieve the first part of the mission, then maybe he could use this force to achieve the intent of the second mission? Stopping German reinforcements from reaching Carentan by holding at Graignes could secure that intent.

Of course, he had no idea if the invasion was a success or a bitter defeat. He had to see through the confusion and make a decision with very little information.

If only, he thought, he could contact his commander, or any American unit, on the radio.

"We need to decide what to do. What are your orders, sir?" Brummitt asked. "Should I organize the men to head back to the battalion?"

"No. I think we'll defend here," Johnston decided. "Carentan is the key. This may be an opportunity. We shouldn't be here, but here we are. We hold this ground until the rest of the division comes to us."

"Sir, with all due respect," Brummitt replied, "that's crazy. We're miles behind enemy lines. Nobody knows we are here. Most of these men are headquarters troops. How are we going to hold off the German Army here, with this group of miss-dropped troopers?"

"Captain Brummitt," Johnston replied, "we have no choice. It makes military sense to stay here, *now* that we are here. Here we hold the high ground. Here we can create a strong defensive position. Here we can deny the Germans the road to Carentan."

"Major, our mission is to our battalion, way up north." Brummitt answered curtly. "In my capacity as Battalion S-3, I have already formulated a tentative night-march plan. We can go through the flooded swamp areas which we have waded through before, or alternatively go around the swamps to Carentan, link up with the US force there, and continue on to the 82nd Division area."

"Noted. I'm changing our mission," Johnston answered definitively. His tone left no doubt that this decision was final. "We are going to stop the Krauts from moving north along the road to Carentan. We defend here."

Brummitt looked confused, then the look turned to anger.

Johnston pointed to the terrain from his vantage point. "The Germans will be channelized in their movements because of the swamp. They will have to use the road if they intend to get to or from Carentan. We can use this to our advantage."

Captain Brummitt gritted his teeth and silently looked at the map.

"I want you to gather up every man you can find, assign them into units, and place them into positions," Johnston continued. "Set the machine guns in ambush to cover the road with interlocking direct fires. Place the mortars near the church and use this steeple to observe fire. If we can find any mines, I want them placed to stop the Germans from moving along the road and getting into the village... And I want to talk to the mayor of this town and see if he will support us."

"Sir, I disagree with your decision," Brummitt responded. "This place will be our grave if we stay here."

"Well, Captain, it is not your call to make," Johnston answered. "It's mine."

There was a silence between the two leaders.

"How can you be sure this is the right decision?" Brummitt questioned.

"I can't, but I have to take a decision, so there it is," Johnston answered. "We have to work together here. You are second in command. I need your help to set our defense."

"You know that we mostly have headquarters troops here," Brummitt offered again. "These are not rifle platoons."

"They are all paratroopers," Johnston replied. "They will fight."

"All right, sir. I'm on it," Brummitt replied.

Johnston met with the village mayor, Alphonse Voydie, who gathered the villagers and took a vote. They decided to support the Americans. This was a very courageous decision. The villagers of Graignes had lived under German occupation for nearly four years and although the Germans had pretty much left them alone, they knew that the Germans responded cruelly and overwhelmingly to any form of resistance. They knew that entire towns had been devastated and the male population killed, and worse, when other villages in German-occupied France had acted in resistance. The Germans were well known for summarily executing civilians who opposed them. Knowing this, and in spite of this, the brave French families of Graignes opened their homes to the Americans. The women of Graignes prepared hot meals for the hungry American paratroopers and the local grocery store and café—even though they did not have much to share—gave all they had to feed the Americans.

The American paratroopers immediately got to work and the defenses were quickly set and continuously reinforced. As more miss-dropped paratroopers arrived, they were assembled, briefed, and assigned duties. Johnston's force swelled to 182 men as more stragglers arrived, beckoned by the church steeple, which became their guidepost to get out of the swamp. Johnston set up his headquarters in the village's school-house. Field phone telephone wire was laid from the command post in the schoolhouse to the various positions on the perimeter. An aid station was set up and a 24-hour observation post was established in the church belfry. Two 81mm mortars were readied for action, sighted on primary targets along likely avenues of approach, and mortar targets were pre-designated to ensure accurate targeting. Through all this martial preparation, the villagers enthusiastically assisted the Americans. They went out in shallow-bottomed boats to search for ammunition and weapons that had been parachuted into the swamp. The weapons, ammunition, and equipment that the French villagers fished out of the water were cleaned and then distributed along the perimeter to bolster the defense. Soon the village of Graignes was no longer a quiet little farm town, but a fortified military position.

Although the Americans were too far away from friendly forces to make radio contact, one of the communications officers had a carrier pigeon that was used to send messages. Major Johnston sent the following message by pigeon: "Am in position at Graignes coordinate four one five eight zero zero with practically all of hardware blue three four behind enemy lines no contact with friendly forces am remaining in position impossible to get regiment signed Johnston Major [sic]."[1] Johnston never knew if the pigeon made it through. The homing pigeon died en route, but was discovered by a unit of the 82nd Airborne Division near Sainte-Mère-Église before the battle of Carentan and the message was delivered to the Division Intelligence Officer (G2). He notified units in the 82nd Airborne to assist Major Johnston's men. Unfortunately, no units would be anywhere near Graignes until weeks later. Johnston and his men were on their own.

For several days it was quiet and peaceful as the Americans improved their defensive positions in Graignes. Major Johnston and Captain Brummitt set the defenses to trap any Germans that attempted to use the road to Carentan. No large German units moved north until Saturday, June 10, when an unsuspecting column of German SS troops came up the road. The observation post in the church steeple saw the

Germans coming and alerted the defenders. The unsuspecting Germans moved right into Johnston's ambush. The Americans opened fire at close range, surprised the SS troopers, and killed or wounded a half-dozen of the enemy. The surviving Germans withdrew, leaving their dead on the road where they fell. The Americans discovered papers on the dead that indicated that these German SS soldiers were from the 17th SS Panzergrenadier Division "Götz von Berlichingen." This unit was an armored infantry division that was equipped with vehicles, heavy weapons, *Sturmgeschütz* Assault Guns (StuGs),[2] and lots of artillery. The Americans had won the first round, but Johnston realized that the Germans were now alerted to the danger and 180 paratroopers were no match for a German Panzergrenadier division. Johnston also realized that the Germans now knew that the village of Graignes was an American military strongpoint. Soon, the 17th SS would come at his defenses in force.

More SS arrived around 10:00 a.m. on June 10, now mad as hornets for being ambushed. The SS attacked with infantry, hoping to cross the Canal de Vire along a secondary road that led into the village. Johnston's men blew up the bridge across the Canal de Vire just as the Germans were crossing. Dozens of 17th SS troopers were killed in the blast.

On Sunday June 11, while the church priest was holding Mass, the Germans attacked with a large force from the south. The Germans penetrated into the center of Graignes but were forced back by the Americans. Major Johnston ordered all positions manned, understanding that this German attack was a probe and that more attacks would follow. The American observation post reported that more SS vehicles were arriving at the far southern end of the road, out of range of the American guns. The Germans were bringing up mortars, 88mm cannons, and StuG assault guns to pound the defenders. The observation post warned the rest of the defenders.

More Germans arrived. The German force eventually consisted of nearly 2,000 men of the 17th SS Panzergrenadier Division, and the 182 American defenders were outnumbered nearly 10 to 1. The fighting went on for two days. The American defenders held and fought like demons to deny the Germans the avenue of approach to Carentan, but the Germans now were about to write the final chapter of Johnston's defense of Graignes.

Around 4 p.m., after fighting since noon and repulsing every German attack, Major Johnston counted his dead and wounded and reset his defense with what he had left. He warned the French villagers that they should go home and hide as the Americans were running low on ammunition and he was not sure how much longer they could hold off the Germans. From the church steeple in Graignes the American observation post could see German armored vehicles moving into position and saw a battery of German 88mm cannon setting up to fire on the American positions. The observation post reported this to Johnston and he knew that the Germans would soon launch a major assault. The American 81mm mortars had been particularly devastating, especially since they had a perfect observation platform in the belfry of the church.

Sensing the Americans were running low on men and ammunition, the 17th SS planned one massive, final, coordinated attack and threw everything they had into the fight. The attack started with a mortar and artillery barrage, followed by an infantry assault with StuG assault guns firing in support of the infantry. Rushing to his headquarters building, Johnston directed his mortars to take out the advancing SS. At the same time, a battery of 88mm guns opened fire on the buildings in the village and the church. The 88s blasted the headquarters building while Major Johnston was directing the defense. He and several men in the headquarters were buried when the walls collapsed.

Captain Brummitt was informed that Major Johnston was dead and he immediately took command. He continued the fight using his remaining machine guns to make the Germans pay dearly in casualties as they took the key buildings in Graignes, but the defense was rapidly unraveling. The German 88mm guns targeted the church steeple and destroyed it and the American paratrooper observing fire for the mortars. The mortars were firing at their highest elevation as the German troops closed in.

When the mortars stopped firing, Brummitt's machine guns also ran out of ammunition. The 17th SS, furious at being repulsed and taking heavy casualties, finally cracked the American defensive perimeter. The young captain realized that all hope of continuing the defense was lost and ordered the survivors to form into small groups and exfiltrate northeast toward American lines. As the Germans overran the forward positions, Brummitt fired red flares into the air to signal that the defenders were to abandon Graignes and make their own way as best they could toward friendly lines. The Americans ran into the swamps as the Germans tried to cut them down from the high ground around the smoldering buildings of Graignes.

The Americans ran for their lives and could not carry their wounded into the swamp. During the fighting the wounded had been collected in the church. An American doctor, Captain Abraham Sophian, Jr., was tending the wounded in the church. Before he headed for the swamp, Captain Brummitt ordered Sophian to leave, but the doctor refused those orders, bravely saying that he would stay with the wounded. Brummitt wished the doctor good luck and took off. Sophian hoped to negotiate for clemency with the Germans under the rules of war. The SS, however, were not known for clemency, or for following the rules of war. Incensed and seeking revenge for their heavy casualties and humiliation that the Americans had inflicted on them, the 17th SS executed all 19 American prisoners, including Sophian, and two priests. The SS then rounded up 44 villagers into the damaged church and threatened to kill them all. They brutally interrogated the villagers, wanting to know which of them had helped the Americans, but the Frenchmen would not give up any names. By some miracle the SS did not kill all 44 villagers, but marched them to a nearby hamlet to dig graves for the SS soldiers that the Americans had killed in the battle. In retaliation for the French villagers supporting the Americans, the SS ransacked, looted, and burned Graignes. As darkness fell, the houses of Graignes glowed red and 66 homes burned to the ground. Later, the Germans would kill more villagers.

After the Germans were driven out of France, there were unconfirmed accounts by local French villagers that the Germans had pulled Major Johnston and another officer from the rubble of the schoolhouse. Both men were seriously wounded, but both were reported alive and taken as prisoners of war. According to this account, the Germans brought them to a nearby hamlet, interrogated them, and then executed both Johnston and the other officer. These reports are impossible to confirm, so we may never know.

The defense of Graignes, and the sacrifice of the miss-dropped American paratroopers and the brave French villagers, was not in vain. German Field Marshal Erwin Rommel ordered the 17th SS to move as rapidly as possible to Carentan to defend this critical town and stop the two separated American forces at Utah and Omaha beaches from joining forces. Major Johnston's force delayed the 17th SS for two vital days, June 10–11, 1944, just long enough so that the 17th SS Panzergrenadier Division could not make it to Carentan in time to stop Lt. Col. Robert G. Cole's 3rd Battalion, 502nd PIR from attacking down the causeway and capturing a foothold in the town. This long delay allowed the 101st Airborne to take Carentan before the 17th SS could arrive. By the time the 17th SS finally attacked at Carentan on June 13, the Germans met a stiff defense from the paratroopers of the 101st Airborne and were then repulsed by a strong counterattack by the 2nd Armored "Hell on Wheels" Division, which had raced from Omaha Beach to Carentan. It seems that Allied intelligence had intercepted and decrypted Rommel's message to the 17th SS Panzergrenadier Division and responded by sending in the cavalry in the form of the 2nd Armored Division. Without the stubborn defense at Graignes by Major Johnston and his men, which is now known as the "Alamo of Normandy," the link-up of the American forces at Omaha and Utah beaches could have been delayed and many more American lives might have been lost in taking Carentan.[3]

At least 32 Americans were killed at Graignes during the battle. Several days later, the survivors, about 150 men in small, scattered groups, reached American lines or met advancing American forces. The exact number of casualties that Johnston's paratroopers inflicted on the 17th SS is difficult to know, since the Germans controlled the ground after the battle, but records from the 17th SS Panzergrenadier Division "Götz von Berlichingen" show that as many as 79 dead, 61 missing, and 316 wounded occurred during the battle of Graignes.

Major Charles D. Johnston was typical of many of the officers who volunteered to be paratroopers in World War II. He was born in Knoxville, Tennessee, and was raised by his uncle W. C. Dunn. He did not attend West Point and was not a professional soldier, but was a graduate of the Army Reserve Officers Training Corps (ROTC). Like many of his countrymen, he volunteered when he saw the clouds of war forming, volunteered a second time to join the paratroops, and because of his strong leadership, he was promoted to major and assigned as the battalion executive officer (XO). Unlike others who were decorated for heroism in combat, Johnston never received an award for his heroic leadership at Graignes. Since there was no officer senior to Johnston to witness and report the action, and because the other defenders scattered and exfiltrated back to American lines, Johnston's heroic leadership went unnoticed. Major Johnston's remains were not found until after the war. When his remains were identified, his body was repatriated to the US and he is buried at Lynnhurst Cemetery, Knoxville, Tennessee.

★ ★ ★

Leadership Lesson

Leaders must understand the intent, the bigger picture, of their higher organization in order to make timely decisions when plans must be changed. Understanding "intent" permits the leader to execute disciplined initiative to transform thought into action. Disciplined initiative fosters agile decision making.

Plans are merely a basis for changes. The experienced strategist Field Marshal Helmuth von Moltke said: "No battle plan survives contact

After D-Day and once the beaches were secure, the vast Allied logistical effort kicked into gear to supply the Allied fighting forces in Normandy. In this photo, taken in mid-June 1944, Landing Ship Tanks (LSTs), with barrage balloons afloat above the ships to impede German dive-bombers, unload vehicles and supplies on Omaha Beach in preparation for the breakout from Normandy. In the background, hundreds of other ships are waiting to unload their cargoes. The planning for Operation Overlord, the invasion of Normandy, was detailed and immense. The leadership required to make the invasion a success was even more extraordinary. (US Army photo)

with the enemy." This is true not just in war but for every business, occupation, profession, and walk of life. A plan describes one way to accomplish a mission. Planning is vital, and plans provide a point of departure to get the mission accomplished. Relying only on plans, however, invites failure. Agile leaders are expected to adapt the plan to the changing circumstances. Adept leaders know when to decide to change the plan to fit the situation and do not try to force a plan to work when that plan no longer fits the circumstance. Armies, businesses, and nations have been ruined when a plan is forced to work in a situation that has changed and the plan no longer applies. To overcome this, leaders must understand the situation and make decisions.

Intent can guide these decisions. Intent provides a framework to make decisions to accomplish the mission in all cases, no matter how the situation has changed. Understanding "intent" permits the leader to make successful changes *in time*. Time is a factor in all forms of human endeavor; we never seem to have enough time. In business, winning time is winning business. Coming out with a new product or a killer-app before the competition is the difference between success or failure in the marketplace. Winning time in war is winning the battle. If you beat your competition to the battlefield, or the marketplace, you generate options that can act in your favor. The faster a leader can make a good decision, the better for all.

Understanding intent, therefore, is a key factor in improving decision-making, and decision-making is a key subset of leadership. In the US Army, leaders are trained to operate in uncertain circumstances by understanding the commander's intent.[4] A simple definition of intent, applied to the military and business world is: "The commander's intent clearly articulates the Purpose, Key Tasks, and End (Win) State of the operation or project. Commander's intent is a nested concept based on the higher organization's intent and seeks to fulfill the purpose of that higher intent."[5] Whether this is called "commander's intent" or "CEO's intent," if leaders master how to create and issue intent, they add a powerful tool to the leadership toolbox.[6]

Major Charles D. Johnston, XO, 3rd Battalion, 507th Parachute Infantry Regiment, 82nd Airborne Division, understood the intent of his higher commanders. When the D-Day plan no longer made sense, he acted and decided based upon his best understanding of the new situation, the mission, and his higher commander's intent. His actions depict him as an exceptional leader who was at the right time and place and had the courage to lead. No one would have faulted him if he had ordered his men to make their own way back to their units on the evening of June 6, 1944, as Captain Brummitt suggested. Instead, Johnston saw the bigger picture. He had the courage to make a tough decision on D-Day and this decision made the difference on June 10–11, 1944, by delaying the arrival of German mechanized infantry units to Carentan. Although he did not receive a decoration for his heroic leadership of the paratroopers of D-Day's "Alamo" at Graignes, he nonetheless provides us with an extraordinary example of leadership.

How can you learn from Major Johnston's leadership at Graignes to teach intent to raise your understanding of leadership? Do your emerging leaders take decisions within the parameters of intent, or when the plan fails do they stop and wait for instructions?

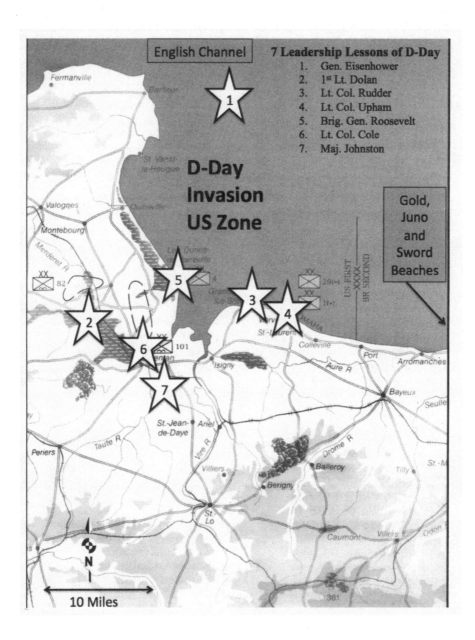

CHAPTER 8

Earn This and Learn

You Will Rise to the Level of Your Leadership

"The men of Normandy had faith that what they were doing was right, faith that they fought for all humanity, faith that a just God would grant them mercy on this beachhead or on the next. It was the deep knowledge—and pray God we have not lost it—that there is a profound moral difference between the use of force for liberation and the use of force for conquest. You were here to liberate, not to conquer, and so you and those others did not doubt your cause. And you were right not to doubt."
President Ronald Reagan, at Pointe du Hoc, June 6, 1984, talking
to the veterans who had stormed the Pointe 40 years earlier

The guns of D-Day, though long silent, still echo to us today. D-Day was a seminal event in World War II and a vital step for the freedom of mankind. America and other free nations stood up against the evil of nazism, recognizing that Hitler had to be defeated. Each generation faces new challenges. Some generations become a beacon to light the way for future generations to follow. The generation that faced down Hitler's legions on D-Day did just that. They exemplify what is great and good about America and about other nations that believe in liberty. Their heroism can inspire us. Their leadership can teach us. After the war, General Eisenhower put the overall leadership lesson of D-Day this way:

> Teamwork wins wars. I mean teamwork among nations, services and men. All the way down the line. From the GI and the Tommy, to us brass hats. Our enemy in this campaign was strong, resourceful and cunning, but he made a few mistakes. His greatest blunder was this: He thought he could break up our partnership. But we were welded together by fighting for one great cause. In one great team.

Teamwork wins. The ability to lead teams in situations of great change and uncertainty is as vital a skill for today's leaders as it was for the leaders on D-Day.

There is tremendous value in studying D-Day in depth to better understand the human dimensions of leadership. Technology has dramatically changed since 1944, but people are basically the same and the leadership lessons of D-Day are timeless. As US Army General Curtis M. Scaparrotti, the North Atlantic Treaty Organization's (NATO) Supreme Commander in Europe, said at a wreath-laying ceremony at the Iron Mike Memorial at La Fière, near Sainte-Mère-Église, during a commemoration of the 73rd Anniversary of D-Day: "There are moments in a nation's history when its future course is decided by a chosen few who walked bravely into the valley of the shadow of death. In such moments, young men and women pledge their lives so that their nation can live." We can learn from their example.

The seven leadership stories in this book offer powerful lessons that you can use to learn how to become a better leader. Their dramatic stories reinforce the summary of the leadership lessons that follow in the next paragraphs. Without reading the stories, the list is useful but not memorable. By reading the stories, the leadership lessons can impact your thinking. When times get tough, imagine if you had to make the decision to "go," as Ike did. Would you buckle under the pressure or measure up to the challenge? Imagine if you had to hold the line at La Fière as Dolan did, or lead under intense difficulty, fear, and confusion as did Rudder, Upham, Cole, Roosevelt or Johnston.

Today, the battlefields of Normandy are a special place. Over 2,300 years ago, a Spartan king said it is not the places that grace men, but men who grace the places. Normandy is a sacred place because it was graced by such leaders as Eisenhower, Dolan, Rudder, Upham, Roosevelt, Cole, Johnston and many, many more. The extraordinary leadership lessons from these leaders are summarized below:

Leadership Lesson Number 1

Leadership is the art of influence. The leader has the opportunity to influence everyone on the team, for better or for worse. A leader

At about 9 a.m. on D-Day, Pvt. First Class James Flanagan, 502d PIR, 101st Airborne Division, center, posed for this photo with other paratroopers of the 101st Airborne Division, in a farm complex near Ravenoville north of Utah Beach. Flannigan had captured a Nazi flag from a command post and a photographer from the 4th Infantry Division saw the group of paratroopers and snapped this famous photo. In days, this photo would adorn the front pages of many newspapers back in the US and quickly became a symbol of the Allied victory on D-Day. (National Archives)

with confidence can influence teammates to believe in success. A leader with courage can inspire courage in others. A leader with skill in interpersonal relations can help the team to work together and overcome difficulties. Most importantly, a leader's focus and selfless dedication to the task at hand influences others to believe that even the most difficult mission, even under severe hardships, can be accomplished. Gen. Eisenhower once said: "Always take your job seriously, never yourself." What Ike meant was that a leader who does not try to shine, but always reflects the credit to his teammates, can influence others to follow him. A leader that can be serious about the team and

American Paratroopers from the 101st Airborne Division hand out food to villagers. The Allied effort to free Europe from Nazi domination and occupation not only won the war, but won the peace for decades to come. (US Army photo)

accomplishing the mission, while still maintaining a sense of humor, is a leader who can help people get over tough times. A leader who understands that leadership is the art of influence, rather than an act of compliance, can inspire people to act together as a team to win. Be this kind of leader.

Leadership Lesson Number 2

To be a leader, first learn how to be a good follower. This may sound counterintuitive, but it is not. The best leaders are also great followers. All of us follow someone. Being a good follower involves giving up some of your own desires and ego for the good of the team. Leadership is not about shouting orders and always being in charge. Leadership requires discipline, dedication, and, most importantly, obedience. All teams require some degree of obedience. If you won't listen to anyone, you cannot lead. Aristotle once told his young student Alexander, the man who would later be called "the Great," that he had to learn to obey before he could learn how to command. Aristotle believed that no one should be allowed to give orders, if they could not obey orders. To be a good follower, you must subordinate yourself to something greater than yourself. If you act selflessly, putting the team first, others will recognize your efforts. Put another way: What kind of person do you want on your team? Someone who is selfless, punctual, trustworthy, skilled, and dedicated? If so, be that kind of person and you will be taking a vital step forward to becoming an effective leader.

Leadership Lesson Number 3

Fear is a reaction and courage is a decision. Many Rangers who served with Lt. Col. James Earl Rudder during World War II believed that he did not know the meaning of fear. To them, Rudder was fearless. Rudder would strongly disagree with that statement. Acting with courage is not fearlessness; it is getting beyond the fear. As Rudder expressed years after the war, he was just as afraid as anyone else, sometimes even more so as he knew the big picture and had more reasons to justify his fears, but he never gave into them. He understood that fear was a normal human reaction. He knew that fear was "good," as it generated awareness of danger. In war, or driving a car, totally fearless people don't last long. Rudder also knew that he had to cycle through the fear as

American, German, and French dignitaries salute as "Taps" is played during a wreath-laying ceremony at the stature of "Iron Mike" at La Fière Bridge near Sainte-Mère-Église, France, June 4, 2017. The ceremony commemorated the 73rd anniversary of the D-Day landings. (US Army photo by Staff Sgt. Tamika Dillard)

fast as possible and arrive at that mental state where he could make a decision and decide on courage. Once he decided on courage, he could act. This is not an easy thing to do and, above all, requires focus. Fear can be gripping. Fear can paralyze. To focus on action in the midst of fear takes a strong mind. Leaders must understand this, move rapidly though the fear, gain situational awareness, and decide. The first step of any leader is to decide to be courageous, whether the situation involves an employee facing the CEO in a stressful briefing, or a soldier facing enemy fire. This is easier said than done, and it is all a matter of the degree of danger and your level of experience—but there are ways to improve your ability to handle fear. Training in decision-making exercises and becoming skilled at the tasks you must perform, can reinforce confidence to help you push through the fear and decide on courage. Be the kind of leader that understands that fear is a reaction and courage a decision. Decide on courage.

Leadership Lesson Number 4

Leaders must adapt, improvise and overcome. A leader has to make a decision based on the best available information. Plans usually offer one way to accomplish a task. Sometimes, if you can control enough of the parameters that influence the plan, a good plan will work. Most likely, however, the friction of operations will impact the plan and the plan will start to unravel. When that happens, leaders must step in, inspire, and direct their team members to adapt the plan, improvise as needed, and overcome the friction. When the plan no longer makes sense, and information is lacking, the only antidote to inertia and defeat is leadership. A leader must act to overcome this friction. In all walks of life, the leader's role is to move the team forward in spite of resistance. Be the kind of leader that can recognize when the plan must change, and then adapt, improvise, and overcome that resistance to accomplish the mission.

Leadership Lesson Number 5

A leader should place himself at the best place and time to make accurate and timely decisions. If all plans went as written, there would be no need for leaders to take any decisions, but as we have learned, few plans work perfectly after first contact with the competition. A leader, at the right place and time, should determine how that path shifts and generate options. When leaders are positioned at the right place and time to make a decision, they can bring maximum authority to complex situations. The skilled leader learns from study and experience where and when to be to make important decisions. With some practice, a leader can learn how to identify the key decision points of any project, determine the times of greatest risk, and know in advance where to be and when. The first step in this process is to understand what decisions will need to be made and then understand where the leader should be to best make those decisions. Through red teaming and war-gaming, a leader can project his thoughts forward in time and space in order to know where to be and how to act. This may sound like a sixth sense, but it is merely a matter of focused thinking about the most likely and most dangerous possibilities. Leaders must be at the point of decision (right place and time) to have maximum effect. Be the kind of leader who is at the point of decision.

Leadership Lesson Number 6

All leadership is by example. Once the leader pushes through the fear and decides on courage, communication becomes the vital force of motivation. This is why leaders must be adept at as many forms of communication as possible. To win, a leader must motivate and impel teammates to act. To do this, leaders must communicate by example and word. Of these two, example is the most powerful. Colorful speeches may be great, but leaders inspire primarily by example. "Follow me" and moving forward with the team means so much more than "Go ahead, I'll be watching you and staying safely behind." When you are a leader, every member of your team watches what you do. In the US Army, there is a saying that an officer is always on parade. This means that the troops are always watching the leader all the time. The people you lead know if you are acting correctly or incorrectly.

Most importantly, the team adopts the character of the leader. If you have an ineffective team, most likely you have an ineffective leader. If you have a successful team, you have a successful leader or a successful leader in that team, even if that leader is not necessarily the person in authority (leadership is not about position). If the leader is cowardly, dishonest, or undependable, the team will reflect those failings. If the leader is courageous, honest and dependable, then it is more likely that the leader will gain the trust of the team and the team will reflect the characteristics of the leader. To earn your teammates' trust, as a leader, you must say what you mean, do what you say, and then lead by example.

Leadership Lesson Number 7

Understand and issue clear commander's intent and expect subordinate leaders to act accordingly when the situation changes and the plan no longer applies. Understanding "intent" permits the leader to minimize confusion and make successful changes to a plan that needs to be changed. As stated earlier, plans are merely a basis for changes. This is true for every business, occupation, profession, and walk of life. When things fail to go according to plan, as they usually do, leaders should quickly know that the plan is failing and act in the proper manner and direction. Knowing the "proper manner and direction" involves a concept called "commander's intent" or, in the civilian world, "business intent" or "CEO's intent." Cutting-edge business leaders understand the value of commander's intent as much as those in the military. As author Chad Storlie wrote in a 2010 article in the *Harvard Business Review* titled "Manage Uncertainty with Commander's Intent": "The role of Commander's Intent is to empower subordinates and guide their initiative and improvisation as they adapt the plan to the changed battle-field environment." The basic framework for this intent is to understand the task, purpose, and end-state/win state of the leader or organization above you. Being clear about the purpose, key tasks, and what a winning end state looks like, can empower your team members to act, adapt, improvise, and overcome when they have to act on their own without the direct supervision of the leader. When the plan is failing, a leader can quickly decide when and where to change the plan to accomplish the mission if he understands the higher intent and has clearly articulated the intent to his team members. Understanding intent assists a leader to adapt his decisions to fit the situation, not to try to force the plan to fit the situation. Armies, businesses, and nations have been ruined when a leader tries to force a plan to work in a situation that has changed and the plan no longer applies. A leader who understands and clearly articulates intent is armed with a powerful leadership skill. Team members that understand and receive clear intent can exercise disciplined initiative. Thinking and deciding faster than the opponent is valuable in war and business. Be the kind of leader that understands and can issue a clear commander's intent.

One example of how the leadership learned on D-Day impacted the civilian world involves the hero of the 2nd Ranger Battalion, Lt. Col. James Earl Rudder. After the war Rudder became the President of Texas A&M. The times were changing and Texas Agricultural and Mechanical College needed to change to support the values that the veterans of World War II had fought for: liberty, equal opportunity for all, and a better world. Rudder became the driving force behind growing Texas A&M from a college to a university. He led the way to make it optional for students to be members in the Corps of Cadets and was a major force in opening the university to women. Rudder served as President of Texas A&M from 1959 until his death in 1970 and became a transformational leader who helped accelerate Texas A&M from a small college to one of the largest, top-ranked universities in the United States.

Rudder was a leader who taught leadership to everyone he met, by his example and through his words and actions. He understood that if you teach, you learn twice. If you are professionally invested in your team members and their leadership development, then your efforts can benefit your own personal growth and also the growth of your team, business or organization. Leadership development opportunities abound and do not require a formal classroom setting. You should always look for opportunities to raise your leadership level and the leadership level of your team. Sometimes a periodic leadership lunch discussion is all that is needed to start growing leadership awareness and improving leadership skills.

A critical first step for every leader is to understand what leadership is. You do not truly understand something unless you can first define it in your own words. If you can define something, you can measure it and improve upon it. Socrates, the great ancient Greek philosopher, said that *all* understanding starts with definition. Definition, therefore, is a great place for a leader to start to develop a personal understanding of leadership. If someone that you lead were to ask you: "What is leadership?" and your reply was: "Not sure; I never really thought about it." Well, that answer would not be very inspiring, would it?

Your personal definition of leadership can act as a guide to improve your leadership and, as you learn and experience more about how to lead, you can modify your definition. I challenge you, right now, to take the time to pause and write down your personal definition of leadership. Most leaders I have met, in the military, business and government, have never taken the time to construct a personal definition of leadership. You should be the exception. Think about it. What is your personal definition of leadership?

Your definition provides you with a personal standard to measure your actions when you are the leader. Do not copy a definition from someone else. Write your definition of leadership in 1–5 sentences and construct your definition with care, word by word. Use both focus and passion in developing your definition. Try to visualize your definition in your mind and feel it in your heart. Imagine explaining this definition to those you lead and using it as a rallying point to increase leadership awareness among your team members. A cynical or cryptic definition such as, "A leader is what a leader does," is not very helpful. Create your definition as if you wanted to persuade someone to believe, trust, and follow you as if everything depended on this. When your definition is complete, test it. Get someone to play devil's advocate and "red team" your definition. Discuss your definition with as many trusted people as possible. Listen, pause, and reflect on their reactions and comments to your definition of leadership. If you find that in the process of this interaction your definition is wanting, then change your definition.

Vow to improve your definition and make it something that you believe in and can be considered part of your personal brand.

My definition of leadership was molded over many years of learning from my parents, in school, sports, my thirty years in the US Army, in business, and, most importantly, in self-study. For me, *leadership is the art of influence and a sacred trust. It is the ability to impel people to work together to accomplish a mission.* For me, leadership is clearly the art of influence. To influence, you must mostly inspire, or impel, and try not to resort to compelling unless there is no other means and then only in dire situations. Most importantly, for me, leadership is a sacred trust. If you

The author, Colonel (US Army, Ret.) John Antal, far right second row, with Reserve Officer Training Corps (ROTC) cadets at the Major Richard "Dick" Winters Leadership Monument near Utah Beach in Normandy, during a five-day D-Day Battlefield Leadership Exercise. Nearly every year the author and a team from How2Lead.US raise money to fund an exercise for US Army college ROTC Cadets from Texas to visit the D-Day battlefields and learn leadership lessons. Also shown in this photo, far left in the second row, is Colonel (US Army, Ret.) J. P. Hogan from How2Lead.US. (Antal photo)

are on my team, I will not let you down. This is the promise I make with my teammates and I strive mightily to keep that promise.

In life, we all rise to the level of our leadership. If your leadership level is high, you can make an extraordinary positive impact. If your leadership level is low, your life will be hard, your ability to work with other people is limited, and your capacity to change things for the better will be less. In any situation where two or more people are involved, leadership is important. Every leader holds in his or her hand the fate of the people he or she leads. In the military, police, firefighters and first responders, the role of the leader can literally affect life or death. In other occupations, the leader is in control of the hours of work of the people in the team. Hours constitute quality of life, and if squandered by bad leadership, can result in waste, abuse and failure. Leaders, therefore, are responsible for the people they lead. For this reason, I believe that leadership is a sacred trust, because it involves people. There is no more precious resource on your team than the people you lead.

In any group, leaders make the difference between success or failure, victory and defeat. Leadership can produce synergy and create teams that can be more than the sum of their parts. Synergy comes from the Greek word meaning to "work together." For example, a flashlight consists of three major components: batteries, a lamp, and a switch. When you put them all together in the right configuration, with the right synergy, you produce light and get four things from three. Leaders do the same thing with teams. They magnify the people in the team to create a greater leverage than the individuals could have if they worked alone.

Being a leader is often a challenge, but the challenge offers great rewards. Leading a team through hardships and disappointment can test your resilience and commitment. Overcoming setbacks to build and lead a winning team can be an electrifying experience. Leadership is a behavioral skill that anyone can develop. Raise your leadership awareness through study and seek opportunities to gain leadership experience. Ultimately, understanding leadership is really a journey about understanding one's self. Self-awareness is key. There is no greater reward than to unlock your ability to influence, motivate, inspire and lead people effectively to succeed.

How2Lead.US holds the "Stars and Stripes" at the Pointe du Hoc, Normandy, in 2017. From left to right: Command Sergeant Major (US Army, Ret.) Edward Braese; the author Colonel (US Army, Ret.) John Antal; Colonel (US Army, Ret.) Richard Jung, Sr.; Lieutenant Colonel (US Army, Ret.) Tim Vane; and Colonel (US Army, Ret.) J. P. Hogan. This group of experienced leaders uses the lessons from leaders who fought on D-Day to teach, coach, and mentor civilian, business, and military groups to raise leadership skills. (Antal photo)

In today's competitive, ever-changing, and hyperactive world of business, the companies and teams that win are those whose people are most skilled, focused and passionate about getting the job done. The key ingredients these successful companies and teams have are leaders; leaders who are on a life-long journey to master the skills of influencing people to succeed. Such leaders, like the leaders of D-Day, will accept nothing less than full victory.

President Franklin Roosevelt's D-Day Prayer June 6, 1944

My fellow Americans: Last night, when I spoke with you about the fall of Rome, I knew at that moment that troops of the United States and our allies were crossing the Channel in another and greater operation. It has come to pass with success thus far.

And so, in this poignant hour, I ask you to join with me in prayer:

Almighty God: Our sons, pride of our Nation, this day have set upon a mighty endeavor, a struggle to preserve our Republic, our religion, and our civilization, and to set free a suffering humanity.

Lead them straight and true; give strength to their arms, stoutness to their hearts, steadfastness in their faith.

They will need Thy blessings. Their road will be long and hard. For the enemy is strong. He may hurl back our forces. Success may not come with rushing speed, but we shall return again and again; and we know that by Thy grace, and by the righteousness of our cause, our sons will triumph.

They will be sore tried, by night and by day, without rest—until the victory is won. The darkness will be rent by noise and flame. Men's souls will be shaken with the violences of war.

For these men are lately drawn from the ways of peace. They fight not for the lust of conquest. They fight to end conquest. They fight to liberate. They fight to let justice arise, and tolerance and good will among all Thy people. They yearn but for the end of battle, for their return to the haven of home.

Some will never return. Embrace these, Father, and receive them, Thy heroic servants, into Thy kingdom.

And for us at home—fathers, mothers, children, wives, sisters, and brothers of brave men overseas—whose thoughts and prayers are ever with them—help us, Almighty God, to rededicate ourselves in renewed faith in Thee in this hour of great sacrifice.

Many people have urged that I call the Nation into a single day of special prayer. But because the road is long and the desire is great, I ask that our people devote themselves in a continuance of prayer. As we rise to each new day, and again when each day is spent, let words of prayer be on our lips, invoking Thy help to our efforts.

Give us strength, too—strength in our daily tasks, to redouble the contributions we make in the physical and the material support of our armed forces.

And let our hearts be stout, to wait out the long travail, to bear sorrows that may come, to impart our courage unto our sons wheresoever they may be.

And, O Lord, give us Faith. Give us Faith in Thee; Faith in our sons; Faith in each other; Faith in our united crusade. Let not the keenness of our spirit ever be dulled. Let not the impacts of temporary events, of temporal matters of but fleeting moment—let not these deter us in our unconquerable purpose.

With Thy blessing, we shall prevail over the unholy forces of our enemy. Help us to conquer the apostles of greed and racial arrogancies. Lead us to the saving of our country, and with our sister Nations into a world unity that will spell a sure peace—a peace invulnerable to the schemings of unworthy men. And a peace that will let all of men live in freedom, reaping the just rewards of their honest toil.

Thy will be done, Almighty God.

Amen.

General Eisenhower's Order of the Day

Soldiers, Sailors, and Airmen of the Allied Expeditionary Force:

You are about to embark upon the Great Crusade, toward which we have striven these many months.

The eyes of the world are upon you. The hopes and prayers of liberty-loving people everywhere march with you.

In company with our brave Allies and brothers-in-arms on other Fronts you will bring about the destruction of the German war machine, the elimination of Nazi tyranny over oppressed peoples of Europe, and security for ourselves in a free world.

Your task will not be an easy one. Your enemy is well trained, well equipped, and battle-hardened. He will fight savagely.

But this is the year 1944. Much has happened since the Nazi triumphs of 1940–41. The United Nations have inflicted upon the Germans great defeats, in open battle, man-to-man. Our air offensive has seriously reduced their strength in the air and their capacity to wage war on the ground. Our Home Fronts have given us an overwhelming superiority in weapons and munitions of war, and placed at our disposal great reserves of trained fighting men. The tide has turned. The free men of the world are marching together to victory.

I have full confidence in your courage, devotion to duty, and skill in battle. We will accept nothing less than full victory.

Good Luck! And let us all beseech the blessing of Almighty God upon this great and noble undertaking.

Dwight D. Eisenhower

Gen. Dwight D. Eisenhower shares a light-hearted moment with his staff and Gen. Omar N. Bradley in Normandy, France, shortly after D-Day. Gen. Bradley would later say about the fighting in Normandy on D-day that, "Every man who set foot on Omaha Beach that day was a hero." Gen. Eisenhower, in his order on D-Day, declared to his troops: "We will accept nothing less than full Victory!" The heroes of D-Day delivered just that and then went on to defeat Nazi Germany and win the war in Europe.

General Eisenhower's "In Case of Failure" Note

General Eisenhower recognized more than anyone that the invasion involved big risks. Although great effort, planning, training, and rehearsal had been conducted to make the invasion a success, anything could go wrong and might cause the invasion to fail. In this case, Gen. Eisenhower wrote a note and put it in his pocket, putting it in reserve for the worst case:

> Our landings in the Cherbourg-Havre area have failed to gain a satisfactory foothold and I have withdrawn the troops. My decision to attack at this time and place was based upon the best information available. The troops, the air and the Navy did all that bravery and devotion to duty could do. If any blame or fault attaches to the attempt it is mine alone. July 5

Demonstrating the immense pressure Gen. Eisenhower must have felt, he mistakenly dated the "in case of failure" note July 5, instead of June 5. He stuck the note in his pocket and did not remember much about it for several days after the invasion was a success. The leadership lesson from this note is that a leader takes full responsibility for everything his team does or fails to do. In addition, this note is an example of Eisenhower's humility. He was a leader who believed that leaders don't shine—they reflect.

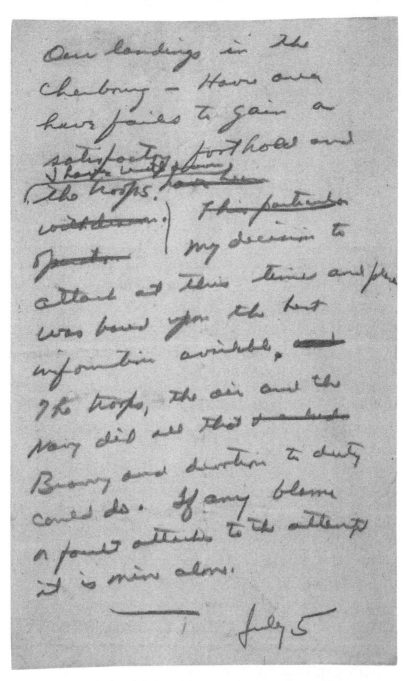

Eisenhower "In Case of Failure" note. (NARA 186470)

The Senior Leaders of D-Day

Courtesy of www.eucom.mil

*"You have got to have something in which to believe. You have got to
have leaders, organization, friendships, and contacts that help
you to believe that, and help you to put out your best."*
*Dwight D. Eisenhower, from remarks to the Leaders
of the United Defense Fund, 1954*

Some of history's greatest military leaders helped secure an Allied victory, and D-Day was certainly an important test of that leadership. Here are some facts about those fascinating Allied leaders.

General Dwight Eisenhower, Allied Expeditionary Force Supreme Commander. During World War II, Eisenhower earned his fifth star as Supreme Commander of the Allies—one of only nine men to ever hold a five-star rank. As the Allied Commander, Eisenhower was considered the most powerful military man in the world. Ironically, his Jehovah's Witness parents had been strict pacifists.

Air Chief Marshal Sir Arthur Harris, 1st Baronet, Commander of the Royal Air Force Bomber Command. He believed that strategic bombing alone would defeat Germany. Unfortunately, this strong conviction, and his reluctance to allow his aircraft to be diverted from this role, brought Harris into conflict with fellow Allied commanders, including Chief of the Air Staff and Prime Minister Winston Churchill. In January 1946, he was ignored and omitted from the Victory Honours List and resigned later that year.

Air Marshal Arthur Tedder, 1st Baron Tedder, Deputy Commander of Allied forces. A colleague Eisenhower respected considerably, Tedder was to "paralyze" the French railway on the eve of *Overlord*. He identified over 70 railroad targets in France and Belgium, directing traffic away from lower Normandy. Historians generally agree Tedder was key to the success of the Allied air forces. By destroying bridges over the Seine and Loire rivers, they effectively isolated Normandy, imposing long detours and endless delays on the Germans.

General Bernard Law Montgomery, 1st Viscount Montgomery of Alamein.

During the Normandy landings and for several months afterwards, Montgomery commanded all Allied troops in France. But in September 1944, Eisenhower took over, with Montgomery reverting to command of 21st Army Group, much to his chagrin. His arrogance was well known, and the "Montgomery cocktail," a martini mixed at a ratio of 15:1, is a facetious reference to his alleged refusal to go into battle without at least that numeric advantage. Reportedly, severe internal injuries from World War I prohibited his own drinking and smoking.

Admiral Sir Bertram Home Ramsay, Allied Naval Expeditionary Force commander. Ramsay was responsible for Operation *Neptune*, which was primarily a Royal Navy effort—only 346 American of 2,468 major vessels were involved on D-Day. Ramsay did not live to see victory in Europe. On January 2, 1945, his aircraft crashed upon take-off, on his way to see General Montgomery, .

Lieutenant General Omar Bradley, Commander of US First Army. General Bradley was the last of only nine people to hold a five-star rank in the US Armed Forces. In 1949, he was named first chairman of the Joint Chiefs of Staff. For D-Day, Bradley was chosen to command the US First Army, which alongside the British Second Army made up General Montgomery's 21st Army Group.

Lieutenant General Miles Dempsey, Commander of British Second Army. In North Africa, Sicily, and Italy, Dempsey gained a reputation for expertise in combined operations such that Gen. Montgomery selected him to lead the Second Army (the primary UK force, plus Canadians) in January 1944.

Air Marshal Trafford Leigh-Mallory, Commander in Chief of the Allied Expeditionary Air Force. Leigh-Mallory was the most senior British officer killed in World War II. For D-Day, he led the Allied aerial push to stop German troop movement. His success led to his appointment as Air Commander in Chief of South East Asia Command. Unfortunately, on his way there in November, he died when his plane crashed in the French Alps.

Lieutenant General Carl Spaatz, Commander of Strategic Air Forces in Europe. Spaatz was under direct command of Gen. Eisenhower. Spaatz was noted for his Oil Plan which prioritized those targets. After the war, Eisenhower was reported as saying Spaatz and Gen. Bradley were the two American general officers who contributed most to the victory in Europe.

Lieutenant General Water Bedell Smith, Chief-of-Staff at Supreme Headquarters, Allied Expeditionary Force. "Beetle" Smith began his military career as an enlisted soldier but ultimately became one of Eisenhower's most trusted strategic advisers.

The D-Day Beaches

Courtesy of www.eucom.mil

The armed forces used codenames to refer to planning and execution of specific military operations to prepare for D-Day. Operation *Overlord* was the codename for the Allied invasion of northwest Europe. The assault phase of Operation *Overlord* was known as Operation *Neptune*. This operation, which began on June 6, 1944, and ended on June 30, 1944, involved landing troops on beaches and all other associated supporting operations required to establish a beachhead in France. By June 30, the Allies had established a firm foothold in Normandy—850,279 men, 148,803 vehicles, and 570,505 tons of supplies had been landed. Operation *Overlord* also began on D-Day, and continued until Allied forces crossed the River Seine on August 19. The battle of Normandy is the name given to the fighting in Normandy between D-Day and the end of August 1944. Allied codenames for the beaches along the 50-mile stretch of Normandy coast targeted for landing were Utah, Omaha, Gold, Juno, and Sword.

Utah Beach. Utah was the most western beach between Pouppeville and La Madeleine, 3 miles long, assigned to the US First Army, VII Corps. Casualties were the lightest of all landings—out of 23,000 troops, only 197 men were killed or wounded. It was divided into zones assigned Tare Green, Uncle Red, and Victor.

Omaha Beach. Omaha was between Sainte-Honorine-des-Pertes and Vierville-sur-Mer, 6 miles long (largest). Taking Omaha was the

US First Army, V Corps' responsibility, with sea transport from the US Navy and elements of the Royal Navy. The movie *Saving Private Ryan* portrays some events here. The 1st Infantry assault experienced the worst ordeal of D-Day operations. The Americans suffered 2,400 casualties, but 34,000 Allied troops landed by nightfall. Divided into Charlie, Dog, Easy, and Fox zones.

Gold Beach. This beach ranged from Longues-sur-Mer to La Rivière, 5 miles long, and included Arromanches, where Mulberry Harbor was established. British Second Army, XXX Corps, landed here, and by nightfall, 25,000 troops had landed and pushed the Germans 6 miles inland. The British had just 400 casualties. Divided into How, Item, Jig, and King zones.

Juno Beach. Juno spanned either side of the port of Courseulles-sur-Mer from La Rivière to Saint-Aubin-sur-Mer, 6 miles wide. Out of the 21,400 men from the Canadian 3rd Infantry Division and British Second Army, I Corps, who landed, 1,200 were injured. Divided into Love, Mike, and Nan zones.

Sword Beach. Sword stretched 5 miles from Saint-Aubin-sur-Mer to Ouistreham at the mouth of the River Orne. Nine miles north of Caen, it was a major route hub of Northern France. With help from French and British commandos, the British landed 29,000 men from its Second Army, I Corps, and suffered just 630 casualties. Divided into Oboe, Peter, Queen, and Roger zones.

D-Day by Numbers

Total Allied troops who landed in Normandy: 156,115
Total Allied airborne troops (included in figures above): 23,400
American: 73,000 (Omaha and Utah beaches + airborne)
British: 61,715 (Gold and Sword beaches + airborne)
Canadian: 21,400 (Juno Beach)

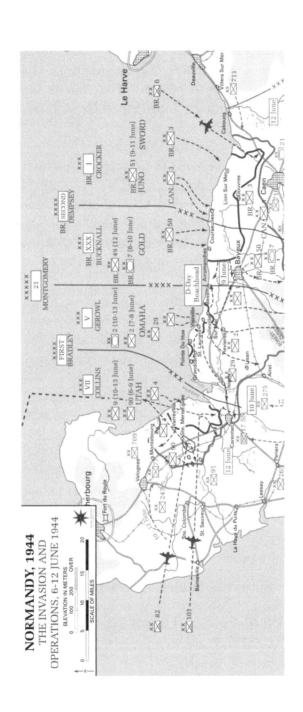

NORMANDY, 1944
THE INVASION AND
OPERATIONS, 6-12 JUNE 1944

Total Allied aircraft that supported landings: 11,590
Naval combat ships: 1,213
Landing ships/craft: 4,126
Ancillary craft: 736
Merchant vessels: 864

Total naval vessels in Operation *Neptune*: 6,939
Of the 6,939 ships involved in D-Day, 80 percent were British, 16.5 percent US, and the rest from France, Holland, Norway, and Poland.

Soldiers' home nations: United States, Britain, Canada, Belgium, Norway, Poland, Luxembourg, Greece, Czechoslovakia, New Zealand, and Australia (+177 French commandos)

Involved Allied army divisions:
3rd British Infantry—Sword Beach
3rd Canadian Infantry—Juno Beach
4th Infantry—Utah Beach
1st & 29th Infantry—Omaha Beach
50th British Infantry—Gold Beach
6th Airborne—Dropped on east bank of the Orne River
82nd & 101st Airborne—Night drop on Cotentin Peninsula behind Utah Beach
2nd Ranger Regiment—Pointe du Hoc

German Order of Battle and Unit Locations on D-Day

From Cross Channel Attack, US Army

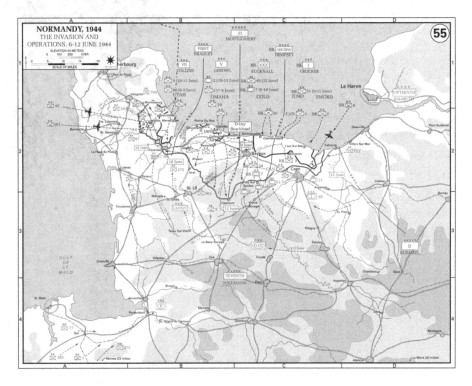

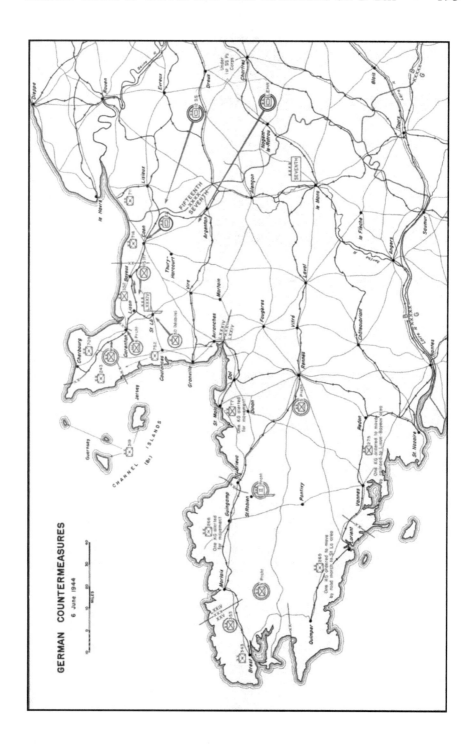

President Ronald Reagan at Pointe du Hoc on the 40th Anniversary of D-Day, June 6, 1984

We're here to mark that day in history when the Allied armies joined in battle to reclaim this continent to liberty. For four long years, much of Europe had been under a terrible shadow. Free nations had fallen, Jews cried out in the camps, millions cried out for liberation. Europe was enslaved, and the world prayed for its rescue. Here in Normandy the rescue began. Here the Allies stood and fought against tyranny in a giant undertaking unparalleled in human history.

We stand on a lonely, windswept point on the northern shore of France. The air is soft, but 40 years ago at this moment, the air was dense with smoke and the cries of men, and the air was filled with the crack of rifle fire and the roar of cannon. At dawn, on the morning of the June 6, 1944, 225 Rangers jumped off the British landing craft and ran to the bottom of these cliffs. Their mission was one of the most difficult and daring of the invasion: to climb these sheer and desolate cliffs and take out the enemy guns. The Allies had been told that some of the mightiest of these guns were here and they would be trained on the beaches to stop the Allied advance.

The Rangers looked up and saw the enemy soldiers—the edge of the cliffs shooting down at them with machine guns and throwing grenades. And the American Rangers began to climb. They shot rope ladders over the face of these cliffs and began to pull themselves up. When one Ranger fell, another would take his place. When one rope was cut, a Ranger would grab another and begin his climb again. They climbed, shot back, and held their footing. Soon, one by one, the Rangers pulled themselves over the top, and in seizing the firm land at the top of these cliffs, they began to seize back the continent of Europe. Two hundred and twenty-five came here. After two days of fighting, only 90 could still bear arms.

Behind me is a memorial that symbolizes the Ranger daggers that were thrust into the top of these cliffs. And before me are the men who put them there.

These are the boys of Pointe du Hoc. These are the men who took the cliffs. These are the champions who helped free a continent. These are the heroes who helped end a war.

Gentlemen, I look at you and I think of the words of Stephen Spender's poem. You are men who in your "lives fought for life... and left the vivid air signed with your honor."

I think I know what you may be thinking right now—thinking "we were just part of a bigger effort; everyone was brave that day." Well, everyone was. Do you remember the story of Bill Millin of the 51st Highlanders? Forty years ago today, British troops were pinned down near a bridge, waiting desperately for help. Suddenly, they heard the sound of bagpipes, and some thought they were dreaming. Well, they weren't. They looked up and saw Bill Millin with his bagpipes, leading the reinforcements and ignoring the smack of the bullets into the ground around him.

Lord Lovat was with him—Lord Lovat of Scotland, who calmly announced when he got to the bridge, "Sorry I'm a few minutes late," as if he'd been delayed by a traffic jam, when in truth he'd just come from the bloody fighting on Sword Beach, which he and his men had just taken.

There was the impossible valor of the Poles who threw themselves between the enemy and the rest of Europe as the invasion took hold, and the unsurpassed courage of the Canadians who had already seen the horrors of war on this coast. They knew what awaited them there, but they would not be deterred. And once they hit Juno Beach, they never looked back.

All of these men were part of a rollcall of honor with names that spoke of a pride as bright as the colors they bore: the Royal Winnipeg Rifles,

Poland's 24th Lancers, the Royal Scots Fusiliers, the Screaming Eagles, the Yeomen of England's armored divisions, the forces of Free France, the Coast Guard's "Matchbox Fleet" and you, the American Rangers.

Forty summers have passed since the battle that you fought here. You were young the day you took these cliffs; some of you were hardly more than boys, with the deepest joys of life before you. Yet, you risked everything here. Why? Why did you do it? What impelled you to put aside the instinct for self-preservation and risk your lives to take these cliffs? What inspired all the men of the armies that met here? We look at you, and somehow we know the answer. It was faith and belief; it was loyalty and love.

The men of Normandy had faith that what they were doing was right, faith that they fought for all humanity, faith that a just God would grant them mercy on this beachhead or on the next. It was the deep knowledge—and pray God we have not lost it—that there is a profound, moral difference between the use of force for liberation and the use of force for conquest. You were here to liberate, not to conquer, and so you and those others did not doubt your cause. And you were right not to doubt.

You all knew that some things are worth dying for. One's country is worth dying for, and democracy is worth dying for, because it's the most deeply honorable form of government ever devised by man. All of you loved liberty. All of you were willing to fight tyranny, and you knew the people of your countries were behind you.

The Americans who fought here that morning knew word of the invasion was spreading through the darkness back home. They fought—or felt in their hearts, though they couldn't know in fact, that in Georgia they were filling the churches at 4 a.m., in Kansas they were kneeling on their porches and praying, and in Philadelphia they were ringing the Liberty Bell.

Something else helped the men of D-Day: their rockhard belief that Providence would have a great hand in the events that would unfold here; that God was an ally in this great cause. And so, the night before the invasion, when Colonel Wolverton asked his parachute troops to kneel with him in prayer he told them: Do not bow your heads, but

President Ronald Reagan salutes at the Pointe du Hoc, Normandy, as the surviving members of the US Army 2nd Ranger Battalion, who stormed the cliffs on D-Day, look on. June 6, 1984. (US Government photo)

look up so you can see God and ask His blessing in what we're about to do. Also that night, General Matthew Ridgway on his cot, listening in the darkness for the promise God made to Joshua: "I will not fail thee nor forsake thee."

These are the things that impelled them; these are the things that shaped the unity of the Allies.

When the war was over, there were lives to be rebuilt and governments to be returned to the people. There were nations to be reborn. Above all, there was a new peace to be assured. These were huge and daunting tasks. But the Allies summoned strength from the faith, belief, loyalty, and love of those who fell here. They rebuilt a new Europe together.

There was first a great reconciliation among those who had been enemies, all of whom had suffered so greatly. The United States did its part, creating the Marshall plan to help rebuild our allies and our former enemies. The Marshall plan led to the Atlantic alliance—a great alliance that serves to this day as our shield for freedom, for prosperity, and for peace.

In spite of our great efforts and successes, not all that followed the end of the war was happy or planned. Some liberated countries were lost. The great sadness of this loss echoes down to our own time in the streets of Warsaw, Prague, and East Berlin. Soviet troops that came to the center of this continent did not leave when peace came. They're still there, uninvited, unwanted, unyielding, almost 40 years after the war. Because of this, allied forces still stand on this continent. Today, as 40 years ago, our armies are here for only one purpose—to protect and defend democracy. The only territories we hold are memorials like this one and graveyards where our heroes rest.

We in America have learned bitter lessons from two World Wars: It is better to be here ready to protect the peace, than to take blind shelter across the sea, rushing to respond only after freedom is lost. We've learned that isolationism never was and never will be an acceptable response to tyrannical governments with an expansionist intent.

But we try always to be prepared for peace; prepared to deter aggression; prepared to negotiate the reduction of arms; and, yes, prepared to reach out again in the spirit of reconciliation. In truth, there is no reconciliation we would welcome more than a reconciliation with the Soviet Union, so, together, we can lessen the risks of war, now and forever.

It's fitting to remember here the great losses also suffered by the Russian people during World War II: 20 million perished, a terrible price that testifies to all the world the necessity of ending war. I tell you from my heart that we in the United States do not want war. We want to wipe from the face of the Earth the terrible weapons that man now has in his hands. And I tell you, we are ready to seize that beachhead. We look for some sign from the Soviet Union that they are willing to move forward, that they share our desire and love for peace, and that they will give up the ways of conquest. There must be a changing there that will allow us to turn our hope into action.

We will pray forever that some day that changing will come. But for now, particularly today, it is good and fitting to renew our commitment to each other, to our freedom, and to the alliance that protects it.

We are bound today by what bound us 40 years ago, the same loyalties, traditions, and beliefs. We're bound by reality. The strength of America's allies is vital to the United States, and the American security guarantee is essential to the continued freedom of Europe's democracies. We were with you then; we are with you now. Your hopes are our hopes, and your destiny is our destiny.

Here, in this place where the West held together, let us make a vow to our dead. Let us show them by our actions that we understand what they died for. Let our actions say to them the words for which Matthew Ridgway listened: "I will not fail thee nor forsake thee."

Strengthened by their courage, heartened by their value [valor], and borne by their memory, let us continue to stand for the ideals for which they lived and died.

Thank you very much, and God bless you all.

"You can manufacture weapons and you can purchase ammunition, but you can't buy valor and you can't pull heroes off an assembly line," remarked D-Day veteran Sergeant John Ellery, 1st Infantry Division. At the American Cemetery at Colleville sur Mer, 9,387 American dead are buried. The Cemetery is located on the bluff overlooking Omaha Beach. Many Americans, like this one in the photo above, lie in graves as unknown soldiers with the inscription on their cross: "Here rests in honored glory, a Comrade in Arms, known but to God. (Antal photo)

Notes

Introduction

1 World War 2 Today: http://ww2today.com/chamberlain-announces-peace-for-our-time.

Chapter 1

1 Gordon A. Harrison, *Cross Channel Attack, US Army in WW II: European Theater of Operations, Center or Military History* (Washington, D.C., 1993), Appendix B, p. 457.
2 See Appendix C: General Eisenhower's Note "In Case of Failure".

Chapter 2

1 This horrible accident occurred when someone in the stick accidently set off a Gammon Grenade inside the aircraft. The Gammon Grenade was a notoriously unreliable explosive grenade with a finicky triggering mechanism. Several men were killed instantly – Private First Class Robert L. Leaky, Private Pete Vah and Corporal Kenneth A. Vaught. All members of the stick were wounded, except Corporal Mervin J. Fryer. One of the wounded, Private Eddie O. Meelberg, died a few hours later in the hospital.
2 Richard P. Hallion, *The U.S. Army Air Forces in World War II, D-Day 1944, Air Power Over the Normandy Beaches and Beyond* (Washington, D.C.: Air Force History and Museums Program, 1994), p. 2. Defeating the Luftwaffe in preparation for the D-Day invasion was a bitter and costly fight. Air casualties by the 8th US Army Air Force alone, during all of World War II, were more than 47,000 casualties, with more than 26,000 dead.

3   *Soldier: The Memoirs of Matthew B. Ridgway*, as told to Harold H. Martin (Harper & Brothers, 1956), p. 4.

4   TSgt W. E. "Bing" Wood, a note on June 6, 1944 in the diary Woods kept as the aerial engineer of C-47A Skytrain Serial Number: #42-92841, in the collection of the Air Mobility Command Museum, Dover Air Force Base, DE. 5301http:// amcmuseum.org/at-the-museum/aircraft/c-47a-skytrain/.

5   S. L. A. Marshall, *Regimental Unit Study Number 5*, p. 21. Note: This manuscript was prepared during World War II by the deployed combat historians assigned to the History Section, United States Army European Theater of Operations (ETO). The original is on file in the Historical Manuscripts Collection (HMC) under file number 8-3.1 BB 4. The author was S. L. A. Marshall, who compiled it using the oral interview techniques which he had invented.

6   S. L. A. Marshall, *Night Drop: The American Airborne Invasion of Normandy* (Little, Brown Publishers, 1962).

7   Letter from Captain John J. Dolan to Lt. Gen. James Gavin, dated March 15, 1959. In this letter, Dolan explains his actions at La Fiere. See: Murphy, R.M., *No Better Place to Die, The Battle for La Fière Bridge, Ste. Mère-Eglise, June 1944*, (Pennsylvania: Casemate Publishers, 2009), p. 146.

Chapter 3

1   *2nd Ranger Battalion: The Narrative History of Headquarters Company, April 1943– May 1945*, compiled by George M. Clark, William Weber, and Ronald Pardis, US Army, 1945. US Army War College Research Library, OCLC Number: 10758267, p.6.

2   In an address to the officers attending the US Army's Command and General Staff College in 1951, General Huebner said: "One of the things to remember is that the American soldier is essentially a civilian. He is stubborn and individualistic, and no matter what he indicates he feels sure that he can find a better way to do it than anyone else. Even if he can't he still prefers to do it his own way." Clarence R. Huebner, Address to the 1950–51 graduating class of the Army War College, Ft. Leavenworth, Kansas, June 29, 1951.

3   Thomas M. Hatfield, *Rudder: From Leader to Legend* (Texas A&M University Press, 2011), p. 116.

4   Royal Navy, Operation Neptune, The Normandy Invasion June 6, 1944, Royal Navy, UK Ministry of Defense, 13_472 NHB, p. 2.

5   The USS *Ancon* would eventually serve in the Pacific Theater of Operation (PTO) and, in preparation of the Japanese surrender in World War II, was anchored between USS *Missouri* (BB-63) and USS *South Dakota* (BB-57) in Tokyo Bay in September 1945. Its crew witnessed the official Japanese surrender on September 2, 1945.

6   Patrick O'Donnell, author of *Dog Company*, interviewed by Bucky Fox in, "Army's Earl Rudder Climbed to a Hero's Peak On D-Day," *Business Daily*, June 4, 2015.

http://www.investors.com/news/management/leaders-and-success/james-earl-rudder-led-rangers-to-d-day-triumph/.

7   Small Unit Actions. France: 2nd Ranger Battalion at Pointe du Hoe. Saipan: 27th Division on Tanapag plain. Italy: 351st infantry at Santa Maria Infante. France: 4th Armored Division at Singling, CMH Pub 100-14. Center for Military History, US Army, Washington, DC, 1991. p. 5. Note: A D-Bar ration was the World War II equivalent of an energy bar. The D-Bar was produced by Hershey Chocolate Corporation and consisted of a very hard, not very sweet, four ounces, 600 calories, chocolate food bar. By the end of World War II, Hershey had produced nearly three billion ration bars.

8   *Small Unit Actions, France: 2nd Ranger Battalion at Pointe du Hoc*, American Forces in Action Series, Historical Division, War Department, Washington, D.C., Facsimile Reprint, 1982, 1986, 1991, CMH Pub 100-14, Center of Military History, United States Army, p. 4.

9   Interview with 1st Sgt. Leonard Lomell and Staff Sgt. Jack Kuhn, HistoryNet.com, June 12, 2006. See: http://www.historynet.com/d-day-interview-with-two-us-2nd-ranger-battalion-members-who-describe-the-attack-at-pointe-du-hoc.htm. Hereafter: Lomell.

10 Col. Robert W. Black, *The Battalion, The Dramatic Story of the 2nd Ranger Battalion in World War II* (Stackpole Books, 2006), p. 101.

11 Lomell.

12 Black, 110.

13 Lomell.

14 Lomell. Note: 1st Sgt. Leonard Lomell was awarded the Distinguished Service Cross and Staff Sgt. Jack Kuhn the Silver Star for their actions in destroying the German guns near the Pointe du Hoc on D-Day.

15 Black, 134.

16 Stephen E. Ambrose, *D-Day Illustrated Edition: June 6, 1944: The Climactic Battle of World War II* (New York: Simon and Schuster, 1994), p. 477.

17 Daniel E. Sumey, "Rangers, Lead the Way! – How the Rangers at Pointe du Hoc Turned Disaster into Victory during the D-Day Invasion," *Discerning History*, June 6, 2016. http://discerninghistory.com/2016/06/rangers-lead-the-way-how-the-rangers-at-pointe-du-hoc-turned-disaster-into-victory-during-the-d-day-invasion/.

18 Thomas M. Hatfield, "The First Night on Pointe du Hoc: An Excerpt from Thomas M. Hatfield's *Rudder: From Leader to Legend*," *Humanities Texas*, June 2011. http://www.humanitiestexas.org/news/articles/first-night.

Chapter 4

1   It might be difficult to remember that on June 6, 1944, with the Allied juggernaut readying to hurl itself against Hitler's Atlantic Wall, only five years earlier, on September 1, 1939, when the Nazi Führer ignited the war in Europe by attacking Poland, the US Army possessed only 240 M1 combat cars and M2 light tanks,

and only one medium tank equipped with a 37mm gun. All of these armored vehicles were already obsolete in 1939 and no match for the Germans. In addition, in 1939, the US had no major tank production program. Now, on the eve of the invasion of Normandy, the US Army had 16 Armored Divisions (with 269 tanks in each division) and 41 independent tank battalions (74 tanks and assault guns per independent tank battalion) deployed worldwide. By the end of World War II, the US would prove its ability to innovate and manufacture tanks by producing a total of 49,234 M4 Sherman tanks.

2   One of the early designers of the amphibious tank was a British citizen and an immigrant from Hungary named Nicholas Straussler. Using the principle of buoyancy developed by Archimedes, Straussler postulated that if he could make the mass of a tank in water greater than its weight, it would float. In March 1943, the energetic, persistent, and brilliant British Major General Sir Percy Cleghorn Stanley Hobart embraced Straussler's idea to develop a swimming tank. Hobart had served in the British Army in World War I, saw the future of the tank in warfare, and transferred to the Royal Tank Corps in 1923. He studied and was influenced by the writings of the prominent British historian and military philosopher B. H. Liddell Hart. Liddell Hart was one of the early proponents of combined-arms tank warfare and his writings had influenced many armor enthusiasts before World War II. Studying Hart's writings and experimenting with his own ideas concerning armored warfare, Hobart became one of the foremost tank experts in Great Britain and often quarreled with his superiors who held a less positive view of the use of tanks in war. Never flinching in his belief in the employment of tanks, Hobart was promoted to brigadier and commanded the first permanent armored brigade in Britain and was Inspector Royal Tank Corps. In 1937, he was promoted to Major General. In 1938, on the eve of the outbreak of World War II, he was sent to Egypt to train the "Mobile Force," which eventually became the 7th Armored Division. The 7th, nicknamed the "Desert Rats," would later fight Field Marshal Erwin Rommel, "The Desert Fox," in the African campaign. When World War II broke out, Hobart stubbornly clashed with his superiors again and was dismissed. He left the Army in 1940 and joined the Home Guard, a form of local militia. News of Major General Hobart serving as a private in the Home Guard reached Prime Minister Winston Churchill. Churchill pulled Hobart "out of exile" in 1941 and assigned him to train the newly formed 79th Armored Division. "The High Commands of the Army are not a club. It is my duty," Churchill announced concerning Hobart, "... to make sure that exceptionally able men, even those not popular with their military contemporaries, should not be prevented from giving their services to the Crown." It did not hurt Hobart's cause that he was also the brother-in-law of Britain's rising star, General Bernard Montgomery. Churchill saw the potential of Hobart's views concerning tank warfare and supported his efforts to experiment with armored vehicles. After the disastrous Allied defeat

during the raid on Hitler's Atlantic Wall at Dieppe in August 1942, Hobart's unit was renamed and redesigned as "79th (Experimental) Armored Division Royal Engineers." The specific purpose of this unit was to create innovative new armored vehicles that would make the next attempt to crack the German's beach defenses more successful. Empowered, Hobart proposed, invented, and manufactured a family of specialized tanks that would prove very useful on the beaches of Normandy. "Hobart's Funnies," as they came to be called, included the Armored Vehicle Royal Engineers (AVRE) to destroy obstacles and bunkers; the Duplex Drive (DD) swimming tanks; a Crab flail tank that detonated mines; and the flamethrower Crocodile tank.

3   The DD tank was designed to swim from ship to shore. Turning a 36-ton steel tank into a boat was a tall order, but Hobart was able to make it happen. In order to swim, each DD tank was equipped with a 6-foot-high canvas and rubber flotation screen that was held up by metal struts and inflatable tubes. This screen displaced enough water to provide the buoyancy needed to keep the tank from sinking in calm seas. The screen was erected by the crew and could be taken down once the tank reached land. To propel the tank through the water at a top speed of six knots, two large propellers were fitted to the DD tank engine. The canvas screen was about a foot higher than the turret and the tank commander had to stand on the back deck of the tank and steer his "36-ton floating bucket" with the aid of a wooden rudder.

4   In the study, *Destroyers at Normandy, Naval Gunfire Support at Omaha Beach*, the "*Carmick* saw American tanks stalled in the Vierville draw and, in cooperation with the tankers, knocked the first hole in the defenses." Later, in the USS *Carmick* official *After Action Report*: "Early in the morning, a group of tanks were seen to be having difficulty making their way along the breakwater road toward Exit D-1 [the Vierville draw]. A silent cooperation was established wherein they fired at a target on the bluff above them and we then fired several salvos at the same spot. They then shifted fire further along the bluff and we used their bursts again as a point of aim."

5   Ambrose, *D-Day Illustrated Edition*, p 493.

Chapter 5

1   Joseph Balkoski, *Utah Beach: The Amphibious Landing and Airborne Operations On D-Day, June 6, 1944* (Stackpole Books, 2005), p. 179.

2   Rick Atkinson, *The Day of Battle: The War in Sicily and Italy, 1943–1944* (Macmillan, Henry Holt & Company, 2007), pp. 159–160.

3   Braim, Paul F., *The Will to Win: The Life of General James A. Van Fleet* (US Naval Institute Press, 2001), p. 79.

Chapter 6

1   *Osttruppen* (eastern troops) were employed in several of the German static divisions in Normandy. One unit, the 795th Georgian Infantry Battalion (*Ost-Bataillone*) was assigned to the 709th Division and fought in the area of the village of Turqueville, near Saint-Côme-du-Mont. Some of these units fought well, but many were not dependable and surrendered. The German Army in World War II had nearly 427,000 soldiers pressed into serving in Osttruppen units and fielded a total of 30 divisions.

2   Marshall, S. L. A, *Men Against Fire: The Problem of Battle Command* (University of Oklahoma Press, originally published in 1947, reprinted in 2000), p. 72.

Chapter 7

1   Margaret R. O'Leary and Dennis S. O'Leary, *Tragedy at Graignes: The Bud Sophian Story* (Bloomington, IN: iUniverse Books, 2011), p. 228.

2   The *Sturmgeschütz*, or StuG as it was called for short (with the G in the name always capitalized), was a German self-propelled assault gun that featured a high-velocity 75mm cannon that was powerful enough to knock out most Soviet tanks, especially if hit in the flank or rear. The cannon was mounted on an old tank chassis, a Panzerkampfwagen III, as German industry struggled mightily to provide upgraded versions of older vehicles to the front-line troops. As a self-propelled assault gun, the StuG had no turret and therefore was cheaper and faster to produce. Without a turret the StuG also had a much lower silhouette compared with a tank. This increased the StuG's survivability as it was difficult to target and hit. The StuG had another advantage in that it only required four men to crew the vehicle: commander, gunner, loader, and driver. Other tanks, like the German Panther or Tiger, required a five-man crew. This meant that Germany could produce more armored assault guns for less cost and manned by fewer men. The StuG, however, had some major drawbacks over a tank. Without a turret, the gun often had to be aimed by moving the StuG's tracks. The gunner could only traverse the gun 24 degrees. It took time to move the vehicle for the gunner to target the enemy, much slower than a tank with a turret. In spite of its limitations, however, the StuG was a successful tank killer and by January 1944 was credited with destroying a whopping 20,000 Soviet tanks on the Russian Front.

3   For additional information on the battle of Graignes, read Martin Morgan, *Down to Earth: The 507th Parachute Infantry Regiment in Normandy, June 6–July 15, 1944* (Atglen, PA: Schiffer Publishing Ltd., 2004).

4   Commander's intent is a nested concept that "succinctly describes what constitutes success for the operation. It includes the operation's purpose and the conditions that define the end state. It links the mission, concept of operations, and tasks to subordinate units." Understanding the intent of your superiors can provide you

with a guide to decide to move in the right direction and act when the plan fails and a decision is required. Clearly articulating intent to your subordinates empowers them to make decisions within your intent rather than waiting for guidance when the plan fails. For today's US Army, understanding commander's intent is a crucial element of mission command. According to the 2012 edition of *US Army Field Manual Army Doctrine Publication 6-0*, "mission command is the exercise of authority and direction by the commander using mission orders to enable disciplined initiative within the commander's intent to empower agile and adaptive leaders in the conduct of unified land operations." In short, mission command is a culture of leadership that attempts to empower every member of the team to think and execute disciplined initiative. Rather than micro-manage soldiers or employees, and waste time while subordinate leaders hesitate and wait for orders, the right leadership culture (mission command) and the use of commander's intent can empower subordinates to act to take advantage of unforeseen opportunities or unplanned disruptions and act *in time*. See: Army Doctrine Reference Publication No. 6-0, Headquarters, Department of the Army, Washington, D.C., 17 May 2012, pp. 2–3.

5   This is the author's personal definition of "commander's intent" that has been successfully used in the military and in business.

6   For business, you can replace "commander" with CEO/director/program manager or any appropriate leadership title. The latest US Army manual defines commander's intent as: "The commander's intent is a clear and concise expression of the purpose of the operation and the desired military end state that supports mission command, provides focus to the staff, and helps subordinate and supporting commanders act to achieve the commander's desired results without further orders, even when the operation does not unfold as planned. Commanders establish their own commander's intent within the intent of their higher commander. The higher commander's intent provides the basis for unity of effort throughout the larger force" (ADP 6.0 May 17, 2012).